CAPITALISM

—— AND ——

JUSTICE

CAPITALISM
—— AND ——
JUSTICE

ENVISIONING SOCIAL
AND ECONOMIC FAIRNESS

John Isbister

KUMARIAN
PRESS

Capitalism and Justice: Envisioning Social and Economic Fairness

Published 2001 in the United States of America by Kumarian Press, Inc.
1294 Blue Hills Avenue, Bloomfield, CT 06002.

Production, design, indexing, and proofreading by ediType,
Yorktown Heights, N.Y., and Charleston, S.C.
The text of this book is set in 10/13 Adobe Sabon.

Printed in Canada on acid-free paper by Transcontinental Printing and Graphics, Inc.
Text printed with vegetable oil–based ink.

∞ The paper used in this publication meets the minimum requirements of the American National Standard for Information Sciences—Permanence of Paper for Printed Library Materials, ANSI Z39.48–1984.

Library of Congress Cataloging-in-Publication Data

Isbister, John, 1942-
    Capitalism and justice : envisioning social and economic fairness / John Isbister.
    p. cm.
    Includes bibliographical references and index.
    ISBN 1-56549-123-8 (cloth : alk. paper). — ISBN 1-56549-122-X (pbk. : alk. paper)
    1. Capitalism — Moral and ethical aspects. 2. Social justice. 3. Distributive justice.
    I. Title.

    HB501 I665 2001
    174 – dc21
                                                            00-046222

10 09 08 07 06 05 03 02 01   10 9 8 7 6 5 4 3 2 1   First Printing 2001

For my son David

CONTENTS

"O.K., guys, now let's go and <u>earn</u> that four
hundred times our workers' salaries."

PREFACE

The highest calling is to do justice — to trouble the comfortable
and comfort the troubled.   — STEVE BANKS, homeless advocate

WE LIVE in a capitalist world. The capitalist economic and social
system has taken over almost the entire globe. Two exceptions
exist — Cuba and North Korea — but every other country has turned
to capitalist markets. Precapitalism and postcapitalism have both disappeared. Capitalism has almost completely destroyed the more personal
and organic social forms that preceded it. What were once thought to
be the faces of postcapitalism — socialism and communism — have collapsed almost entirely. Some countries like China and Vietnam still have
ruling parties that call themselves communist, but the economies over
which they preside are increasingly based on private ownership and the
market. The triumph of capitalism may not be permanent, but it is likely
to last through our lifetimes and the lifetimes of our children and grandchildren; it is hard to see on the horizon any social force strong enough
to dislodge it.

We have a great deal of experience working for justice within the
capitalist system. The labor movement, the civil rights movement,
the welfare system, the environmental movement, the women's movement — these and other struggles have occurred within capitalism and
have typically had the goal of making it more just, not overthrowing it.
They have had many victories but not complete victory, since they have
run into the boundary conditions of capitalism. The capitalist system is
elastic, but not infinitely so. That, at any rate, is my contention and the
reason for this book.

Part I sets out the foundations of the discussion. Chapter 1 describes
the components of social justice, which I think are equality, freedom,
and efficiency. Chapter 2 outlines the defining features of capitalism and
shows why capitalism is the only game in town. With these preliminaries
taken care of, the rest of the book asks what justice entails in particular

situations, and how close we can get to it without encountering the binding constraints of our social system.

Part II deals with problems of social justice that occur at the national level. Chapter 3 considers the distribution of incomes that would exist in a just society. Would everyone have equal incomes, or would there be a spread? If a spread, what should be the ratio between the highest and the lowest? Once the argument of chapter 3 is set out, the next three chapters discuss ways of achieving a just income distribution. Chapter 4 is on the features of an equitable system of income taxation. Chapter 5 discusses the taxation of wealth and inheritances. Chapter 6 turns to the welfare system and policies to eliminate poverty. Chapter 7 closes the section on national dilemmas by developing an argument in support of programs of racial preferences in hiring, admissions, and contracting.

Part III expands the scope of the discussion to include international issues. Chapter 8 sets out the broad problem of globalization. Chapter 9 considers the boundaries of justice: Do foreigners have the same moral standing as people of our own country, and do we owe them equal treatment? Chapter 10 is on foreign aid: What do the rich countries owe the poor countries in aid, and what do rich people owe poor people? Chapter 11 considers the conflicts of justice generated by immigration and develops the idea that immigration should be thought of as an issue of civil rights. Chapter 12 asks where environmental justice lies.

The book does not come close to exhausting the problems of social justice that arise in a capitalist society. They are endless, including problems in the areas of labor relations, market structure, the sharing of commercially valuable ideas, scientific research, trade and investment, national sovereignty, education, health care, the family, gender and sexual-preference discrimination, and many more. The problems on which the book focuses are centrally important, however.

Each of the problems is broad, and each has an extensive scholarly and popular literature devoted to it. The chapters that follow concentrate on the arguments about justice and provide only enough empirical information to give the arguments some grounding. The endnotes include references to sources that contain much more factual material, for readers who wish to explore a topic further.

The book lies on the boundary of economics and moral philosophy. I have tried to adopt some of the methods of the rapidly developing field of applied ethics, a field in which writers attempt to construct cogent arguments about the rights and wrongs of pressing issues that confront us.[1] As in much of applied ethics, the approach I take is practical: the book focuses upon specific economic issues such as income distribution, tax structure, and foreign aid, rather than upon the structure of economic theory or upon the complex interrelations between capitalism and such subjects as power, identity, culture, race, class, gender, and imperialism.[2]

Every one of us, I venture, has ideas about justice. Certainly children do. One of the most frequent phrases I heard from my children when they were young was, "It's not fair." They were intensely sensitive to injustices they believed were perpetrated upon them. So was — and am — I. They and I are perhaps less sensitive to the injustices we inflict upon others, but we are not oblivious to them. Part of the process of growing up has been to learn to distinguish between getting what we deserve, on the one hand, and being unfair to people, on the other.

We all have ideas about justice, and those ideas conflict. Some think high-income earners should be taxed to provide for a generous welfare system, while others think taxes should be cut because people deserve to keep what they have earned. Some think people in rich countries should welcome immigrants from poor countries, while others think foreigners should be kept out. These and countless other disagreements are not only about self-interest but about justice, about what people deserve.

We are sometimes able to work out solutions to our disagreements. The key to arriving at good solutions, I think, is democracy. Democracy is the political expression of the most important principle in this book, that we are of equal worth. We are of equal worth and we deserve, therefore, to have an equal say when we disagree about justice or about anything else. Democratic decision making cannot ensure justice, of course. In most democratic processes, decisions are made by majority vote, and majorities frequently impose injustices on minorities. Political representatives may deny adequate support to people who are poor through no fault of their own. They may close the gates against homeless refugees. Mindful of democratic abuses, we often agree to restrictions on majority rule: constitutions with bills of rights, requirements for supermajorities or consensus, checks and balances among different branches of government, and so forth. None of these restrictions forces legislative bodies to act justly, however.

An ideal democracy would give a voice to everyone who is affected by a decision. The real democracies with which we are familiar cannot reach this standard. Poor children are affected by the welfare system, for example, but children cannot vote. Foreigners are affected by the policies of a country like the United States, but foreigners have no vote. Future generations of people have an interest in the environmental policies undertaken today, but they have no way of expressing that interest. Even the best possible democracy leaves relevant people out of the decision-making process. In any case, our actual democracies are not fairly representative even of the people who are eligible to be members of them. Political decisions are influenced heavily by campaign contributions that come largely from people at the top of the income range who have an interest in the status quo. Higher-income people are more likely to vote than lower-income people, so for this reason alone they have a disproportionate influence over decisions.[3]

Our democracies are imperfect, but they are still the best forum we have for decision making when our interests and our conceptions of justice differ. It is in the democratic political sphere that we should confront our disagreements and work out solutions.[4] This book is intended as a voice in the democratic discussion of justice.

Throughout, I have tried to develop coherent arguments based on defensible premises. I hope to persuade, but I am under no illusion that I will be completely persuasive. The questions raised by this book are so difficult that they will never be settled, and perhaps that is just as well. As far as I can tell, part of what it means to be human is to struggle continuously over the meaning of justice and how to achieve it.

I wrote the book at the Robarts Library of the University of Toronto, where I was a visiting scholar in the economics department. I appreciate very much the invitation of economists Jon Cohen and Nancy Gallini to spend a year in Toronto. I would like to thank two moral philosophers, William H. Shaw and Richard Wasserstrom, who introduced me to their subject. My friends Kevin DeLapp, Jennifer Hansen, and Katie Lambden at the University of California, Santa Cruz, and Fred Weaver at Hampshire College read the manuscript closely and gave me hundreds of suggestions. It is a privilege to have such attentive and insightful readers. My son Peter Isbister accompanied me on the journey of this book and provided a great deal of help. I am particularly grateful to my wife, Roz Spafford, who has a way with both words and ideas that is frequently stunning, and who challenged and guided me from beginning to end.

Notes

1. A comprehensive introduction to applied ethics is found in *The Encyclopedia of Applied Ethics* (San Diego: Academic Press, 1998).

2. Another book that takes a practical approach to the ethical implications of economic policies, although in a different way from this book, is Harlan M. Smith, *Understanding Economics* (Armonk, N.Y.: M. E. Sharpe, 1999). A good survey of the relationship between economic theory and moral philosophy is Daniel M. Hausman and Michael S. McPherson, *Economic Analysis and Moral Philosophy* (New York: Cambridge University Press, 1996).

3. For a discussion of ways in which capitalist values seep into and distort democratic processes, see David Copp, "Capitalism versus Democracy: The Marketing of Votes and the Marketing of Political Power," in *Ethics and Capitalism,* ed. John Douglas Bishop (Toronto: University of Toronto Press, 2000), 81–101.

4. Amy Gutmann and Dennis Thompson discuss how democracies can be better forums for the discussion and resolution of moral conflicts in *Democracy and Disagreement* (Cambridge, Mass.: Belknap Press of Harvard University Press, 1996).

Part I

Foundations

Chapter 1

JUSTICE

T HE TALE of the little red hen is familiar to many. The little red hen finds some grains of wheat in the farmyard. She asks the other animals — the cat, the rat, and the pig — who would like to help her plant the grains, then reap the harvest, then carry the wheat to the mill for grinding into flour, and then bake the flour into bread. "Not I," says each of the animals, each time it is asked. Finally, when the bread is baked, the little red hen asks who would like to help her eat it, and the cat, the rat, and the pig all volunteer. The little red hen declines their help and eats the bread herself.

Is she justified in keeping all the bread?

The Architecture of Justice

To answer the question, we need some ideas about what justice is. Justice, according to a long tradition in Western thought, is the quality of getting what one deserves. This definition dates at least to the *Institutes* of the Roman emperor Justinian in 533, a compilation of Roman law as it existed at that time. The *Institutes* begins: "Justice is the constant and perpetual wish to render everyone his due."[1]

Justice is a broad idea, used for assessing behavior in many different situations. Aristotle, writing almost a millennium before the *Institutes,* identified different kinds of partial justice: distributive justice, relating to who gets honors and money in the society; rectificatory justice, relating to compensation for criminal acts and injuries; justice in exchange, relating to the conventions that govern trade in the marketplace; and political justice, relating to the principles by which people rule others.[2] The issue confronting the little red hen, and the subject of our inquiry, is the first of these, social or distributive justice.

In any society, people are connected with each other in complex ways — by markets, by businesses, by governments, by schools, by families, and by many other institutions — and through these connections they may or may not get what they deserve. "Justice is the first virtue of social institutions," wrote philosopher John Rawls, "as truth is of systems of thought."[3]

Justice is not the only human virtue. Among the long list of virtues are compassion, love, sympathy, honesty, altruism, courage, integrity, responsibility, and understanding. A fully comprehensive treatment of ethics would deal with all of them and more. Justice is the bedrock social virtue, however, because we have a right to it. We may wish to be treated with love, sympathy, and understanding and find it delightful when we are, but we do not necessarily have a right to such treatment. We have a right to justice.

Justice consists of giving people what they deserve, but how do we know what they deserve? The literature of moral philosophy is rich with different ways of thinking about the subject, among them approaches associated with utilitarianism, natural rights, the social contract, Marxism, liberalism, feminism, ecology, communitarianism, and libertarianism, all of them traditions that overlap and enrich each other.[4] I will draw on some of these philosophies in the pages that follow. For the most part, though, the conception of justice advanced here is situated in the liberal tradition, a tradition holding that people are of equal moral value and that the rights of the individual are prior to the rights of the community.

I assert in this chapter — and try to support — the idea that social justice has three components: equality, freedom, and efficiency. People deserve to be treated as equals, they deserve to be free, and they deserve to get the best they can out of their limited resources.

The three components of justice can conflict with each other. Maximum freedom may lead to inequality, for example. Complete equality may lead to inefficiency. When conflicts arise between the components of justice, we must reason the problem out as best we can, by using our judgment. This way of proceeding was recommended by the philosopher W. D. Ross, who argued that moral obligations are contingent, or prima facie, obligations.[5] Some principles are applicable in some situations but not in others. It is essential to think about the principles of justice, not in order to follow them blindly but in order to provide a basis for what must ultimately be our own thought processes.

Some scholars go so far as to say that no independent standards of justice exist, since ideas about justice are culturally specific.[6] What is impermissible in one culture, they maintain, is fine in another. Slavery was right in ancient Greece, for example, but is wrong in modern America.

The inquiry into justice, according to some who hold this view, is a matter not for philosophers and theorists but for historians, anthropologists, and social scientists.

Moral relativism has a certain attractiveness because it helps to make us sensitive to our own cultural biases. As a matter of empirical fact, it is certainly correct that people in some cultures view morality differently from people in other cultures.[7] This fact does not in itself constitute much of an argument in support of the view that there should be no independent standards of justice, however. To reason by analogy, the fact that some cultures believe that disease is spread by offended gods rather than by bacteria is irrelevant to whether antibiotics are effective.

Moral relativism is ultimately impossible, I think, as a foundation of our search for justice. It is an example of what philosopher G. E. Moore called the naturalistic fallacy — converting an "is" statement into an "ought" statement.[8] For most of US history, most white Americans were unashamedly racist; they were part of a racist culture. Yet many of us believe they were ethically deficient — ethically deficient in their own time, not just according to the ideas of a later time — and we honor not them but the small minority who regarded racism as inherently unjust. That minority of people, in struggling against racism, were inspired by principles they regarded as universal, not emanating from their own racist society. Ethical relativism provides no foundation upon which to challenge prevailing norms, so it is not of much use to people who are seeking justice.

We will, in the end, disagree about the principles of justice, but I do not believe we should be, or are, willing to concede that those principles are only sociological or personal constructs. As human beings, we search for principles of justice that transcend our local experience. The fact that we do not agree does not, and should not, stop the search. Let us consider, therefore, the three principles of justice that this chapter advances. The hen, the cat, the rat, and the pig deserve, I maintain, to be treated as equals, to be free to pursue their goals, and to get the best results they can from their efforts.

Equality

Why should equality be central to our concept of justice? Why do we deserve to be regarded as equal with each other?

Some philosophers have attempted to derive equality from a more basic ethical axiom. In the most seminal contribution to moral philos-

ophy in the twentieth century, *A Theory of Justice,* John Rawls began
with an imaginary "original position" in which people are excluded
from knowledge of their own position in the world — whether they
will be rich or poor, male or female, and every other relevant personal
characteristic — by a "veil of ignorance."[9] Behind the veil of ignorance,
Rawls claimed, people would necessarily agree upon equality of what
he called primary social goods — liberty and opportunity, income and
wealth, and the bases of self-respect — as one of the foundations of
justice. Rawls's only exception to equality was his famous "difference
principle," about which more later. His derivation of the principles of
justice from an imaginary original position is interesting but in the end, I
think, unconvincing. If people in the original position agree upon equality as a foundation of justice, it must be because they share certain
motivations or believe they will share certain motivations in the world
to come — in spite of the fact that knowledge of their psychological
makeup is supposed to be hidden from them by the veil of ignorance.

Other philosophers have based human equality upon a characteristic that they allege all human beings, and only human beings, share: a
characteristic such as the ability to make moral judgments, or to feel,
or to engage in dialogue.[10] These attempts fail also, however, because
some human beings — for example, infants in some cases or people in
comas — do not possess these characteristics. Hence if moral standing is
based on an inherent characteristic, it follows that people have unequal,
not equal, moral standing.

Perhaps equality can be derived from a more basic ethical axiom, but
it is hard to see how, and in any case one would then be confronted with
the problem of justifying that particular axiom. It is sufficient, instead,
to begin with equality as a foundation of justice. This was the view of
Thomas Jefferson, who wrote in the Declaration of Independence: "We
hold these Truths to be self-evident, that all Men are created equal, that
they are endowed by their Creator with certain unalienable Rights, that
among these are Life, Liberty, and the Pursuit of Happiness."

Students of history are all too aware of the limitations of this sentence. It was not intended in 1776 to extend to African and Native
inhabitants of the United States, and the word "Men" excluded half the
population. Yet if we replace "Men" with "people," the words echo
to us over the centuries as expressing universal truths. The truths are
"self-evident," not derived from something more basic.

In fact, Jefferson's statement *cannot* be derived from experience or
data, since in terms of our attributes we are unequal. Each person is

unique, with his or her own characteristics, and is emphatically not the same as everyone else, indeed anyone else. Jacobus tenBroek explains: " 'All men are created equal' is not a declarative sentence; it is an imperative. It is not a statement but an exhortation. It is not an affirmation or description. It is a command. Whatever its form, its function is directive."[11]

Whatever our individual attributes, and they are enormously diverse, the Declaration of Independence instructs us that we are to treat each other as having equal moral standing, equal worth. Political theorist Bruce Ackerman puts it nicely. In a debate about conflicting rights, he says, each person is entitled to respond to a challenge to his standing from another person by saying, without fear of contradiction, "because I'm at least as good as you are."[12]

This is where people in the liberal tradition begin in trying to sort out the principles of justice. Equality is so basic to justice that one is pressed to imagine what meaning justice could have if it did not imply equality. "Unequal justice" is an oxymoron, a self-contradicting expression. "Every modern theory of justice begins from the premise that citizens must be treated as equals in some respect," writes economic philosopher John E. Roemer.[13]

Let us grant, therefore, along with Jefferson, that we are morally equal. Hardly anything is solved by this concession, however; our problems have just begun. Two major issues emerge. First, in what respects are we to be treated as equals, and, second, who exactly is to be equal? The first issue is dealt with next, the second in chapters 9 and 12.

What does the fact of moral equality entitle us to? The answers that have been advanced by philosophers, economists, and other theorists are many: equal income, equal wealth, equal welfare, equal happiness, equal resources, equal opportunity, equal capacity, equal liberty, equal standing before the law, and more. The choice of what is to be equalized matters because, as Amartya Sen points out, since people are diverse, if one insists upon equality in one dimension, one inevitably gets inequality in others.[14] For example, some of us get more happiness from wealth than others do. If we are made equal in wealth, therefore, we will be unequal in happiness. Alternatively, if we are made equal in happiness, we will have unequal wealth.

Most of the answers to the question of what should be equalized lie more or less in one of two camps: equality of opportunity or equality of resources, on the one hand, and equality of outcomes or equality of welfare, on the other.[15] Equality of opportunity means that we all begin at the same starting line in the journey of life, while equality of outcomes means that we get equivalent benefits from our life efforts. Since we have diverse personal characteristics, the two concepts of equality cannot both be honored at the same time. If our opportunities are equal, then because some are more skilled or energetic than others, we will necessarily garner different results. If results are to be equal, people will have to be given different opportunities, to compensate for their differences in characteristics. Does justice require one or the other version of equality?

Let's get back to the question of whether the little red hen is justified in keeping all the bread. If you believe that justice requires only equality of opportunity, the answer is yes — provided that each of the four animals had an equal chance to produce the bread, either alone or cooperatively with the others. Only the hen chose to do so, and she deserves to benefit from that choice. She made the bread and it is justly hers. If you believe in equality of outcomes, the answer is no: the hen has all the bread, while the others have none. Justice requires that each animal have an equal share.

I am going to advance the following argument. Equality of opportunity is fundamental to justice, although it can never be achieved because of differences in our inherited characteristics. The best we can do is approach it. Equality of outcomes is not fundamental to justice; in fact it violates the norm of justice to a certain extent. Nevertheless, unequal outcomes, if perpetuated over time, themselves create unequal opportunities. So even if a state of perfect social justice — that is, perfect equality of opportunity — could be achieved, it would be unstable; over time it would descend into a state of unequal opportunity. Therefore, in the real world in which we live, the cause of justice can be advanced by working for greater equality of outcomes. Still, at times, and this is one of the indeterminacies of justice, equality of opportunity and equality of outcomes conflict, and we must use our judgment.

Without equality of opportunity, we cannot get what we deserve. The cat, the rat, and the pig are equal in moral standing with the little red hen. If they are prevented from making bread, they can claim an injustice because they are entitled to say, as Ackerman might suggest, "we are just as good as the hen is." If they are not prevented from making bread, if their failure to make bread is their own fault, not someone else's, they have no claim to an injustice. This seems to be what Jefferson had in mind. Men who are created equal have an equal right to "the Pursuit of Happiness," he wrote, not to the achievement of happiness.

Justice requires "a level playing field" without artificial restrictions. It requires an absence of discrimination and restriction related to race, class, gender, sexual orientation, faith, political opinion, or anything else. It requires the absence of monopolies, restrictive licenses, and cliques, anything that would predetermine the outcome of one's life journey. It requires that the rules of the game be fair not only at the beginning of the journey, when each person starts, but throughout the journey. The rules must apply to everyone, including the rules that determine acceptance to a field of endeavor, promotion, on-the-job training, salary levels, club membership, or anything else that is relevant to one's success. All this is what is sometimes called formal equality of opportunity.

True or fair equality of opportunity requires more than formal equality, more than just the absence of unequal restrictions on one's actions. It also requires equality of resources at the beginning of the journey: equal education, equal technology, equal community support: whatever resources are necessary for the achievement of the goal must be distributed equally to everyone in the race. Without equal resources, opportunity cannot be really equal.

Social arrangements can be structured in such a way as to remove many of the impediments to equal opportunity, although with great difficulty. Not, however, all the impediments. Inequality of opportunity results in part from characteristics that we inherit, including different kinds of intelligence and physical abilities, and also from the differences in child rearing practices we have experienced. It is important, therefore, to take every possible measure to make opportunities more equal, while conceding from the start that complete equality is impossible.

The impossibility of achieving complete equality of opportunity might lead one to abandon the goal altogether and turn to equality of outcomes as the way of measuring justice. Some moral philosophers and political theorists hold that since we are all of equal moral standing, we deserve to get equal benefits from the social system. This is a mistake; equality of outcomes is not a fundamental component of justice.

One problem with establishing equal outcomes as the criterion of justice is that equal outcomes are almost impossible to identify. For many purposes we use money or wealth as a common metric, a way of comparing apples and oranges, but it will not do to say that people are equal in their life outcomes if they are equally wealthy. The reason is that some people value wealth more than others. Some people devote their lives to amassing as much of it as they can, while others have different goals: leisure, perhaps, or power, or doing good for others. If the hen enjoys both work and bread while the cat enjoys idleness, they may each achieve their goals even though the bread goes only to the hen. It would be a mistake to think that justice requires everyone to be equally wealthy if everyone does not equally share the goal of wealth.

Economists and philosophers have wrestled with this problem.[16] One possible solution is to say that the yardstick of outcomes is not money but happiness or utility or welfare or preferences. A just world, one could say, is one in which all of us are equally happy, or in which we are equal in terms of meeting our goals, whatever those goals are. The business school graduate gets to be chief executive officer (CEO), and the seeker after enlightenment finds wisdom. This way of thinking of equality has merits, but it has obvious problems. Some people have a greater capacity for happiness than others do. Does this imply that they deserve to be more happy, or perhaps less happy in the sense of being further from their goals? It is not clear.

This is a serious problem, but it is not the most serious problem connected with using equality of outcomes as the measure of justice. Let us wish it away; assume for the sake of argument that all people have the same preferences and that their preferences can be measured by a common yardstick, say, loaves of bread. All that this heroic assumption does is bring us face-to-face with the central problem in using equality of outcomes as a measure of justice. People who have equal opportunity but who perform differently deserve to be rewarded differently. The standard of equal outcomes is likely to lead to injustice, therefore, not justice. Surely the little red hen, who went to all the trouble of producing the bread while her companions did nothing, deserves a greater share of the bread, if not all of it.

At least, I think so. This is a controversial assertion, however, and an understanding of the controversy can lead to a fuller understanding of distributive justice. Rawls believes that people should not be rewarded because of successful performance. He writes that

> no one deserves his place in the distribution of native endowments, any more than one deserves one's initial starting place in society. The assertion that a man deserves the superior character that enables him to make the effort to cultivate his abilities is equally problematic; for his character depends largely upon fortunate family and social circumstances for which he can claim no credit. The notion of desert seems not to apply to these cases.[17]

The philosophical basis of strict egalitarianism, equality of outcomes, is that we do not deserve a reward for meritorious behavior because we are not responsible for the traits that lead us to behave meritoriously.[18] The fact that the hen is industrious while the cat, the rat, and the pig are lazy does not mean that the hen has a just claim to more than an equal share of the bread. I think this view is mistaken.

The issue of the responsibility we have for our actions is one of the oldest to trouble our species. In religious disputation it is the question of free will: if God created us, are we entirely God's puppets, or do we have independent capacities with which we can acknowledge or deny God's sovereignty? In secular terms, it is a question of environmental and genetic influence on our lives. We develop ourselves through a complex interplay of nature and nurture. Does this mean that we have no independent agency, that our behavior is completely determined by the influences on our lives, or do we have at least some capacity to make independent choices? If the former, there is no justice in rewarding us differently because of differences in our behavior.

As a matter of empirical truth, the issue is probably unresolvable. If we are to maintain a measure of self-respect, however, we must insist that we are responsible for *some* things in our lives; if we were not, we would not be moral beings, people for whom questions of right and wrong and good and bad are relevant. This is what distinguishes real people from real hens; the former can make independent choices and are properly held accountable for them, while the latter cannot and are not. If we deny this, we deny what is most central to our humanity. Augusto Pinochet did evil and should have paid the consequences of his actions; Mother Teresa did good works and justly deserved the honors and recognition she received. Doubtless each was influenced by genetic endowments and child-rearing practices, but we cannot allow this to absolve them completely of responsibility for their lives.

Let us distinguish between personal attributes, on the one hand, and willpower, on the other. The distinction between the two is that we are not responsible for our attributes — let us say for our intellectual capacity, for our parents' influence on us, for the gifts we have been given, for our race and gender, for our basic personality. Beyond the attributes we have been awarded in the lottery of life, we have independent willpower, which we choose to use to greater or lesser degree. If we have been dealt a good hand of attributes, we can ride easily on our laurels or we can make the most of the good hand. If we have been dealt a bad hand, we can succumb to it or we can struggle to overcome it. Our attributes are important, but they are not everything.

To draw a distinction between attributes and will is to be guilty, perhaps, of overly rigid, binary thinking. We have no practical way of identifying the different influences upon our behavior.[19] Our performance in life results, no doubt, from a continuous and complex interplay of attributes and will. The distinction is theoretically important to an understanding of justice, however, even if it cannot be made empirically. We can agree with Rawls that we should not be rewarded on the basis of our attributes, for which we bear no responsibility. We do, however, deserve to be rewarded for the use of our will. Philosopher Robert C. Roberts writes,

> we are inclined to give greater credit for actions... which result from moral struggle.... Some acts are morally praised not just because they are good, but also because they are difficult.... The greater the moral obstacles (that is, contrary inclinations) a person has overcome in doing something the more his action seems to be his own *achievement,* his own *choice,* and thus to reflect credit on him as an *agent.* It seems to show that his action is *his* in a special way.[20]

In some cases, attributes dominate completely. We may think, for example, that the best place for psychopaths is a mental hospital rather than a prison, because they do not deserve to be punished for the attributes they cannot control. On the positive side, some saintly people may just have been born that way; they may never have had to work to achieve virtue, and consequently they do not deserve any particular praise. Most of us, however, struggle on a daily basis, setting our will in some tension with our inclinations.

If this is a correct account of our moral responsibility for our behavior, what are we to say about rewards? If we receive rewards and penalties solely on the basis of our behavior, no doubt we will receive some rewards and penalties that we do not deserve, because some portion of our behavior is governed by our attributes. If our rewards are completely unrelated to our behavior, we will be treated unjustly because our use of willpower will be ignored. We should therefore receive some rewards independently of our behavior and some rewards dependent upon our behavior. It is beyond our skills to devise a compensation system that separates out the contributions of attributes and will, so our rewards cannot be structured in such a way that they are perfectly deserved. Actual behavior and achievement should count, however, because we are in charge of our wills. Strict equality of outcomes is unjust.[21]

The fictional hen in our parable may not have a just claim to the entire loaf. Because she has worked and the other three have not, however, she deserves a greater share. In this tale, justice would be violated by insisting upon an equal distribution of the bread, because we conceive of the four animals as beings *who are responsible for their actions.*

We could amend the story so that the circumstances are a little different. The cat has been denied an education in bread making because of antifelinist discrimination, the rat is physically disabled, and the pig is a single mother with infant piglets. They would like to help but they cannot. In this story, we are back in the realm of unequal opportunity. The cat, the rat, and the pig are handicapped by characteristics for which they should not be penalized. They are of equal moral worth, and justice requires that they get some of the bread. The point of the amended story is to caution against assuming too easily that actual differences in outcomes are justified by differences in behavior for which the participants are responsible. Equality of opportunity is difficult to achieve.

In fact, equality of opportunity is impossible to achieve over a continuous period of time. Consider a second amended version of the story of the little red hen. This time, as in the original version, all four animals are equally capable of making bread and are not prevented from doing so. They enjoy equal opportunities, but only the hen takes advantage of those opportunities. The hen makes a loaf of bread every day, while the cat, the rat, and the pig decline to do so. The hen eats each day's loaf and refuses to share, the consequence being that she is well fed and prosperous, while the other three decline in health. The animals are all fertile, and within a year we find in the barnyard a new baby hen, cat, rat, and pig. The new hen is happy and healthy, having been well fed by her mother. The new cat, rat, and pig are malnourished. Within a short time (farm animals grow quickly), the new hen is out on her own collecting grains of wheat. When she asks her contemporaries who would like to help her make bread, they all decline, as their parents had, but for a different reason. They would like to help, but they are too weak to undertake the rigors of hard work.

In the second generation we have unequal opportunity, a severely tilted playing field. It is surely unjust, this time, for the younger hen to keep all the bread. The other animals have equal moral standing, and they were denied the opportunity to make bread as a consequence of a personal characteristic that was no fault of their own, poverty. The unequal distribution of outcomes in the first generation was justified because of the autonomous choices made by the four parents, but the unequal distribution that this led to in the second generation was unjust because it violated the principle of equal opportunity.

When we think of justice not at a moment in time, therefore, but over the generations, the assumption that equality of opportunity can be conceptually separated from equality of outcomes dissolves. Some of us are born into families that can afford to feed us bread and more, nurturing all our capacities, while others are not. Some are born into rich countries with advanced technology, while others are not. These sorts of differences make us unequal at the start.

This reasoning leads to the possibility that equality of opportunity actually *requires* equal outcomes. This possibility exists because we live our lives over a period of years, our generations overlap, and our societies continue over time. My opportunities are determined in large measure by the resources — including economic, educational, technological, and moral resources — given to me by my parents and by my society. If my parents and my society are vastly different in their access to these resources from yours, you and I will be unequal at the starting blocks. Until each person has an equal opportunity to develop his or her talents — something that cannot exist while the distribution of outcomes in the world remains unequal — we cannot be equal at the starting line.

The state of distributive justice is therefore highly unstable over time. Even if it could be achieved at some point, it would disappear within a generation. This means that a state of perfect justice would never appear in real time, except by the remotest of coincidences. One could imagine a deus ex machina intervening in the world and establishing perfect equality of opportunity, but that state could not last. Since in the real world we have no deus ex machina, and since each generation is shaped by previous overlapping generations, the unequal distribution of goods, services, and other endowments ensures that we live in a world of far from perfect justice, at all times. The second amended version of the story is egregiously misleading in beginning with a golden age, in imagining there was an earlier generation characterized by perfect equality of opportunity. There never was.

We seem to have gotten ourselves into a bit of a muddle at this point, but it is a muddle that reflects the complexity of justice in the real world. Justice requires equality of opportunity, not equality of outcomes. Equality of opportunity cannot be achieved, however, for two reasons. First, even if all the external constraints on our success could be equalized, we still would have diverse internal constraints, such as health. Second, even if equal opportunity could be achieved at a certain point in time, it would be unstable; it would contain the seeds of its own destruction. It would lead to unequal outcomes, and the unequal outcomes in turn would create unequal opportunities for the children who make up the next generation. Unequal outcomes are therefore a mark of injustice, not because it is wrong for people to receive different rewards for differences in their behavior, but because unequal outcomes in time create unequal opportunities.

It follows, therefore, that the struggle for justice will normally include reducing inequalities in outcomes. To take part in this struggle is sometimes to run the danger, however, of preventing people from receiving their just rewards. This is one of the conflicts that can arise in the search for justice; when we find ourselves dealing with real social problems, we will have to make difficult judgments. In the case before us, and thinking only, so far, in terms of the principle of equality, the hen is obliged to distribute some of the bread she has made to the other animals, at least enough to provide basic nutrition for them and their families. *preventing harm by one to another*

Freedom

The second component of social justice is freedom. As in the case of equality, we begin with this intuition, rather than derive it from something else. Who could deny that freedom is central to justice? To be unfree is to be subject to the control of someone else, someone who has more power than you, someone who has power to determine your fate. The great struggles for social justice — the revolutions and the movements for national rights, for civil rights, and for human rights — have all been centered on the achievement of freedom. For Jefferson, it was a self-evident truth that people were endowed by their creator with the right to liberty.

For libertarians, freedom is the only social virtue. Using the word "liberal" in its nineteenth-century sense as one who holds the value of freedom above all else, Milton Friedman wrote in *Capitalism and Freedom,* "As liberals, we take freedom of the individual, or perhaps the family, as our ultimate goal in judging social arrangements."[22] Not only do Friedman and other libertarians regard freedom as the preeminent social virtue, as being superior in importance to equality and everything else, they see it as necessarily being in conflict with equality. To work for equality, they hold, is to work against freedom, since this must involve taking away assets that people have justly acquired.

This section develops a contrary argument. Freedom is of central importance, but it can reach its fullest potential only in the presence of equality; the ideal state of freedom is equal freedom. Rawls is correct in holding that "each person is to have an equal right to the most extensive basic liberty compatible with a similar liberty for others."[23] To be less than equally free is to be in some respects unfree. Moreover, true freedom requires something close to equality of outcomes.

It is customary, in discussions of freedom, to distinguish between "freedoms-to" and "freedoms-from." Freedoms-to are freedoms to do various things, some of which are summarized in the First Amendment to the US Constitution, which guarantees the freedom to worship, speak, publish, assemble, and petition the government for redress of grievances. The Fourth Amendment includes the right to hold property against unreasonable seizures. Freedoms-from are different, and they are not mentioned in the Constitution. They include, according to many, the freedom from such afflictions as hunger, poverty, illiteracy, sickness, and homelessness.

The conflict between these two conceptions of freedom was, in a way, the major political conflict of the twentieth century, the capitalist powers emphasizing freedoms-to and the communists freedom-from. In the opinion of many in the communist world, freedoms-to were decadent or "bourgeois" concepts and were actually barriers to the real freedoms, which were freedoms-from. A state that gave too much emphasis to freedoms-to, they believed, thereby gave too much power to individuals, power that would be used to prevent the achievement of the freedoms-from for the majority of the people.

The conflict between the two kinds of freedom is real, but to focus only on the conflict is to miss the ways in which the two complement each other. The absence of resources prevents us from doing what we want to do in much the same way that restrictive laws do. To cite a common example: in order to publish my views, I need not only freedom of the press but also a press. Anatole France famously remarked upon "the majestic equality of the laws, which forbid rich and poor alike to sleep under the bridges."[24] The laws similarly allow rich and poor to feast on caviar, but the law is not the relevant restriction. Political philosopher Philippe Van Parijs writes, "real freedom is not only a matter of having the right to do what one might want to do, but also a matter of having the means for doing it."[25] Freedoms-to and freedoms-from are both essential to full freedom.

Freedoms come in conflict one with another in an additional, interpersonal way. I should have freedom of speech, but not freedom to shout "fire" in a crowded theater, because I would thereby impinge on the freedom of other people to be safe. In his classic 1859 essay *On Liberty,* John Stuart Mill wrote that "the only purpose for which power can be rightfully exercised over any member of a civilized community, against his will, is to prevent harm to others."[26] For a person who thinks that the only restrictions on freedom are legal or formal restrictions, the condition that A's freedom be maximized so long as it does not interfere with B's freedom will allow the state to impose only minimal constraints on people. The state is permitted only to enforce laws prohibiting murder, robbery, assault, shouting "fire" in a crowded theater, and similar infractions. For a person who thinks that real freedom is restricted also by the failure to have access to adequate resources, the conflicts between people's freedoms are more severe, and the permitted scope of the state's intervention is more extensive. Total resources are limited, so in many circumstances if I am to have more resources, in order to be able to increase the scope to do what I want, you will have fewer, and we will therefore be in a relationship of conflict.

In practice, the optimum state of freedom is difficult, perhaps impossible, to identify. The problem is much the same as the problem of identifying equal outcomes in the previous section on equality. We differ so much in what we want to do and in the barriers we face in doing those things that we have no real way of measuring and comparing the restrictions we face. We can presume, however, that access to wealth and income often helps people to reach some of their goals. It follows that, other things being equal, the goal of maximum equal freedom would be facilitated by a more egalitarian distribution of income and wealth.

Note how equality of outcomes has figured in the discussion so far. The section on equality did not begin from the assertion that justice required equal outcomes, only equal opportunity, but we were led from this position to the conclusion that unequal outcomes gravely threaten equal opportunity over the long run, and therefore also threaten justice. In thinking about freedom, we have not begun from the assertion that freedom is best defined as "freedom-from" a variety of afflictions, but we have been drawn to the conclusion that unless people are protected from poverty and other hardships, they will have difficulty exercising their freedoms to pursue their goals. It is one of the conclusions of the reasoning so far, not its starting point, that social justice is advanced by seriously reducing if not eliminating the inequalities in income and wealth that mark our societies.

This is not to say that freedom and equality are the same or that they can never come in conflict. Libertarians, as we will see in chapter 4, argue that it is impermissible for the state to take away even the smallest portion of a person's property against his will if he has acquired the property legitimately. This is an extreme interpretation of freedom and is surely incorrect, for a number of reasons, one of them being that it neglects the impact that inequality of resources has on some people's freedom.

In a less extreme version, though, this interpretation has a kernel of truth to it. Freedom implies that we have some security in our possessions and that the state is not allowed simply to confiscate what we have. Chapter 2, on capitalism, will note that private property is the heart of the capitalist system. It is more than this, however. To at least a limited extent, security in one's property is essential to freedom, whatever the social system, be it capitalist, socialist, or anything else. Taxation of some of our income and property is justified for a number of reasons — to be discussed in chapters 4 through 6 — but a state that completely confiscated all our possessions would violate our freedom. If such confiscation were necessary to bring about equality, two important components of justice, freedom and equality, would be in conflict.

The little red hen may have legitimate concerns about her freedom. She may believe that, since she made the bread, she has the right to dispose of it as she will and that an attempt to force her to give any of it away is an attack on her freedom. This extreme view is hard to maintain, but suppose there were 100 animals and the barnyard state required that the bread be shared equally, the consequence being that she had to give up 99 percent of the loaf. This would be confiscation, pure and simple, a serious infringement of her freedom.

Efficiency

Efficiency means getting the best out of the available resources. This is a virtue if resources are limited and if the demands on those resources are greater than can be met, that is, if a situation of scarcity exists. Efficiency is a criterion much used by economists in comparing economic outcomes. Since most economists are of the opinion that resources are always scarce, relative to the use that could be made of them, they think that efficiency is always a virtue.

They may not be right. Anthropologist Stuart A. Schlegel describes the world of the Teduray in the rainforest of the southern Philippines, a world in which resources are ample and the concept of scarcity is absent.[27] In such a world, efficiency is irrelevant. The Teduray's world is not our world, however. In the world in which we live, it seems that everything is scarce, in relationship to our desires. We want more goods, more leisure, more information, more conveniences, more clean air. If by chance we have enough of some things (although I like ice cream, I would tire of it after a while), we only want more of others. So efficiency matters to us.

Human beings, taken together, have an enormous sum of legitimate needs and desires, well exceeding the capacity of the earth's resources and our technology to provide them. Some of our wants are trivial or harmful, of course, and the satisfaction of them does us no good. Many people eat too much fat, for example. Even if we had a way of eliminating the trivial and harmful wants, however, and even if the world's goods were distributed more equitably than they are now, we would still live in a world of scarcity. We do not currently produce enough to provide everyone a decent, comfortable standard of living, including among other things food, clothing, housing, recreation, leisure, first-rate medical care, stimulating education, and the opportunity to travel and to investigate. Justice is the quality of getting what one deserves, and we deserve all this, and more. If social arrangements are inefficient, therefore, we suffer an injustice.

A serious problem with the pursuit of efficiency is that it can change, in ways we do not like, the distribution of resources and incomes going to individuals in the society. For example, a concentration on high-technology industries might increase the country's overall productivity but put unskilled workers at a disadvantage and lower their incomes. Two different and conflicting criteria have been developed to deal with this problem, Pareto efficiency and the difference principle. Neither, in my opinion, is fully satisfactory.

The criterion of Pareto efficiency, much used by economists, is that a situation is fully efficient, and cannot be made more efficient, if the only way one person can get more is if another person gets less.[28] A situation can be made more efficient, on the other hand, if one person can get more without reducing the amount going to anyone else. Improvements in efficiency should be made. Once a situation is fully efficient, in the Pareto sense, no further changes can be recommended on the grounds of efficiency — although changes on the grounds of equity may be called for.

The problem with Pareto efficiency is that it privileges too much the status quo. Suppose there is one slave-owner and a million exploited, malnourished slaves. If the slaves were freed and allowed to work for themselves, they would raise the country's output and their own standard of living many fold. The former slave-owner, on the other hand, would suffer a decline in fortune. The Pareto criterion would not count the freeing of the slaves and the resulting increase in production as an improvement in efficiency because of the loss to one person, and that the most favored person in the status quo. This is not a very helpful concept of efficiency. Surely we are correct in thinking that the society without slavery is more efficient than the one with.

John Rawls's difference principle is a constraint on his prescription that justice requires an equal distribution of primary social goods.[29] A difference in the possession of primary social goods is justified, Rawls claims, only if that difference has the effect of increasing the amount available to the least-favored person. In the language of game-theory strategy, it is the principle of maximin. Suppose each person has the same income, regardless of whether she works. In this circumstance, no one might think it worthwhile to work, so nothing would be produced and everyone would have an equal income of zero. In contrast, if people are allowed to keep some portion of what they earn — with the result that incomes are unequal — some people are motivated to produce, and some of what they produce goes to the lowest-income person. The justification of inequality is that it permits the lowest-standing person to be better off. This is as far as Rawls is willing to go in allowing that efficiency has a role in social justice. What matters is not the total production in a society, or the average production, or the welfare of the typical person, but *only* the well-being of the least-advantaged person.

The difference principle has a certain attractiveness, but I think it fails to give sufficient weight to our legitimate interest in making the best possible use of our scarce resources. A social or technological change may improve the well-being of millions of people while leaving the welfare of the least-fortunate person unaltered. Such a change is unjust, according to the difference principle. I think it more reasonable to say that the change improves efficiency, while at the same time it makes the distribution of income more unequal. By improving efficiency, it advances justice, while by increasing inequality it moves the society in an unjust direction. We have two criteria that conflict, and we must use our judgment in assessing the change's overall impact on justice. We should not, however, automatically presume that the change is unjust, as the difference principle does.

The little red hen improves the efficiency of the farmyard: she makes bread when there was none before, so she increases the goods available in her community. This is so whether she shares the bread with the other animals or not. In either case, the Pareto standard would judge her actions as improving efficiency, since some of the animals (perhaps just the hen) are better off, and none is worse off. The difference principle would condemn her behavior unless she gave as much as possible (up to a limit of one-quarter loaf) to each of the other three animals. According to the difference principle, the only reason she could retain more than the other three would be if this were necessary as an incentive to persuade her to make the bread in the first place. This is a strange way of thinking of the situation, however. It is clearer to think of the hen as increasing efficiency — where efficiency is a virtue — and then to ask whether efficiency conflicts with equality.

In thinking about efficiency, we should not be bound by the restrictions of either the Pareto doctrine or the difference principle. Instead, I think, we should understand efficiency as anything that improves the welfare of people in general, or a majority of the people, or the typical person. The next section will make this vague statement a little more precise. Efficiency is only one component of justice, and it can conflict with the other components.[30] It would be a mistake, however, to say that efficiency is irrelevant to justice; in a world of scarcity we deserve to have the relationships among us established in such a way that we get the best out of our limited resources.

Utilitarianism, Efficiency, and Justice

Utilitarianism, as first propounded by Jeremy Bentham, James Mill, and John Stuart Mill, has become one of the foundations of modern economics and modern ethics.[31] In economics it is partly a positive theory of human motivation: people are thought to act in such a way as to maximize their utility or the satisfaction of their preferences. It is, however, as a normative theory (a theory of what should be, not what is) that utilitarianism is relevant to justice.

Utilitarianism as a normative or ethical theory holds that the best actions are those that create the greatest total amount of happiness or utility. A stylized example can show how utilitarianism works. Suppose the happiness of one person can be compared to the happiness of another; suppose there are two people in the world; and suppose there are two actions under consideration, actions that are expected to have different outcomes. The first action will produce an outcome in which you and I each have two units of happiness, while the second action will produce one unit of happiness for you and ten for me. The first action leads to four total units of happiness in the world and the second to eleven. Hence utilitarians prefer the second action, in spite of the fact that your happiness has fallen in half and you are now far behind me.

This example shows that utilitarianism is a narrower theory of ethics or justice than the approach developed in this chapter. All that matters to utilitarians is the total amount of happiness, not its distribution. As Rawls says, utilitarianism "does not take seriously the distinction between persons."[32] Utilitarianism is therefore only a theory of efficiency, with nothing independent to say about equality or freedom. Equality and freedom are part of the utilitarian calculus only if they are part of individuals' preferences.

Utilitarianism is, however, a good basis for thinking about efficiency. What is to be maximized, according to the utilitarians, is not income, wealth, loaves of bread, or any particular material thing, but rather utility — defined sometimes as happiness but more generally as preferences. The most efficient outcome is the one that gives us the most of what we want. We may want riches, we may want solitude, we may want self-knowledge, we may want excitement, we may want love, we may want to be productive: whatever it is, the utilitarian criterion is that together as a group we should maximize the achievement of our preferences. Efficiency has to do with getting the best out of our limited resources, best in terms of what we most value.

It must be said that with two added assumptions, utilitarianism has a bias toward equality of outcomes. Suppose each person's capacity for happiness is the same (the assumption of identical utility functions), and suppose further that for each person the marginal utility of income declines. In other words, your first dollar of income gives you an enormous amount of happiness, the second a lot but less than the first, the third quite a bit but less than the second, and so forth. Begin with a situation in which I am rich and you are poor. If the state taxes a dollar away from me and gives it to you, the sum total of happiness in the society will increase. This follows from the fact that I have so many total dollars that the loss of one does not reduce my utility by much if anything, while you are so poor that the addition of one dollar improves your well-being a lot. The transfers should not stop with just one dollar; they should continue until our incomes are equal, because only at that point will our marginal utilities of a dollar be the same — and when they are the same the sum of human happiness cannot be increased by further transfers.[33]

In some circumstances a utilitarian may favor equality, therefore, but note that the conditions that would lead him in this direction are restrictive. Each person's capacity for happiness must be identical. We know this is not so in the real world; people's capacities for happiness, as for everything else, differ a great deal. Since this is the case, utilitarianism must call for those fortunate people with a well-developed capacity for happiness to be given more than their less fortunate companions. Hence utilitarianism is a defensible basis for understanding efficiency, but not equality.

Efficiency — getting the best out of the available resources — is a component of justice, and utilitarianism is a good way of conceiving of efficiency. Efficiency is only one component of justice, however, and it may conflict with the others.

Who Must Provide Justice?

Justice is what we deserve; we have a right to it. Does it follow that we must also provide justice? Must we give people what they deserve? Suppose you and I are unequal at the starting line of life because you have fewer resources than I do. You deserve to be equal with me. Does it follow from this that I must give some of my resources to you, so that you have more than you had and I have less and we become equal?

It is a difficult question, one that will occupy us throughout the book, particularly in part III. We will find situations in which the correct answer is not entirely clear. Here it is enough to argue that the advantaged have a prima facie obligation to provide justice to the disadvantaged. It is an obligation that may be overridden in some circumstances, but it must be taken seriously. Many reasons can be cited in support of the obligation. This section considers three: rectification, self-interest, and common humanity. It argues that the first two are only partially satisfactory and that the third is transcendent.

Rectification

We saw at the beginning of this chapter that rectification, as a principle of justice, can be traced back to Aristotle. A person who has benefited from the unjust treatment or the unjust situation of another person may owe that person money, goods, honor, or something else of value.[34]

Consider three circumstances. First is the case in which you have less than me because I have exploited you. Perhaps I have stolen from you. In this case, I must repair the damage by making you equal, and in addition I may face punitive damages. Second is the case in which I am not responsible for your lack of fortune, but still you have contributed to my good fortune. Perhaps you are a poor farm laborer whose low wages permit me to enjoy cheap food. In this case, I should contribute to your welfare as a matter of just payment for the good fortune I enjoy. Third is the case in which I have not exploited you, nor have you contributed to my good fortune, but rather either one or both of these facts were true about people in a previous generation, perhaps our respective parents. As a consequence of their interaction, I have chanced into a position of good fortune and you have chanced into bad. If you and I owe our unequal situation to the unjust relationship of others, I do not deserve my fortune and should contribute to yours.

Many situations fall naturally into these categories. Whites may owe African Americans compensation because of the history of slavery. Rich countries may owe poor countries foreign aid because of the history of imperialism. Distributive justice is not exactly the same as criminal justice, however, and exclusive reliance upon the principle of rectification will sometimes lead us astray when we are thinking about distributive justice. Rectification calls for justice to be given not because of the relative status of different people but because of wrongs that have been committed.[35] To understand the problems this can lead to, think of the following cases.

First, a third world colony was terribly exploited by an imperial power, but since independence it has succeeded in raising the standard of living of its people to one of the highest in the world, while the former imperial power has slipped into a relatively low-income category. Rectification would call for the former imperialist to transfer resources to the former colony, but this would make no sense in terms of their current status. The transfer of funds would contribute to inequality in the world, not equality.

Second, consider a group of people who have emerged from a completely isolated, traditional life in a rainforest, because their habitat was destroyed by an earthquake. They are ill equipped to survive in the modern world in which they now live. No one living or dead caused them harm, yet they are destitute and in danger of starvation. If we stick to the principle of rectification, no one owes them anything, yet most people would think they are owed some help.

Rectification is a basic principle of criminal and civil justice, but criminal justice is not the same as distributive or social justice, the subject of this book. One of the foundations of social justice, I have argued, is equality. An important cause of inequality is often that the fortunate have treated or are treating the unfortunate improperly. In such cases, rectification is a good motive for providing social justice. When improper treatment is not the cause of social inequality, however, rectification is irrelevant to the obligation to provide justice.

Self-Interest

Perhaps I owe you justice because I will benefit from improving your lot in life. If you are equal at the starting blocks with me, there is less chance that you will contaminate me with your infectious diseases, that you will rob me or in other ways reduce my quality of life. If you have a higher income, you will be able to buy some of the goods I produce.

In some sense, we all benefit from living in a world that is characterized by justice rather than injustice, so this sort of reasoning carries some weight. Self-interest is not the same as morality, however, and it is a weak foundation on which to base justice. What if I am rich and you are poor, and I honestly can see no benefit to myself from transferring some of my resources to you? If self-interest is the only basis for providing justice, you are out of luck.[36] Often we will provide justice as a matter of self-interest, but we must go beyond self-interest.

Common Humanity

What about cases in which my good fortune is unconnected to your lack of fortune and in which I can discern no benefit to myself from transferring any of my fortune to you? Do I nevertheless have an obligation to do so? I believe I do, and the reason is applicable whenever injustice exists.

The reason has to do with the community of human beings. We are related to each other. Our community may be completely obvious in some cases, less so in others. When I walk down the main street of my town and see homeless people shivering in the winter cold, I am in no doubt of this. We share the same actual space, the same sidewalk. The homeless person is part of my visual universe, as I am of hers. When she asks me for change we have a human connection; however

I respond to her, I cannot avoid the fact that we have a relationship. I do not ever see most of the world's unfortunate, but we inhabit the same planet and we respond to many of the same impersonal forces. The economy in which we are both entwined is global in scope; it is the same economy, bound by ties of trade and investment. The media bring me images of people throughout my country and around the world. We are all part of the same community, and we are responsible for our community. This is the most fundamental basis of our obligation to provide justice.

It is not a new idea. In 1624, John Donne wrote:

> No man is an island, entire of itself; every man is a piece of the Continent, a part of the Main. If a Clod be washed away by the sea, Europe is the less, as well as if a Promontory were, as well as if a Manor of thy friends or of thine own were. Any man's death diminishes me, because I am involved in Mankind. And therefore never send to know for whom the bell tolls. It tolls for thee.[37]

The little red hen cannot be indifferent to the fate of the cat, the rat, and the pig. She is connected to them.

Notes

1. Justinian, *Institutes*, trans. Thomas Collett Sandars (London: Longmans, Green and Co., 1922).

2. Aristotle, *The Nichomachean Ethics*, trans. David Ross, rev. J. L. Ackrill and J. O. Urmson (Oxford: Oxford University Press, 1980), book 5.

3. John Rawls, *A Theory of Justice* (Cambridge, Mass.: Harvard University Press, 1971), 3.

4. For introductions to modern theories of justice, see James P. Sterba, "Recent Work on Alternative Conceptions of Justice," *American Philosophical Quarterly* 23 (1986): 1–22; Tom Campbell, *Justice* (London: Macmillan Education, 1988); and Sirkku Hellsten, "Theories of Distributive Justice," in *Encyclopedia of Applied Ethics* (San Diego: Academic Press, 1998), 1:815–28.

5. W. D. Ross, *The Right and the Good* (London: Oxford University Press, 1930).

6. Among the proponents of moral relativism, see Gilbert Harman, "Moral Relativism Defended," *Philosophical Review* 84 (1975): 3–22; and David B. Wong, *Moral Relativity* (Berkeley: University of California Press, 1984). For critiques of moral relativism, see Bernard Williams, *Morality: An Introduction to Ethics* (New York: Harper and Row, 1972), 13–39; and James Rachels, *The Elements of Moral Philosophy* (Philadelphia: Temple University Press, 1986), chapter 2. The subject is surveyed in John Hospers, *Human Conduct: An Introduction to the Problems of Ethics* (New York: Harcourt, Brace and World,

1961), 577–94; and in J. Carl Ficarrotta, "Moral Relativism," in *Encyclopedia of Applied Ethics*, 3:275–88.

7. For a brief survey of ways in which justice is viewed in different cultures, see Laura Nader and Andree Sursock, "Anthropology and Justice," in *Justice: Views from the Social Sciences*, ed. Ronald L. Cohen (New York: Plenum Press, 1986), 205–33.

8. G. E. Moore, *Principia Ethica* (Cambridge: Cambridge University Press, 1903), chapter 1.

9. Rawls, *A Theory of Justice*.

10. For a short survey and critique of this strategy, see Wong, *Moral Relativity*, chapter 13.

11. Jacobus tenBroek, *Equal under the Law* (New York: Collier, 1969), 19.

12. Bruce Ackerman, *Social Justice in the Liberal State* (New Haven, Conn.: Yale University Press, 1980), 19.

13. John E. Roemer, *Theories of Distributive Justice* (Cambridge, Mass.: Harvard University Press, 1996).

14. Amartya Sen, *Inequality Reexamined* (Cambridge, Mass.: Harvard University Press, 1992), 1.

15. For surveys of the literature on these concepts, see Daniel M. Hausman and Michael S. McPherson, "Taking Ethics Seriously: Economics and Contemporary Moral Philosophy," *Journal of Economic Literature* 31 (1993): 671–731; Daniel M. Hausman and Michael S. McPherson, *Economic Analysis and Moral Philosophy* (New York: Cambridge University Press, 1996); and Louis Putterman, John E. Roemer, and Joaquim Silvestre, "Does Egalitarianism Have a Future?" *Journal of Economic Literature* 36 (1998): 861–902.

16. For a survey of this subject, see Roemer, *Theories of Distributive Justice*.

17. Rawls, *A Theory of Justice*, 104.

18. The relationship of responsibility and reward has been studied intensively. In addition to Rawls, *A Theory of Justice*, see Ronald Dworkin, "What Is Equality? Part 1: Equality of Welfare" and "Part 2: Equality of Resources," *Philosophy and Public Affairs* 10 (1981): 185–246 and 283–345; Thomas Scanlon, "Equality of Resources and Equality of Welfare: A Forced Marriage?" *Ethics* 97 (1986): 111–18; R. Arneson, "Liberalism, Distributive Subjectivism, and Equal Opportunity for Welfare," *Philosophy and Public Affairs* 19 (1990): 159–94; G. A. Cohen, *Self-Ownership, Freedom, and Equality* (Cambridge: Cambridge University Press, 1995); and Roemer, *Theories of Distributive Justice*.

19. Andrew Levine argues that it is so difficult to identify and reward autonomous choices that the idea of doing so is nonoperational and meaningless. See his "Rewarding Effort," *Journal of Political Philosophy* 7 (1999): 404–18.

20. Robert C. Roberts, "Will Power and the Virtues," *Philosophical Review* 93 (1984): 227–47.

21. This argument against equal outcomes and for equal opportunity is related to, but somewhat different from, Roemer's argument: "Were equality of welfare the goal rather than equality of opportunity for welfare, then society would be mandated to provide huge resource endowments to those who adopt terribly expensive and unrealistic goals.... Calling for equality of opportunity for welfare, on the other hand, puts some responsibility on [one] for choosing

welfare inducing goals that are reasonable" (John E. Roemer, *A Future for Socialism* [Cambridge, Mass.: Harvard University Press, 1994], 12). For a critique of Roemer, see Richard J. Arneson, "What Do Socialists Want?" in John E. Roemer, *Equal Shares: Making Market Socialism Work,* ed. Erik Olin Wright (London: Verso, 1996), 209–30.

22. Milton Friedman, *Capitalism and Freedom* (Chicago: University of Chicago Press, 1962), 12. The phrase "or perhaps the family" is not a minor or innocent addition to this sentence. Much feminist scholarship is directed at the family as an institution of oppression for many, perhaps most, women. To the extent that Friedman removes relationships among individuals within families from his purview, he appears to acquiesce in a great deal of gender discrimination. For a sampling of the literature on this subject, see Virginia Held, *Feminist Morality: Transforming Culture, Society, and Politics* (Chicago: University of Chicago Press, 1993); and Carole Ulanowsky, "The Family," in *Encyclopedia of Applied Ethics,* 2:233–47.

23. Rawls, *A Theory of Justice,* 60.

24. Anatole France, *The Red Lily,* trans. Frederic Chapman (London: Bodley Head, 1921), 95.

25. Philippe Van Parijs, *Real Freedom for All: What (If Anything) Can Justify Capitalism?* (Oxford: Clarendon Press, 1995), 4.

26. John Stuart Mill, *On Liberty,* ed. Currin V. Shields (New York: Liberal Arts Press of New York, 1956), 13.

27. Stuart A. Schlegel, *Wisdom from a Rainforest: The Spiritual Journey of an Anthropologist* (Athens: University of Georgia Press, 1998).

28. The doctrine, which became the foundation of twentieth-century welfare economics, was first propounded in Vilfredo Pareto, *Cours d'économie politique a l'Université de Lausanne* (Lausanne: Rouge, 1896–97).

29. Rawls, *A Theory of Justice.*

30. An influential theory of justice sometimes known as "economic analysis of law" holds that efficiency is the only criterion of justice and therefore cannot come into conflict with other criteria. This, it seems to me, is untenable, since it ignores the valid intuition that we deserve both equal treatment and liberty. See Richard A. Posner, *The Economics of Justice* (Cambridge, Mass.: Harvard University Press, 1981).

31. The classic statement, published first in 1861, is John Stuart Mill, *Utilitarianism,* ed. Oskar Priest (New York: Macmillan Publishing Co., 1957).

32. Rawls, *A Theory of Justice,* 27.

33. Those who are mathematically inclined will recognize this paragraph as describing the first-order condition for a maximum in calculus.

34. On the distinction between rectification and compensation, see Andrew Valls, "The Libertarian Case for Affirmative Action," *Social Theory and Practice* 25 (1999): 299–323.

35. Some philosophers take the view, contrary to the position I have argued, that distributive justice is similar to criminal justice, consisting of the righting of past wrongs. Robert Nozick's libertarian views — in *Anarchy, State, and Utopia* (New York: Basic Books, 1974) — will be considered in chapter 4. See

also Brian Barry, *Democracy, Power, and Justice: Essays in Political Theory* (Oxford: Clarendon Press, 1989), chapter 16.

36. I must acknowledge here the influence on me of my freshman philosophy professor at Queen's University in Kingston, Ontario, A. R. C. Duncan, who lectured for an hour in 1960 on the moral vacuousness of the phrase "honesty is the best policy."

37. From John Donne, *Devotions upon Emergent Occasions*, in *Complete Poetry and Selected Prose*, ed. John Hayward (London: Nonesuch Press, 1967), meditation 27 (1624), p. 538.

Chapter 2

CAPITALISM

The Structure of Capitalism

SINCE THE SEARCH for social justice is constrained by capitalism, we need to understand its structure. This is a difficult undertaking, since capitalism is anything but neat and well defined. It has evolved over centuries in different parts of the world, attended often by enormous conflict. Karl Marx was right in holding that capitalism requires constant change:

> The bourgeoisie cannot exist without constantly revolutionizing the instruments of production, and thereby the relations of production, and with them the whole relations of society.... Constant revolutionizing of production, uninterrupted disturbance of all social conditions, everlasting uncertainty and agitation distinguish the bourgeois epoch from all earlier ones.[1]

In spite of this constant change, capitalism has at least eight continuing characteristics. It has not abandoned them nor, I think, will it do so. The search for justice must proceed within these constraints:

- Most property, including most of the means of production, is privately owned.

- Economic activity is organized on a global scale.

- The ratio of financial to real assets is higher than in other systems.

- Most people earn their living by working for wages or a salary.

- Most goods and services are distributed by being bought and sold in impersonal markets.

- Income and wealth are unevenly distributed, with a gap between rich and poor.

30

- Over time the economy expands, but with periods of instability and decline.

- Governments at the national, state, and local levels are active participants in the economy.

Private Ownership of Property

The origin and justification of private property are matters of ideological dispute. To seventeenth-century English philosopher John Locke, private property was a natural right.[2] To nineteenth-century French philosopher Pierre Joseph Proudhon, property was theft.[3] What is not in dispute is that private property is the heart of capitalism.

This is not to say that every last piece of property is owned privately. Governments typically own parklands and wildernesses, buildings and monuments, highways, airports and harbors, and military assets. Some types of assets are found sometimes in one sector, sometimes in the other. Electrical power generation is typically in the private sector, for example, but sometimes in the public. Prisons are typically in the public sector, but sometimes in the private. Schools are found in both. Most of the productive economic assets, however — the farmland, the factories, the machinery, the communications links — are held privately. "Privately" does not always mean "individually." Industrial assets are typically owned by large groups of people, through their direct or indirect ownership of stocks, but nevertheless the assets are owned by people in their private capacity, not by the government.

It is helpful to distinguish between property in consumption and property in production. The former consists of such assets as homes, automobiles, and appliances, the latter of plant, equipment, and other assets that are used in the production of goods and services. Both are owned privately in capitalism, but it is the private ownership of productive assets that defines capitalism and creates its principal class division: the capitalist class, which owns the productive assets, and the working class, which does not own productive capital and is employed by the capitalists.

Global Scope

The capitalist system has always been international in scope. Immanuel Wallerstein showed that, from the beginning of the European commercial revolution in the sixteenth century, the core capitalist areas traded for food with peripheral areas, at first in southern and western Europe and later in the regions that became the third world.[4] Most of the peripheral areas gained little from the new capitalist system, but they were part of it.

Capitalism was the driving force behind the great European empires from the sixteenth century through the first part of the twentieth century. The formal and informal control that the Europeans exerted over most of the rest of the world went hand in hand with the development of trade routes. International trade provided cheap food for the new industrial labor forces and also the raw materials for the new factories. Without access to these cheap sources, capitalism might never have succeeded or might have grown only on a limited scale. Accompanying international trade, administration, and settlement was vast international investment. Huge sums were sent to all corners of the world to build the mines and plantations, the harbors and the railroads. The remarkable railroad system in the United States was financed in the nineteenth century almost entirely by money borrowed in London.

Globalization is therefore not a new phenomenon; it has been a central part of capitalism since the beginning. It did, however, intensify in the latter part of the twentieth century. The depression and the Second World War had brought with them a certain economic isolation for most countries, as traditional trade routes and investment channels were disrupted. These were carefully rebuilt after the war, with the help of new international institutions like the International Monetary Fund, the World Bank, and the General Agreement on Tariffs and Trade, all founded for the purpose of reestablishing the international market capitalist system and permitting it to grow to new heights. With the new wealth of the postwar era came massive new foreign investments, some of them connected to the quickly growing multinational corporations. The interconnectedness of the system was demonstrated with sometimes terrifying results in the 1980s and 1990s as financial crises in parts of Latin America and Asia spread rapidly to other regions and deepened into full economic crises that shattered living standards.

Policymakers at both the national and international levels have struggled with the question of how best to control the global sweep of economic affairs. The current fashion — getting out of the way of international markets and letting them pursue their own course — may not last. The fact of globalization, however — the interconnectedness of most of the world — is here to stay, and this fact constrains attempts to achieve social justice.

Financial Assets

In a capitalist economy, people typically own the productive assets in-directly, not directly. Rather than own a company outright, they hold stock certificates, which represent an ownership share in the company, or they own bonds, which represent a debt of the company. The companies that are owned directly tend to be small; with few exceptions, the great industrial enterprises of a mature capitalist economy are owned by their stockholders.

When thinking about a country's wealth, therefore, one should distinguish between financial wealth and real wealth. Financial wealth is the value of pieces of paper like stocks, bonds, and dollars, while real wealth is the value of such tangible assets as plant, equipment, highways, and inventory, as well as knowledge and technology. Almost all financial wealth represents an asset to some people and a liability to others. For example, if my company sells a bond to you, the bond is your asset and my liability: it represents what you own and what I owe. Since bonds, stocks, and other similar pieces of paper are both assets and liabilities, they do not add to the net wealth of a country. The true wealth of a country consists only of its real assets.

John G. Gurley and E. S. Shaw demonstrated that in capitalist economies over time, financial assets typically grow faster than real assets or national product.[5] They estimated, for example, that financial assets — the sum total of stocks, bonds, and the liabilities of financial institutions — were about one-half the level of real national wealth in the early 1880s in the United States, rising to about twice the level of real wealth in the early 1960s.

Reliance on finance is a mark of a capitalist economy. Gurley and Shaw showed that socialist economies had a much lower ratio of financial to real assets. Finance represents a separation between savers and investors. The people who engage in enterprises are not the people who provide the funds for them. When capitalist firms expand and build up their capital stock, they fund some of the expansion from their own profits, or "retained earnings." These are seldom sufficient, however, so the firms turn to outside sources, by issuing bonds or stocks.

Among the many consequences of the growth of finance in a capitalist economy, the one most important for our inquiry is the increasing mobility of capital. Fixed assets are hard to move. A steel mill in Gary, Indiana, is not going anywhere. Over time it may depreciate and even eventually disappear, and its owners may decide to rebuild elsewhere, but this is a process that occurs over decades. Financial wealth, on the other hand, can be disposed of — bought, sold, and moved — almost instantaneously. National financial crises are typically associated with and even caused by the rapid movement of liquid, or easily transferable, capital. With a simple computer command, billions of dollars of financial assets can be switched from one institution to another and from one country to another. These days, the international movement of financial capital vastly exceeds in dollar amount the volume of international trade in real goods and services.

This mobility of capital restricts the ability of governments to pursue their own economic policies. A government of a low-income country that wanted to reduce foreign imports by raising tariff rates might find that it had thereby lost the confidence of foreign investors, who react by moving their funds out of the country's financial assets. The value of the local currency plunges and a financial crisis erupts, a crisis that can be resolved only when the country opens its trade to international markets once more. Financial markets exert a stern discipline.

Wage Labor

The classic definition of capitalism is that it is a system of wage labor. The workers do not own the land, the tools, and the factories; these are owned by the capitalists. Production requires labor along with capital, however. Capitalists pay wages or a salary to workers, in return for the temporary use of their labor.

Not every worker in a capitalist economy is an employee. Small businesses are operated by sole proprietors, partners, or franchise owners — people who are in business for themselves. Writers and artists are sometimes self-supporting. The great majority of the labor force in economically advanced capitalist countries, however — and an increasing proportion in poor countries — are employees of firms and organizations.

Even when wages are well above the subsistence level, the wage relationship leads to dependency of the worker upon the employer. Of course other forms of labor organization create their own forms of dependency; no one could argue that serfs and sharecroppers are free agents. Even self-employed farmers are dependent to a large extent — upon their suppliers, their bankers, their markets, and the unpredictable variations in weather. Moreover, wageworkers are not completely dependent; in a free labor market they are able to quit their jobs and look for others. Still, in the capitalist labor market, the wageworker is dependent to a large extent on his or her employer. The level of compensation, the job duties, and the conditions of employment are all set by the employer. The most fundamental dependency in the wage-labor system is that the worker relies on the employer for a job. The job can disappear and the worker can be unemployed.

The relationship between employer and employee is so uneven in relative power that both workers and governments have needed to do a great deal to rectify the balance. Workers formed labor unions, initially over the total opposition of employers and often at serious risk to themselves, in order to bargain collectively, rather than individually, with employers over wages and conditions of work. At the urging of workers, governments have imposed many constraints on the employer-worker relationship, including minimum-wage and maximum-hour laws, requirements to bargain collectively in good faith, occupational safety measures, and many other provisions. Still, the constraints are imperfect, and they are often in danger of dissolving in the face of unregulated international competition. They also weaken as companies turn increasingly to temporary employees.

In other words, the wage-labor relationship is subject to continuous contention and bargaining in the capitalist system. The fact of wage labor, however, the fact that most people work for an employer in return for wages or a salary, is a given.

The Market

In capitalist societies, most goods and services are distributed in markets, where they are bought and sold for a price. Not everything is distributed through markets. Most goods and services produced by governments — schooling, military protection, highways, and other things — are funded by tax revenues and simply allocated to people, outside the market. A lot of distribution in the private sector occurs outside markets as well, for example within families and within companies. Economic relationships between producers and customers that occur outside individual firms, outside families, and outside the government are generally mediated by the market, however.

Some people claim that the market is the defining feature of capitalism,[6] but this is going too far. Most noncapitalist economic systems have made extensive use of the market. Ancient Greece and Rome — both slave, not capitalist, economies — had thriving markets. Still, while some noncapitalist societies had markets, all capitalist societies depend upon them as the principal mechanism for economic distribution. While markets do not necessarily imply capitalism, capitalism implies markets.

The Rich and the Poor

Every capitalist society is marked by a wide range of incomes and an even wider range of wealth. This is a continuous subject of political and ethical discussion, and virtually every capitalist state takes some measures to modify the distribution that would result from the purely unregulated operation of the market. Public policy may change the array of incomes, but it cannot alter the fact that in a capitalist system some people are rewarded much more generously than other people.

The reason for this is that incomes are generated in a wide variety of unregulated ways in capitalism. The neoclassical theory of marginal-productivity pricing tells us that workers of a certain type will be paid just as much as the last worker hired contributes to the revenue of the firm. To the extent that this theory represents reality, more productive workers will be paid more than less productive workers, and also workers in labor markets where workers are scarce will earn more than workers where the supply of labor is plentiful. Since both skills and relative supplies vary widely, so do earnings. The predictions of marginal productivity are probably violated in many, perhaps most, cases. Earnings may be affected not just by productivity but by traditions, by discrimination, by longevity on the job, by union-management bargaining, by political influence, by family connections, and by many other factors. Moreover, the distribution of wages and salaries is only part of the overall distribution of income, and likely the most equitable part. At the top end of the income stream, many of the rich enjoy income from investments — from stocks, bonds, and other financial instruments — and also from family connections and inheritances. At the bottom end, many of the poor and the near-poor are not even in the labor force — the sick, the disabled, the mothers with dependent children, and others. The capitalist economy, left unregulated, would provide many of these people with nothing, so ways have been found to keep them from starvation, but often not much more.

We know of no capitalist system that has not had a major gap in incomes. In fact we know of few social systems of any sort that have not had some sort of economic inequalities. On the whole, though, income distribution was more uneven in capitalism than in socialism, at least during the 1970s and 1980s when a fair number of socialist systems still existed and we had comparative data. As countries moved from socialism to capitalism, they usually paid the price of increasingly unequal incomes. Part II considers how large the gap should be and what can be done to modify the income distribution of a capitalist economy — but whatever is done, as those chapters show, a substantial gap will remain.

Uneven Expansion

[handwritten: because of born abilities]

The capitalist economy expands over time, but the expansion is not steady; it proceeds in fits and starts, with sometimes a backward move. Over time, however, the economic trajectory is inexorable: more and more and more.

From its modest beginnings in Europe, capitalism spread around the world, and it raised the level of production to unheard-of heights in many places. It permitted a population explosion, providing food and consumer goods for many more people than the world held at the start of the capitalist era. Each year, most capitalist economies still expand faster than their populations grow. In the United States in recent decades, for example, production has risen at a rate of about 3 percent a year, while the population has grown at just over 1 percent, leaving roughly a 2 percent increase in output per person.

This expansion is normal and expected. A year of zero growth is counted as an economic failure in capitalist economies. From time to time output does fail to grow or even falls. The world as a whole sustained a catastrophic fall in production in the 1930s, and since that time individual areas have experienced depressions. Still, the world has never experienced a capitalist economy that was permanently stagnant. Capitalism, as many have observed, is an engine of growth.

[handwritten margin note: Good not Bad]

Capitalism has to grow because of the competition between firms: most firms are constantly in danger of losing market share to rivals. They must do everything they can to improve their products and attract more customers; if they fail to do this they are likely to find themselves defeated or devoured by firms that are more aggressive. One consequence is that many firms invest heavily in research and development of improved products. In addition, governments in most capitalist countries support basic scientific research as well as applied technological research. Technology is constantly improving, therefore, spawning new products and improved products and allowing more output to be produced with cheaper and fewer inputs.

Some critics have argued that it would be best, for ecological reasons, if the American and other highly productive economies approached a steady state, or zero economic growth.[7] It is hard to see how this could happen in an actual capitalist economy. Zero economic growth would imply very low levels of investment in new plant, equipment, and technology, just enough investment to replace the depreciated capital stock and no more. A low level of investment, however, would reduce the level of aggregate demand in the economy and send it into a downward spiral. As long as capitalist firms are free to operate and seek profits, they will never allow this to happen over a long period of time, because they can improve their profitability by investing and seeking a higher market share.

This brings us face-to-face with one of the most serious indictments against capitalism. The earth, which is fixed in size and resources, may not be able to sustain a constantly growing economy. In the long run, economic expansion is likely to come up against rigid limits. If so, it will mean the end of capitalism and its conversion to a more centrally managed system. There is no evidence that this will happen soon, however.

Just as inevitable as capitalism's growth is the unevenness of that growth. Capitalist economies know periods of surging advancement as well as periods of stagnation and decline. Economists and policymakers have devoted a lot of energy to constraining the wildness of the capitalist ride, to tempering the booms and buoying up the depressions. We understand now that governments can influence the stability of a capitalist economy, but they cannot permanently insulate it from ups and downs. The reason is that capitalism is a global, decentralized system. It consists of millions of people making decisions that are uncoordinated but that affect each other. To a large extent, perhaps even miraculously, the market can mold these separate decisions into a smoothly running whole, but it cannot prevent every catastrophe.

Government Participation

Every capitalist system depends in a major way upon government involvement in the economy. It is a serious misunderstanding of capitalism to think that it consists of a private sector alone or that it stands in opposition to government. Capitalist firms may oppose particular government policies, but they depend for their well-being in large measure upon the government.

There are different ways to understand the relationship of governments to the private sector in capitalist countries. For Marx, the government was an extension of the ruling capitalist class: "The executive of the modern State is but a committee for managing the common affairs of the whole bourgeoisie."[8] For liberal economists and social scientists, the state is a means by which the society as a whole can compensate for the lapses and injustices generated by private actions and can provide public goods. Thus, for example, the social system requires trained, educated people, and the private market cannot provide education in efficient, equitable ways to all the people, so the state steps in and provides it. Similar arguments justify the state's provision of military protection and of highways. Governments are needed to change the distribution of incomes that would be generated by a purely private economy and to stabilize its rough business cycles.[9] John Kenneth Galbraith saw the state as a "countervailing power," a strong institution that is set up to counter the strength of massive capitalist firms, not to stymie them but to keep their impulses under a certain check, so as to promote the benefit of the people as a whole.[10] In contrast, the tradition of public-choice economics sees politicians and bureaucrats inside government structures as self-seeking utility maximizers, attempting to influence matters so as to benefit themselves.[11] Whatever the reasons for government participation in the capitalist economy, the fact of it is clear. In the United States, governments at all levels are responsible for almost one-third of the country's output, and government regulations influence the way in which the remaining two-thirds is produced.

Libertarians argue that the state should be kept to a minimum, that its only legitimate function is to enforce contracts and perhaps to provide military protection.[12] This is an arguable position, but it bears no relationship to any successful capitalist society, all of which have much more intrusive, comprehensive governments than the libertarians would prefer. The impracticality of the libertarian position is shown dramatically by the experience of Russia in the 1990s, a country that came pretty close to attempting the libertarian program. It abolished its communist economic organization abruptly and attempted to turn to the market, with almost none of the public institutional controls that mark capitalism in other countries. Without those controls, the market quickly turned to criminal activities, and by most accounts the Russian economy came to be dominated by Mafia-like groups. No one could claim that the Russian economy was a model of capitalism after the demise of communism in 1991.

These are the essential characteristics of capitalism: private ownership, global scope, finance, wage labor, decentralized markets, unequal income distribution, unstable growth, and government participation. None of them is a rigid characteristic. Each has assumed different forms throughout the history of capitalism, and each will certainly be stressed and reshaped in the future, as social forces change. They can be bent quite far in some cases, but they cannot be broken as long as capitalism survives.

Is Capitalism Just?

Capitalism left to its own devices fails to produce social justice. It does not give us equality, freedom, or efficiency. It produces inequalities of both opportunities and outcomes. It expands the freedom of some people at the expense of others. It produces economic growth, but erratically. Each of the eight defining characteristics of capitalism presents obstacles to the achievement of social justice.

Private property. Since the ownership of property is for the most part in private hands, it is inherently unequal. Some own while others do not, while among the owners, some have a lot and others little. Consequently some are freer to pursue their goals than others. The institution of private property makes the achievement of equality, of either opportunity or results, impossible.

Globalization. The global scope of capitalism stands in contrast to the national scope of political control. Within countries, governments have made some progress in their attempts to tame the worst excesses of capitalist firms. No transnational government exists that can do the same on a global scale, so globally the injustices are greater than nationally.

Finance. Since capital is increasingly financial in form, it is increasingly mobile throughout the world. It can escape the attempts of national public entities to constrain its actions. Regulating capital is like squeezing a balloon. You can get it under control in one place, only to discover that it is pursuing its own ways in another.

Wage labor. The institution of wage labor puts workers at a disadvantage to the owners of capital, in terms of both freedom and equality, a disadvantage that can be partially but not entirely countered by labor organization and by government regulation.

The market. The market parcels out its rewards according to many forces, including but not confined to the pressures of supply and demand, forces that often have little to do with desert.

Income distribution. The unequal distribution of incomes, caused partly but not entirely by the system of wage labor, is both a manifestation of injustice and also a cause of further injustice since it precludes equality of opportunity.

Unstable growth. Economic growth increases the options available to people in the short run but may cause catastrophic ecological imbalances in the long run. The unevenness of the growth produces major social dislocations and inequities.

Government intervention. Democratic governments are the best source of power to face capitalist power and mold it in ways that can enhance rather than diminish justice, but capitalist power typically breaks through the boundaries of the political sphere, exerting influence that diminishes the power of democracy.

These themes will all be developed in greater detail in later chapters. The next section briefly considers the opposite point of view, the argument that capitalism promotes justice. It has been made by many people, never more forcefully than by Milton Friedman in *Capitalism and Freedom.*

Friedman's Defense of Capitalism

For Friedman, the only social goal is freedom, not equality.[13] Capitalism produces individual freedom in the economic sphere, he argues, and it also is a necessary (although not sufficient) condition for political freedom, that is to say, democracy.

Capitalism creates individual freedom, according to Friedman, because it decentralizes economic power. In socialism, fascism, or other noncapitalist forms of social organization, economic decisions are made centrally, by the state or by a small group of people. Because ordinary people do not own or control property, they lack the freedom to pursue their own goals. They are completely subject to the whims of the people who control the resources. In a system of decentralized markets with private ownership of property, on the other hand, people are free to do what they want. They can enter into any market they want or withdraw from it, since exchange in free markets is voluntary. They engage in market transactions, therefore, only to the extent that they believe they will benefit from those transactions.

Capitalism is a necessary condition for political freedom, Friedman maintains. In a society in which resources are controlled centrally by the state, the state will have no interest in providing resources to dissident political groups that wish to challenge those who are in control. Under capitalism, however, since the state does not control all the resources, diverse political groups are free to find their support where they will and communicate with their fellow citizens in an attempt to persuade them to their point of view. Friedman makes much of the fact that Marx was able to write and have a political career in a capitalist country, Britain, since an industrialist, Friedrich Engels, was willing to support him.

Friedman's arguments are not silly; they are half-right. Capitalism does have some advantages over socialism in promoting freedom. The collapse of socialism on a global scale at the end of the twentieth century was caused in major part by people seeking to enhance their freedom. If the question is capitalism versus socialism, and if the only criterion for making the choice is freedoms-to, narrowly defined, capitalism probably comes out on top.

This is far from identifying capitalism with freedom in its fullest meaning, however — that is, freedom as the equal ability of each person to pursue his or her goals. It is even further from identifying capitalism with justice. For one thing, even if it were true that participation in each particular transaction were voluntary (and there are some exceptions to this general rule), it does not follow that participation in the market system is voluntary. A farmer can sell his wheat in Chicago or in Kansas City to Broker X or to Broker Y, but he cannot decide not to sell it. It would be impossible for him to forgo his cash income and live directly on the wheat he grows. Similarly a laborer can work for one employer or another, but not for none. Our participation in capitalist markets is involuntary. Since we have no alternative but to participate in capitalist markets, it is incorrect to assert that markets necessarily expand our freedom of choice. For such an assertion to make sense, we would have to have an alternative to markets, and we do not.

Friedman regards equality as the enemy of freedom, so the fact that capitalism creates inequalities is no mark against capitalism for him. If one takes an expanded view of freedom, however — the view that true freedom requires not only the absence of restraints but also the resources necessary to pursue one's goals — then the relationship between capitalism and freedom looks entirely different. The fact that capitalism generates serious inequalities in people's holdings means that people have differing degrees of freedom to pursue their goals. A millionaire has much more of this sort of freedom than does a welfare mother. There is nothing in the capitalist system to ensure that people have the material means to pursue their goals. Capitalism implies the absence of most legal constraints, it is true, but it confers strikingly unequal degrees of freedom on people.

In terms of political freedom, Friedman celebrates the possibility that dissident groups can find funding in diverse places in a capitalist system, but he ignores the fact that capitalist values flood into the political sphere. Yes, occasionally an Engels can be found to support a political opponent of the capitalist system. More often, however, the money from capitalist sources supports candidates and parties that are procapitalist, leaving the political groups that are critical of capitalist excesses starving for funds. Voters are bombarded with messages from one side and find it hard to hear messages from the other; this hardly creates the conditions for unbiased decision making in a democracy.

The argument that capitalism necessarily promotes freedom is not, therefore, persuasive. Capitalism may permit freedom, up to a point, but it does not automatically ensure freedom. Freedom, like the other components of justice, must be struggled for.

Alternatives to Capitalism

Many who have arrived at roughly this position have concluded, reasonably enough, that if capitalism can guarantee neither freedom nor equal treatment, it should be replaced. This is no longer a viable position, however. There is no point seeking alternatives to capitalism, for two separate reasons.

The first reason is that noncapitalist systems have been tried and for the most part have been found to be even less just than capitalism. In view of the bloody and tumultuous history of the twentieth century, we have no excuse for thinking that the world could be made more just by abandoning capitalism.

The second reason is that capitalism is all we have. Precapitalist social formations — tribes, isolated villages, feudal arrangements, and the rest — are almost gone, destroyed by capitalist imperialism, trade, investment, and technology. Socialism and communism were once thought to be the natural successors of capitalism, but as forms of social and economic organization they too have almost disappeared. Capitalist relationships characterize most local communities, almost all states, and certainly the international relationships between states. The next two sections advance this argument in more detail.

Precapitalism: The Organic Community

Capitalism arose in Europe in the sixteenth century and spread by means of commerce and imperialism (often the two were indistinguishable) to the rest of the world. Everywhere it expanded it destroyed what had come before: manorial, feudal systems of different sorts in Europe and a variety of tribal, communal, and imperial systems in the rest of the world. The old systems did not disappear easily; their going was attended by conflict and bloodshed.

Consider, for example, the enclosure movement that lasted over centuries in England. On the old precapitalist feudal manors, no one "owned" the land; that is, no one had legal title to it and was able to sell it. The king held the land in trust from God, the great nobles held it in trust from the king, the lesser nobles held it in trust from the greater nobles, and so on down to the serfs, who did not own the land but had the right to work it and to keep a portion of its product. Serfdom was a lowly and unfree status, but it had its rights, including the right to raise crops and to graze animals on the commons, to use the tools of the manor, and to be protected against marauders by the lord. In turn, the serfs were obliged to provide goods and/or labor to the lord. The serfs were not free to move and seek alternative opportunities; they were required to stay on the manor. In return, and this is critical, they were guaranteed a place on the manor: a home, land, pasture, tools, and protection. Their birthright was a humble one, but it was guaranteed. The enclosure movement was the process by which the feudal lords converted themselves into capitalist farmers and destroyed the manorial community. They claimed the common land of the manor as their private property and denied the serfs access to it. They wanted it in order to graze sheep, not for their own use but to sell the wool in international markets. The serfs were left with nothing — no land, no animals, no tools — only their own bodies. Some were hired by the newly capitalist farmers for wages, while others migrated to the towns and cities.

The particulars were different in different parts of the world and in different periods, but the general story was the same. In most parts of the precapitalist world, at most times, people were members of an integrated, organic community in which they had both rights and responsibilities, guaranteed by the fact of being born. These were typically spiritual as well as secular communities, in which the gods were thought to be present and active in all aspects of life. In many precapitalist communities, people's principal tasks were to emulate their ancestors and to please the spirits.

Was it a just world, just in a sense that might have meaning for us today? Can we turn to the precapitalist world to give us a vision of how to live our lives? For the most part, no. Few precapitalist societies had ideas of justice that are congenial to us today. The caste or class system was generally rigid; one's fate in life was largely determined by the accident of birth. People enjoyed virtually none of the freedoms associated with, say, the Bill of Rights. Rulers ruled and subjects obeyed. Wars were endemic and punishments often cruel. The European feudal world was an organic community in which people belonged and were not abandoned, but it was a world of exploitation and harshness for most of its members.[14] Few of us would want to live in the Aztec culture, to take another example, or in most of the precapitalist societies of which we have some knowledge.

We know of some precapitalist cultures that are attractive from a modern perspective, cultures that were nonviolent, egalitarian, and respectful of their members. Anthropologist Ashley Montagu published studies of cultures he called "unaggressive," among them the Fore of New Guinea, the !Kung of Botswana, the Inuit of the Arctic, and the Tasaday of the Philippines.[15] Colin M. Turnbull gave us a marvelously enticing picture of the BaMbuti Pygmies of the Ituri rainforest in Africa, an egalitarian people with a joyous nature and deep concern for the forest and for each other.[16] Stuart A. Schlegel's portrait of the Teduray of Mindanao in the southern Philippines, among whom he lived for two years in the 1960s, is particularly compelling.[17] The Teduray were gentle, cooperative, and loving people, living in harmony with the forest and with each other. They taught him, he says, to treat everyone as an equal, to take each person's concerns seriously, to shun violence, and to infuse his life with love as much as possible.

We cannot return to the Teduray world, however, not even as visitors in the way that Schlegel once did. The rainforest world of the Teduray is gone. Every single person in the village where Schlegel lived was slaughtered in 1972. A group of Muslim insurgents, fleeing into the forest from government troops, came to the village demanding food and also women for sexual use. The Teduray were willing to share their food, but they regarded the demand for women as the equivalent of slavery, and to avoid slavery, if nothing else, they were willing to fight. They had only primitive weapons, however — bows and arrows, blowguns, a few homemade shotguns — while the intruders had automatic assault weapons. The battle turned into a killing frenzy, and the villagers were destroyed.

The story of other rainforest Teduray villages is less dramatic, but they too are disappearing. The forest is slowly being cut down, partly because of the overseas demand for timber and partly because of the pressure to increase farm acreage. As their habitat decreases, the people move farther into the heart of the forest, but eventually they run out of room. Schlegel describes how, when a group of Teduray decide to leave the forest and join a settled community on the outside, they abandon their culture overnight. They go to church, send their children to the mission school, begin speaking a new language, and take their place at the bottom of the social hierarchy in their new home. Within a generation, they lose almost all memory of the forest.

The Teduray experience can stand for most precapitalist cultures that have come in contact with capitalism. The cultures could not survive. Sometimes the people were destroyed outright. To understand the magnitude and effect of the killing, we need look no further than the contact between Native Americans and European settlers. In some cases the killing was done by the direct agents of capitalism and in some cases not. The destroyers of Schlegel's village were not capitalists; they were engaged in a battle against capitalism and Christianity, on behalf of a fundamentalist vision of Islam. They were equipped, however, with the weaponry that capitalist technology had created, so they prevailed. More common is the experience of the other Teduray who were simply absorbed into the world economic system. In a short period of time they lost their environment, their entire world. Around the globe, capitalism has driven tribespeople to become peasants, peasants to become day laborers, and day laborers to become the urban underemployed. The precapitalist cultures disappear, replaced perhaps by what Oscar Lewis called the culture of poverty.[18]

Some in the capitalist world try to retain or re-create the best parts of precapitalism. Some Amish and Mennonite communities are based on precapitalist values, as are some other faith-based groups. The 1960s and 1970s saw the creation of secular alternative rural communes, communities whose members tried to eliminate all marks of distinction between them, to be self-sufficient, and to live simply. The communes had some successes, but most eventually collapsed. Communities such as these have attempted to embody precapitalist values, but none has succeeded in cutting itself off from capitalist influences: from the market, from the media, from the legal system, and from other influences of the modern world. While we can learn from our antecedent societies, we cannot return to them. That door has been closed.

Postcapitalism: The Transcendent Dream

The most serious challenges to capitalism have come not from those who wanted to return to a simpler world but from people with an alternate — socialist or communist — vision of an economically advanced society. Marx and the early socialist thinkers accepted what they understood as the virtue of capitalism — that it had produced unprecedented economic growth and thereby had created the potential for a high standard of living for everyone. Capitalism had, however, brought with it exploitation, alienation, and injustice, all of which they believed could be overcome in the new socialist world that would replace capitalism. For a later generation, communism was not the successor to capitalism but its substitute, a more humane and efficient system for transforming nonindustrial societies like Russia and China.

As Michael Ignatieff argues, many communists understood their movement as embodying the science of history, but communism was really the opposite; it was a dream.[19] It was a dream held by nineteenth- and twentieth-century people who were intensely aware of the injustices of the capitalist system in which they lived. They were revolted by the crassness of capitalism, by the huge gap between the rich and the poor, by the way in which the system used up and discarded millions of people, by the replacement of human values with the values of money and accumulation, and by the warfare that they understood as a direct consequence of capitalist competition. Against the inhuman face of capitalism, they posited the image of "the new man," the socialist man (not until its later years was socialism at all infused with feminism), the man whose values were focused on a concern for his community and for his fellows, not distorted and narrowed by competition and accumulation. In the socialist dream, the community's resources and assets were to be owned collectively by the people and used to fulfill the people's real needs. The new economic principle was to be, in the words of Marx and Engels, "from each according to his abilities, to each according to his needs." The state was a pure democracy, or in some versions there was no state at all. With the end of capitalism would come the end of nationalism, and with the end of nationalism the end of war.

It was an extraordinary dream, a dream so powerful that for many people it persisted long after the evidence showed that it was failing. In the middle years of the twentieth century, some communists abandoned the dream as the government of the Soviet Union committed one atrocity after another — but others stayed faithful, presumably because the dream had such meaning for them and also because the alternative, the continuation of the advanced capitalist system, seemed so ghastly.

Nevertheless, the dream failed. In many ways, the communist regimes of the twentieth century brought the opposite of justice. Lenin and Stalin in the Soviet Union, Mao Zedong in China, Kim Il Sung in North Korea, Pol Pot in Cambodia, and many of their subordinates and imitators were responsible for far more deaths among their innocent countrymen than even Hitler. While the Nazis can be held accountable for about 25 million deaths, the latest scholarship attributes between 85 and 100 million deaths to eighty years of communist rule.[20] Millions were consigned to labor camps without the niceties of a fair trial. Democracy was abandoned, as a vestige of corrupt and bourgeois capitalism.

Many of the communist regimes produced remarkable economic growth, but in the end even this could not save them from collapse. The major communist revolutions occurred in precapitalist societies. The economic function of the Soviet state, to take the leading communist example, was to create a modern industrial system. In just two generations, despite the terrible burdens of two world wars, it succeeded in turning a backward, rural society into an urbanized, industrial society with a relatively healthy, literate, and productive population, with substantial social services and with world-class scientific and cultural establishments. But it was not enough. The human costs were monstrous,[21] and in the end the Soviet economic system could produce neither the food nor the consumer goods demanded by an urbanized population. Marxist orthodoxy was that capitalism was the engine of economic growth and that once capitalism had done its work of raising productive capacity it would be replaced by a socialist system concerned with the needs not of the capitalists but of the people. The actual history of twentieth-century Russia looks much the opposite: communism was the engine of industrial growth, but it could not meet people's needs for consumer goods, for freedom, and for human rights, so once it had done its work of economic growth it was replaced by a version of capitalism. Whether Russian capitalism will be more respectful of the people's needs is yet to be seen.

Perhaps the failure of communism to last, in any substantial way, into the twenty-first century can be attributed in part to the Cold War, to the massive opposition the communist countries faced from the capitalist countries, and to the consequent diversion of billions of dollars of resources into armaments rather than to the provision of goods for their people. Certainly the hostility of the United States to socialism in its own hemisphere — in Chile, Cuba, and Nicaragua — is the obvious explanation of the downfall of two of those regimes and the economic difficulties of the third.

Some who remained true to the dream in the face of the actual performance of many of the communist regimes argued that those regimes did not represent true communism, that Stalin, Mao, and the others had betrayed communist and socialist principles. The "democratic socialists" in the West, a group of people on the whole honorable, visionary, and compassionate, held that if it was to be responsible to the real needs of the people, socialism had to answer to the people. This principle informed most of the Western socialist parties, including the British Labor Party and the New Democratic Party and its antecedents in Canada. They accepted the constraints of democratic, electoral systems. To gain power in a genuinely democratic system, however, the democratic socialists had to give up most of their socialist principles, including state ownership of the means of production. The Labor government in Britain after the Second World War brought about some real transformations, including the nationalization of a number of the country's most important industries. In subsequent years, however, Conservative governments reversed the nationalizations, and Labor found that it could return to power only if it explicitly rejected its former principles. The story is common to most Western capitalist countries; the socialist parties converted themselves into somewhat left-of-center capitalist parties, arguing for a more generous welfare program, but nothing more radical. One way of understanding the change is to say that the democratic socialists became social democrats. None of the Western socialist parties currently challenges the system of private enterprise. Some academics still make proposals for what they hope might be a humane version of socialism,[22] but these ideas garner little public support.

The communist societies have almost completely disappeared. Not the communist political parties or in some cases the communist totalitarian states — plenty of them still exist, in Vietnam, China, and many other countries. With a few exceptions, however, the communist system of economic and social organization has gone. In Russia, state control of the economy was replaced by a kind of anarchic and unpredictable banditry. The former satellite states of eastern Europe moved in varying degrees toward capitalist markets. The Chinese Communist Party relaxed its control of the economy, encouraging private ownership, entrepreneurship, and foreign investment. In Vietnam, as in China, the party maintained control over the political system, but the economy was increasingly based on capitalist principles. At the beginning of the twenty-first century, only two national societies are still organized on communist principles, North Korea and Cuba. The former is perhaps the world's most disastrous state, its people on or even past the verge of starvation while its regime develops advanced weaponry. The small island nation of Cuba is the one remaining apparently sustainable communist society. In spite of enormous difficulties — including a counterproductive embargo by the United States and abandonment by its former patron, Russia — it has retained a reasonably egalitarian society and has provided for the basic needs of its people. The Cuban political regime has not, however, permitted democracy, so we do not know whether it retains the support of its people and whether it can survive the transition to a new leader.

Not much is left of the dream, therefore. The dream embodied a great deal of what is best about human aspirations — but it failed. While they lasted, most communist societies thoroughly violated human rights and the norms of justice. Moreover, they did not last. Capitalism is not a transitional phase to a utopian world order. The utopian world order has come and gone.

The future is unknowable, and we will surely be surprised by what it deals us. Virtually no one in the mid-1950s expected the European empires to disappear within a few years. Virtually no one in the mid 1980s foresaw the collapse of communism and the disintegration of the Soviet Union. Perhaps the world capitalist system will be gone within a few years as well. Such a change is unlikely, however. Capitalism is growing in power, scope, and achievements. It is hard to see any force on the horizon strong enough even to threaten capitalism, let alone overthrow it. The chances are good that we, our children, and our grandchildren will live in a capitalist system. Moreover — and this is a more controversial statement in view of the evident injustices of capitalism — capitalism should not be overthrown. On the whole, our experiences with the dream — and they have been extensive — have been nightmares. There is no exit; we have to learn to manage what we have.

Is it possible to move some distance toward the dream, to achieve not a utopia but a social system that is more respectful of human beings and of nature, that treats people equally, that is more just, all the while staying within the constraints of modern capitalism?

Notes

1. Karl Marx and Friedrich Engels, *Manifesto of the Communist Party* (Peking: Foreign Languages Press, 1977), 36.

2. John Locke, *The Second Treatise of Government* (1690; reprint, Indianapolis: Bobbs-Merrill, 1952), 36. For a modern defense of private property, on grounds different from those of Locke, see Dan Usher, "The Justification of Private Property," in *Ethics and Capitalism*, ed. John Douglas Bishop (Toronto: University of Toronto Press, 2000), 49–80.

3. Pierre Joseph Proudhon, *What Is Property? An Enquiry into the Principle of Right and of Government*, trans. Benjamin R. Tucker (New York: Howard Fertig, 1966), 11.

4. Immanuel Wallerstein, *The Modern World-System: Capitalist Agriculture and the Origins of the European World-Economy in the Sixteenth Century* (New York: Academic Press, 1974).

5. John G. Gurley and E. S. Shaw, "Financial Structure and Economic Development," *Economic Development and Cultural Change* 15 (1967): 257–68.

6. See, for example, Wallerstein, *Modern World-System.*

7. Herman E. Daly, *Steady-State Economics,* 2d ed. (Washington, D.C.: Island Press, 1991).

8. Marx and Engels, *Manifesto of the Communist Party,* 35.

9. For an influential treatment of the economic role of government, along these lines, see Richard A. Musgrave, *The Theory of Public Finance* (New York: McGraw-Hill, 1959).

10. John Kenneth Galbraith, *The New Industrial State,* 2d ed. (Boston: Houghton-Mifflin, 1971).

11. See, for example, Anthony Downs, *An Economic Theory of Democracy* (New York: Harper and Row, 1957); James M. Buchanan and Gordon Tullock, *The Calculus of Consent: Logical Foundations of Constitutional Democracy* (Ann Arbor: University of Michigan Press, 1962); Donald A. Wittman, *The Myth of Democratic Failure: Why Political Institutions Are Efficient* (Chicago: University of Chicago Press, 1995).

12. Milton Friedman, *Capitalism and Freedom* (Chicago: University of Chicago Press, 1962); Robert Nozick, *Anarchy, State, and Utopia* (New York: Basic Books, 1974).

13. Friedman, *Capitalism and Freedom.*

14. For a wonderfully spirited attack against feudalism, from the perspective of nineteenth-century American republican values, see Mark Twain, *A Connecticut Yankee in King Arthur's Court* (New York: New American Library, 1963).

15. Ashley Montagu, ed., *Learning Non-aggression: The Experience of Nonliterate Societies* (New York: Oxford University Press, 1978).

16. Colin M. Turnbull, *The Forest People* (New York: Simon and Schuster, 1961).

17. Stuart A. Schlegel, *Wisdom from a Rainforest: The Spiritual Journey of an Anthropologist* (Athens: University of Georgia Press, 1998). See also Schlegel's *Tiruray Justice: Traditional Tiruray Law and Morality* (Berkeley: University of

California Press, 1970) and *Tiruray Subsistence: From Shifting Cultivation to Plow Agriculture* (Quezon City, Philippines: Ateneo de Manila University Press, 1979).

18. Oscar Lewis, *La Vida: A Puerto Rican Family in the Culture of Poverty — San Juan and New York* (New York: Random House, 1966).

19. Michael Ignatieff, "The Era of Terror," *New Republic* (August 9, 1999): 37–40. The dream metaphor has been used frequently. See, for example, Walter Lacquer, *The Dream That Failed: Reflections on the Soviet Union* (New York: Oxford University Press, 1994).

20. The most comprehensive accounting of the terror under communism is in Stephane Courtois et al., *The Black Book of Communism: Crimes, Terror, Repression,* trans. Jonathan Murphy and Mark Kramer (Cambridge, Mass.: Harvard University Press, 1999).

21. For a brief account of what is known about the vast network of prison camps that provided much of the labor for the industrialization of the Soviet Union, see Anne Applebaum, "Inside the Gulag," *New York Review of Books* 47 (June 15, 2000): 33–35.

22. See the particularly interesting proposal for a modern version of "market socialism" made by John E. Roemer in two books: *A Future for Socialism* (Cambridge, Mass.: Harvard University Press, 1994) and *Equal Shares: Making Market Socialism Work,* ed. Erik Olin Wright (London: Verso: 1996).

Part II

National Dilemmas

Capitalism
an economic + political system in which a country's trade and industry are controlled by private owner for profit, rather than by the state.

Chapter 3

INCOME
DISTRIBUTION

P EOPLE LIVING in capitalist countries may have equal moral standing, but they do not have equal access to the goods and services provided by their economies. Their incomes are vastly unequal.

A good way of looking at the income distribution in a country is to compare the portion of total national income going to the poorest 20 percent of the population with the portion going to the richest 20 percent. Each group of 20 percent is called a "quintile." According to calculations by the World Bank, in fifteen industrialized countries, including much of western Europe plus Canada, the United States, and Australia, the bottom quintile of households earns an average of about 8 percent of the national income, while the top quintile earns around 39 percent.[1] Of those countries, the United States has the most skewed distribution of incomes, with the lowest and highest quintiles earning 5 percent and 45 percent, respectively. In the United States, the most prosperous one-tenth of the population earn 29 percent of total income. As far as one can tell (data from before the 1970s are skimpy on this topic), the income distribution in the United States became more equal throughout the twentieth century until about 1973, and the proportion of people living in poverty fell. After 1973, however, incomes became less equal, and the proportion of people in poverty fluctuated without a trend. The huge increases in national income since 1973 have gone overwhelmingly to the rich, while the incomes of most Americans, when corrected for inflation, have fallen.[2] Some evidence exists that the poorest began to benefit from the long economic expansion at the end of the 1990s.[3]

Uneven as these figures for household income are, they are egalitarian compared to the figures for the distribution of wealth in the United States (income is what you earn, while wealth is what you own). Ac-

> relating to cr. believing in the principle that all people are equal and deserve equal rights

egalitarian

55

Socialism e conoic
a political e conoic
theory of social organization which advocate that the
means of production distribution and
exchange should be
owned or regulated by the community
as a whole.

cording to data compiled by Edward N. Wolff, the share of wealth held by the top quintile was 85 percent at last count.[4]

The average pay of a CEO in a major corporation was $11.9 million in 2000.[5] The latest estimates are that the poverty line is about $20,000 for a family of four in the United States, and almost 17 percent of families fall below that threshold.[6] The ratio of these two figures — 11.9 million divided by 20,000 — is almost 600, and this of course understates the ratio between the richest and the poorest American, since some earned much more than $11.9 million and many took in less than the poverty threshold. To avoid being accused of alarmism, however, let us take this as the ratio between the "typical" rich and poor families in the United States: 600:1.

What spread of incomes is consistent with social justice? This chapter proposes an answer and then considers whether the answer is compatible with the constraints of capitalism. The reasoning supporting my answer is, I hope, defensible, but in some respects it is unavoidably intuitive. I will try to be explicit about the intuitions; readers with different intuitions may wish to adjust my conclusions.

A factor that seriously complicates the assessment of income distribution in the real world is the relationship between individual and family incomes. If families have the same incomes but different numbers of members, should we regard them as economically equal or unequal? If three people earn equal incomes, but two of them are members of one family while the third is the sole income-earner in her family, should we regard incomes as equal or unequal? Should we peer inside the family structure, to see if the resources that come into the family are shared equitably among its members — and if the answer is yes, does "equitably" mean "equally"? What distribution of income within a family is consistent with justice for women and children? These questions are both important and difficult. They are well worth serious moral investigation, but they are outside the scope of this chapter. The chapter restricts itself to the distribution of incomes among families, without considering the size of families, the number of earners in a family, or the distribution of income within families. Readers may wish to push their own analyses beyond this limit.

Plato's Colony

Economists are typically reluctant to say just what distribution of incomes is morally justified; it all depends, they say, on one's values and assumptions.[7] We do, however, have one carefully thought out and precise recommendation. It comes from Plato's *Laws,* written in the fourth century B.C., a dialogue on the principles to govern a new colony. In book 5 of *Laws,* Plato says that the colony should consist of 5,040 households, each household given a lot of equal size. The purpose of the laws in the new society is "that our people should be supremely happy and devotedly attached to one another, but citizens will never be thus attached where there are many suits at law between them, and numerous wrongs committed, but where both are rarest and of least consequence." This leads him, a few sentences later, to consider the optimal income distribution:

> It had indeed been well that all settlers should further enter our colony with equal means of every kind. But since this cannot be, but one arrival will bring more property and another less, there must be classes of unequal census, and that on many grounds, and in particular because of the equal opportunity our society affords, that so in election to office and assessment of payments to and receipts from the exchequer regard may be had to a man's due qualifications, not only of personal and ancestral virtue, or of bodily strength and comeliness, but of enjoyment of means or lack of them, honors and offices apportioned fairly... and dissensions avoided. On these grounds we must arrange our citizens in four classes according to the amount of their property, a first, a second, a third and a fourth — or they may be called by some other names — whether the members remain in the same class, or shift, as they pass from poverty to wealth, or wealth to poverty, each to the class appropriate to him.
>
> ... In a society which is to be immune from the most fatal of disorders which might more properly be called distraction than faction, there must be no place for penury in any section of the population, nor yet for opulence, as both breed either consequence. Accordingly, the legislator must now specify the limit in either direction. So let the limit on the side of penury be the value of an allotment.... The legislator will take it as a measure, and permit the acquisition of twice, thrice, and as much as four times its value. If a man acquires further possessions, ... he may retain his good name and escape all proceedings by assigning the surplus to the State and its gods.[8]

Plato is clear: no hiding behind the veil of value-neutrality for him. Each man shall have at a minimum a lot of equal size and equal opportunity. Because of different personal characteristics, some will earn more than this. Because of equal opportunity, men may move up and down the income ladder. The maximum allowable is four times the value of the lot, because anything higher will induce jealousy, crime, strife, and conflict. Any income or property earned above this limit is forfeit to the state or to the gods.

It is a good answer (except for the invisibility of both women and the people replaced by the Greek colonists). Equality of opportunity — which we have taken to be the most basic meaning of equality in justice — is provided for. Citizens have a guaranteed income, so they will not fall into dire poverty. They have the right to be rewarded for their hard work and talents, but not so much that they will induce envy, which would rupture the attachment of one citizen to another.[9] It is a reasonable balancing act between different components of justice.

Classical Greece was a different world from today's advanced capitalism. Is it possible that 4:1 is no longer the right ratio and that it should be replaced by something like 600:1?

What Differences in Labor Incomes Are Needed for Efficiency?

In chapter 1, I argued that, since we are of equal moral worth, our incomes should be as equal as possible — not because justice requires equality of outcomes but because if incomes vary from family to family, the children in our families will have unequal opportunities. Let us begin the discussion of an optimal income distribution, therefore, by assuming a utopian society in which all incomes are equal and no barriers of class, race, gender, sexual preference, nationality, or anything else impede equality of opportunity.

Such a society would, unfortunately, be inefficient, because people would have no financial incentive to be productive. Their incomes, being equal, would be unrelated to their contributions to society. People are motivated by many factors, not just money, but money matters. Efficiency, therefore, conflicts with equality, and we must compromise. We should ask what are the *minimum departures from equality* necessary to bring about the efficiency that we really need. The departures should be minimal because every concession to income differences in support of efficiency will take us further down the road of unequal opportunity for children.

People get their income from different sources, principal among them wages and salaries from labor, rents from land and improvements on the land, interest and dividends from investments, profits from entrepreneurship, transfers from the government, and gifts and inheritances. The most important source is wages and salaries, which account for over two-thirds of personal income in the United States. We begin, therefore, by thinking about the relationship between employees' incomes and efficiency. Why might we want firms and other organizations to pay people at unequal rates?

Many of the wage differences that exist in the real world are obviously unjust. Differences caused by discrimination based on race, gender, or other personal characteristics, or by family connections or monopoly power, have no place in a just world. Some of the existing wage differences cannot be so easily dismissed, however, because they are signals that lead to the efficient employment of labor.

Take a simple example. A society has just two jobs, server at a fast-food establishment and high-tech engineer, each with its own employer. It has two workers, Mary and George. Mary is technically adept while George is inept in most pursuits. Both employers would prefer to hire Mary. If the wages in both positions were equal, Mary might choose the less-demanding job of food server, leaving George to take the engineering post, and that would be an inefficient allocation of labor. If, however, the employers are allowed to set their own rates of pay, the high-tech employer will likely raise Mary's rate to such a level that she chooses the engineering job. The fast-food employer will not be able to match the offer, although she would like to hire Mary, because Mary, although she is worth more behind the counter than George is, is not worth as much behind the counter as she is in the lab. The high-tech employer will be able to outbid the fast-food employer for Mary's services. The resulting allocation of labor will be efficient: Mary in the engineering job and George behind the food counter. The story shows that sometimes, not always, wages are an indicator of productivity. When wages differ, and when people try to get jobs with the highest possible wages, they may sort themselves out among the available jobs in such a way as to promote efficiency.

What departures from equal wages should we want, on grounds of efficiency? We probably have different answers — depending upon the weights we give to equality and efficiency — but we can narrow our disagreement by identifying some of the specific reasons for thinking that inequality promotes efficiency.

The first efficiency-related justification for unequal wages is to persuade some people to undertake education, apprenticeships, and training programs so that they will enhance their skills. Consider an eighteen-year-old who has just graduated from high school and is choosing between two careers, one as a clerk, a job she can start immediately, the other as a doctor. In the just world of equal opportunity that we are assuming, she has not already been tracked by her race or class or by her high school counselor into choosing one or the other career; she can make an autonomous choice. If she chooses the medical career, she faces twelve more years of training — four years of college, four years of medical school, and four years of residency — during all of which time, let us assume, she will earn no income at all, before she can start earning a doctor's income. (This is an oversimplification, since residents typically earn a low salary.) If the society wants some doctors, it may have to pay her an income, once she finishes her residency, sufficient to persuade her that she was right to give up the clerical job. How much more does she need to earn?

She expects to retire at age sixty-five, so if she chooses to be a clerk she will have forty-seven years of income-earning work, and if she chooses the medical career she will have thirty-five years. She may reason that she needs to make at least as much during her thirty-five years of doctoring as she would have during her forty-seven years of clerking. On these grounds, the annual income of a doctor would need to be 34 percent above that of a clerk; that is, the ratio of incomes would be 1.34:1. One way to think of this is that she would go in debt for the first twelve years, by the amount of the clerical salary foregone each year, then would pay off the debt during her earning years and still have the same income during those years, net of debt repayments, as the clerk. The two lifetime incomes would be the same, just arranged differently over time.

Actually the ratio would have to be higher than 1.34:1 because of time preference and the interest rate. For a variety of reasons, people prefer to have their income earlier rather than later. Perhaps it is a fear of death, a fear that they may not be around to enjoy the later income, or perhaps it is a failure of imagination, a failure to understand that they will want income as much in the future as they do now. Whatever the reason, it is normal for people to prefer income earlier rather than later. Put differently, if they are going to have to put off their income, they need to be compensated for the wait, by earning interest. So part of the dilemma facing our high school graduate is that if she chooses a clerical career, she will begin earning income now, when she most wants it. To persuade her to choose medicine, a career whose rewards will come later, we will need to sweeten the pot. By how much? Suppose her rate of time preference is 5 percent a year — that is, she would be indifferent between receiving $100 today and $105 a year from now; and suppose also that 5 percent is the interest rate she would have to pay on funds that she borrows while she is in her twelve years of medical education. Under these circumstances, a calculation discounting future income at a 5 percent annual rate demonstrates that the doctor's annual pay rate would have to be roughly double that of the clerk's, or a ratio of 2:1.

It was not by chance that a doctor's career was used in this example, but because medicine has the longest training period of any profession. Even the longest training period can justify an earnings ratio in the neighborhood of only 2:1. In a way, of course, there is no income difference in this example. Thought of in terms of lifetime earnings or, more accurately, in terms of the present value of lifetime earnings when discounted for time preference, the two earnings figures are the same.

A second reason for thinking that earnings differences promote efficiency is that many people need the prospect of higher earnings, or the fear of lower earnings, as an incentive to work hard and effectively. A good deal of evidence on this subject comes from the experience of agricultural communes in communist China and the former Soviet Union. They were very large farms, sometimes with a membership of tens of thousands of workers. In many cases, each worker was paid the same amount, calculated as a portion of the earnings of the commune. When the commune did well, earnings rose, and vice versa. The contribution that any one worker made to the success of the overall operation was too small to be noticed and had no perceptible effect on that worker's compensation. Agricultural economist D. Gale Johnson, writing about the Soviet communes in 1983, said, "The farm worker sees little or no relationship between his or her work and the pay received. Consequently there is little incentive to do any particular job well, to work hard, or to work long hours during busy seasons of the year."[10] The workers were often motivated by factors other than individual material incentives, and the communes did plod along. They were, however, the source of the classic Soviet-era joke, "They pretend to pay us and we pretend to work." The reform of the old communist economic system in both the Soviet Union and China was first marked by the breakup of the communes and their devolution into more individualized, market-based farms.

We know, therefore, that equal wages, unrelated to a worker's effort, cause major problems in overall efficiency. When we try to quantify the effect of merit pay on actual performance, however, we find conflicting evidence.[11] Some studies show a substantial impact,[12] others only a weak one.[13] The difference in findings may be related to the difficulty that organizations have in assessing meritorious performance. In any case, many organizations establish a salary range for each position and attempt to locate people within that range according to their performance.[14] The range varies from position to position and from organization to organization, but it seldom exceeds 50 percent of the base pay for the position.[15]

I have personal experience, however, of a merit range of approximately 100 percent. On the university campus where I teach, tenured full professors are typically promoted to that rank in their early forties and can look forward to twenty to twenty-five more working years before retirement. Since they are in the privileged position of holding tenure, they are in no danger of being fired. What keeps them working hard — and most of them do work hard — over those twenty-five years? Part of the answer is pride in their work. Beyond that, material incentives are provided. Approximately every three years, each professor goes through a rigorous peer review. Success in one of these merit reviews normally results in a pay increase of about 5 percent; there are a number of cases, however, of no increase, on the one hand, or 10 percent or even greater increases, on the other. The net result of all these personnel actions is that, at any time, the gap between the highest and lowest paid full professor is about 2:1. I can report, from many years of having been subject to this system of merit pay and having helped to administer it, that the professors take it very seriously. The increments provide not only income but, equally if not more importantly, recognition of the value of their work.

This is just one observation, and it probably lies at the extreme range of what is needed to keep people working effectively. People with less job security, who face the prospect of being fired if their performance is unsatisfactory, probably need less incentive pay: hence the more typical range of 50 percent or less. In a few cases, the ratio may need to be as high as 2:1.

A third connection between wage inequality and efficiency comes from organizational hierarchies. Most of us work in organizations with many layers of status and function. From the president at the top through all the vice presidents and assistant vice presidents to the section chiefs and the assistant chiefs, the professionals and the quasi professionals, the technicians and the clericals, the custodians and the cleaners, the number of layers is often quite large in big organizations. It seems to be important that each superior layer in the organization carry a higher rate of pay than the layer below it, since most people find it hard to supervise people with higher salaries or to be supervised by people with lower.[16] This is not a universal phenomenon; for example, some professional sports stars play under coaches who earn lower salaries. Still, it is the convention that a higher rank carry higher compensation, and probably for good reason. How much total differential is required? In the real world, the gap between the top and the bottom is often enormous, reflecting a significant difference between each separate position. In a just world that honored the goal of equality as well as efficiency, the gap would not have to be as great. A ratio of 2:1 between top and bottom, for example, would allow for at least twenty separate gradations of 5 percent or fifty gradations of 2 percent.

Some people think the gap needs to be greater; not surprisingly, they tend disproportionately to be people with higher incomes.[17] The *New York Times* records a conversation between its reporter and several top corporate executives, including L. Dennis Kozlowski, CEO of Tyco International:

> Q. It's often said that at a certain level it no longer matters how much any of you make, that you would be doing just as good a job for $100 million less or $20 million less.

> Kozlowski: Yeah, all my meals are paid for, for as long as I'm around. So, I'm not working for that any longer. But it does make a difference in the charities I ultimately leave monies behind to, and it's a way of keeping score.[18]

It does not take an overly active imagination to think of better ways of funding charities and cheaper ways of keeping score.

Combining the reasons for pay differences among employees that we have discussed so far — compensation for training, incentives for hard work, and status differences in the hierarchy — and assuming that the reasons for pay differences are completely independent one from another, we come up with a maximum ratio between the top and the bottom of the labor force of 8:1, that is, 2 x 2 x 2.

Factors exist that could reduce or increase this ratio. There are at least two reasons for reducing it. First, the justifications for pay differentials sometimes overlap. A person who is highly trained is likely to qualify for a more senior position in the hierarchy. One way a person is rewarded for good job performance is often by being promoted to a job at the next status level. To a certain extent, therefore — not totally — the three categories collapse into a single category.

Second, the discussion so far has taken no account of what is sometimes called "psychic income." In a free labor market, people get to choose their jobs, at least to a certain extent, and they often choose them because they like them. The young woman who was deciding between a clerical and a medical career might have had a strong preference for medicine. She might have chosen to be a doctor even if it paid less over her lifetime than a clerical job; the difference is her psychic income. Suppose Michael Jordan — who became the world's greatest and highest-paid basketball player — had figured out at the age of eighteen that he could have had a clerical career paying $30,000 a year or a basketball career paying $20,000. There is a good chance he would have chosen basketball, because he loved it. The same sort of reasoning is true of the other categories. Many of my professor colleagues work hard because they enjoy research and teaching; money is not the main issue. Many people on the communist communes worked hard out of a sense of solidarity and political commitment. Without material incentives it was not enough, but it helped. In organizational hierarchies, many people simply want to be boss; the fact that the next position up comes with a higher salary is an added bonus, but it is not the only incentive. In other words, the added psychic income that usually attaches to higher-status positions reduces although it does not eliminate the need for pay differentials.

On the other side, an argument for increasing the ratio is that we have not exhausted the reasons for thinking that pay differentials signal an efficient allocation of labor. In the first example, both employers preferred Mary over George, not necessarily because she was more highly trained or because she was a more conscientious worker — she may not have been — but because she was more skilled and effective.

In the real world, the gap in effectiveness between some of the most-skilled people like Mary and some of the least-skilled people like George is enormous. Think, for example, about the difference between a Nobel Prize–winning scientist and a typical high school dropout — or, along a different dimension of competency, about the difference between Michael Jordan and an athletic klutz like, say, me. If compensation packages are kept within a ratio of about 8:1, they may be insufficient, in some cases, to direct people to their most efficient employment. In fact, any restriction on the spread of incomes is likely to have some negative effect on efficiency. We must arrive at a compromise, therefore, achieving neither as much equality as we would like nor as much efficiency. If we opt for complete equality, our productive system will collapse. If we opt for the most efficient possible system, we will suffer from extreme inequality, as we do now.

A salary ratio of 8:1 is a good compromise. A range between, say, $20,000 and $160,000 a year would provide a great deal of room for wages to be related to effectiveness. It would probably constrain some labor contracts that would otherwise be efficient, but surely not many, particularly in view of the points made above about the narrowing effects of both psychic income and the overlapping of categories. Moreover, since equality is so important, I think the distribution of labor incomes should be bell-shaped, with many more people in the middle than at the extremes.

Income Differences and Merit

The previous section began with a utopian world in which all incomes were equal — in order to ensure equal opportunity for children — and then asked what minimal departures from equality should be tolerated in order to promote efficiency. Recall, however, the conclusion of chapter 1 that equal outcomes are not a necessary component of justice. We deserve to have equal opportunities, not equal outcomes, and if we have equal opportunities, we will use our talents differently and will therefore garner unequal incomes. Some of the inequality is undeserved, because it is a consequence of personal attributes for which individuals bear no responsibility, but some of it is deserved, because it is a consequence of the autonomous use of willpower. The ideal state of income equality is unclear, because the income differences that result from the use of willpower may create unequal opportunities for the next generation. That being the case, justice is not necessarily compatible with all the income differences resulting from willpower, but still we should consider what influence willpower might have.

Some economists think that a perfectly competitive labor market provides a morally justified answer, but I think they are mistaken. They claim, first, that people's incomes should be proportional to the contributions they make to production and, second, that labor markets in fact reward people according to this principle. Neither claim holds up. The idea that we deserve to be compensated for our productivity is completely different from the argument made in chapter 1 and above, that we deserve equal incomes except for some compensation for the autonomous use of our will. The first claim seems not to be justified, therefore. Neither does the second. Even if it were conceded that people should be compensated in proportion to their productivity, there is no reason to think that the market would accomplish this. This is not the place to enter into a century of disputation over the economic theory of marginal productivity — the theory that claims to show that wages are directly related to a worker's contribution to production — except to say that it holds only under conditions of perfect competition, conditions that are rare in the real world, and that it considers only the marginal or last worker's contribution to production, not the average worker's. Compensation rates in the real, not the introductory-textbook, marketplace are determined by many complex forces, and there is no reason to think that they are closely related to the social value created by workers.

We cannot depend upon the market, therefore, to generate the incomes that workers deserve. We are left, unfortunately, with no firm foundation for making the judgment. All we can do is ask what ratio corresponds to our intuitions about how differences in the use of our will should be rewarded. My intuition is that some reward is justified. We should be compensated for some of our autonomous actions, so an income ratio of 1:1 is too low. The ratio of 600:1 that exists in the actual market is, on the other hand, far too high, since we begin with vastly unequal opportunities, since most of our attributes are doubtless undeserved, and since actual earnings are determined by many factors that are completely independent of our contributions to production. Compensation for all these factors, if it could be done accurately, might or might not lower the ratio to 8:1. Still, we must compromise between the conflicting pulls of equal opportunity: in a world of equal opportunity, people in a single generation will achieve unequal results, but those unequal results will create unequal opportunities for the next generation and should therefore be compressed. Since this is so, an income ratio in the neighborhood of 8:1 seems to me to be about right. This is the roughest and most intuitive of conclusions: that the ratio of labor incomes justified on the grounds of efficiency is roughly the same as the ratio that reflects the rewards we should receive on the basis of our merits.

Differences in Nonlabor Incomes

What about nonlabor income, including interest, dividends, rent, profits, and appreciation in the value of assets? Much of this is income earned by people in return for providing capital. Capital is defined as a means of production that has itself been produced: for the most part, although not entirely, buildings, plant, and equipment. It is essential to the production process, so a way must be found of providing it.

Capital incomes are as tricky to assess as labor incomes. With a free labor market, in the absence of slavery, a person can appropriate the income of only one worker, namely, him or herself. No such restriction applies in the case of capital income. A person can invest no money, a small sum, or a large sum. In the case of labor, since each person controls only one worker, variations in personal income depend entirely upon variations in the rates at which each person is compensated. Variations in capital income, on the other hand, depend largely upon variations in the amount of capital one controls and only secondarily upon differences in the rates at which the use of that capital is compensated. So the principal question becomes, Is there some reason having to do with efficiency why people should own and benefit from different amounts of capital?

The answer to this question depends upon the form of social organization. In capitalism, the capital is owned privately. Suppose we start with a situation of absolutely equal distribution of income. Some people consume all their income and have nothing left at the end of the year. Others consume only half their income, save the rest, and purchase capital with it. In each successive year they do the same. Essentially they are postponing their consumption in the hope of increasing it in the long run. In the first year, they consume only half the goods they might have. In each successive year, though, their income grows if their investments turn out successfully, because they earn increasing amounts of capital income as the capital stock they own grows. Eventually their income is so large, because of the capital income they are adding each year, that not only their income but their consumption exceeds that of their nonsaving neighbors. They save a portion of their income each year and create capital with it because they expect they will be compensated with capital income in the future. If they did not expect this capital income, they would not continue to save. In a capitalist system, therefore, a limit on the income that can be earned from capital will likely reduce the amount of capital available to the society. The citizens may decide that this is a worthwhile limit to impose, but they will have to reckon with the loss in efficiency.

In a noncapitalist society, the answer may be different. If savings were made from the profits of firms structured as worker cooperatives, say, or from the profits of state-owned enterprises, or from the excess of a government's tax receipts over its expenditures, capital would not be in individual hands and the income accruing to capital could be shared in any way. The world in which we live is, however, capitalist.

Profits can be thought of as the return to entrepreneurship, to organization, or, if you will, to risk taking. A person, a group, or a company with a new idea invests some money in developing that idea in the hope that it will be commercially successful. If they fail, they lose their money and time; if they succeed, they reap profits. The prospect of profits is, therefore, an engine of growth. If profits are restricted in a capitalist society, there is a chance that risk taking, innovation, and growth will be reduced.

Freedom, Efficiency, and Incomes

We have uncovered problems with a strict income ratio of 8:1. This sort of spread, or less, is all that is required to compensate us for our merits and to provide most of the incentives that are needed for efficiency. Neither this limit nor any limit, however, will allow us the most efficient possible economy. Some unusual people are so productive that virtually any restriction on their labor income will lead to the possibility that they will not be employed in the most efficient way. Limits on the incomes of capital owners and entrepreneurs may induce some of them to reduce their contributions to economic growth.

A second sort of problem inheres in any limit on incomes. If the limit is applied rigidly, it may violate the norm of freedom, and freedom is an important component of justice. As discussed in chapter 1, freedom requires not just the absence of constraints. In its broadest sense, it moves us toward a fairly egalitarian income distribution, so that everyone can have an equal capacity to do what she wants to do. Therefore, in the name of freedom, one can justify taking some resources from people with means in order to redistribute them to people without. The high-income earners among us do not deserve to keep all their income, as a matter of freedom, because they depend upon so many other people in the earning of it. They do, however, deserve to keep some of it. Confiscation of all their income, or all their income over a fixed limit, would violate their freedom. The concept of freedom surely includes a certain security, a right to be free from arbitrary seizure of one's property. One does not have to go as far as the libertarian philosopher Robert Nozick,[19] who claims that virtually any taxation of one's wealth is a violation of justice, to assert that people have the right to hold on to *some* of what they have created and earned.

It follows that a binding limit on the top incomes that people can earn will create problems of either efficiency or freedom. Consider the example of Bill Gates, who amassed the world's greatest fortune by innovating in microelectronics. Confronted by the news that he would have to forfeit all his annual income above $160,000, he could take one of two steps: he could stop innovating or he could continue. If he stopped, the society would become less efficient. The products he has developed have, after all, improved the productivity and increased the enjoyment of millions of people. We may not care much what income he takes home to his family, but we do care about continued improvements in the quality of our lives. If, on the other hand, he continued to innovate, and thereby earned income above the $160,000 limit only to see all of it confiscated by the tax collector, his freedom to at least some security in his holdings would be violated.

An Ethically Defensible Distribution of Incomes

Let's summarize where we have gotten so far. The idea of equal incomes is initially attractive because it would ensure equal opportunity for succeeding generations. Completely equal incomes would, however, lead to a society that most of us would not be willing to tolerate. We would not be compensated for the autonomous use of our will, we would have no financial incentive to work efficiently, we would suffer from a shortage of capital and entrepreneurship, and our right to some security in our possessions would be violated. So we must retreat from complete equality. We should not, however, retreat as far as the inequality in, for example, the current American economy. The inequality in such a society egregiously violates the standards of both equal opportunity and equal freedom. For almost all of us, a ratio of something like 8:1 in earned incomes should be more than sufficient to recognize the differences in desert among us and to persuade us to work efficiently. Most of us need only a 2:1 ratio. The criteria of equality, freedom, and efficiency conflict, and we should try to arrive at a compromise that honors all of them as much as possible, but none of them completely. In a small number of cases, I think we will want to permit incomes to rise above the 8:1 limit, in the interests of both freedom and efficiency.

So we will have to abandon Plato's idea that we can specify an exact ratio between the highest and lowest incomes that is compatible with justice. Fortunately we have another measure, the share of total personal incomes accruing to different percentiles of the population. Some of the current data were given at the beginning of this chapter. The latest figures for the United States show the lowest 20 percent of the population receiving 5 percent of the income, and the highest 20 percent 45 percent.

No overall distribution of incomes guarantees social justice, of course, since what looks like a defensible array of incomes may hide individual injustices. We can speculate, however, about what the distribution of incomes might look like if justice were achieved.

Begin with an average family income of about $90,000, which is the range that existed in the United States at the end of the twentieth century. This may seem high to readers, but remember it is the average income per family, not per person. The median family income in the United States — the income below which half the families are found — is about half the average, approximately $45,000.[20] The gap between the median and the average is a measure of how skewed the current distribution is, with a small number of exceptionally rich people pulling the average above the median. If the population were concentrated near the center of the income distribution, with symmetrical tails on either side, the median and average would roughly coincide.

A just distribution of family incomes would, I think, follow these principles. First, no family would fall below the poverty line, no matter what the contribution of its members to overall production. Poverty and programs to eliminate it will be discussed in chapter 6; here it is sufficient to say that, in a world of justice, no child suffers the disadvantage of growing up poor. The figure of $20,000 is the poverty cutoff for a family of four; we simplify the discussion by taking $20,000 as the cutoff for all families. Second, most families would be within a 2:1 ratio of incomes. This is sufficient to provide most of the incentives needed for economic efficiency. Third, except for a small number of people, the maximum ratio of incomes would be 8:1. Fourth, a few incomes would rise above the 8:1 ratio.

One expression of these principles is in Table 3.1, which shows 75 percent of the families within a 2:1 ratio, earning between $60,000 and $120,000 a year. Another 10 percent are right at the poverty line of $20,000; most of these are families whose adult members either cannot or choose not to earn the subsistence level of income, and they are brought up to this level by transfers from the government. Ten percent are above the poverty line but below the middle-income range, and 5 percent are above the middle-income range. Among the latter group, 0.1 percent of the families in the country earn incomes above the 8:1 ratio.

In Table 3.1, total personal income is $80,350,000, so with 1,000

Table 3.1
Hypothetical Income Distribution for a Country of 1,000 People

Annual Income (in $ Thousands)	Average Income of Families in Range (in $ Thousands)	Number of Families	Income Earned by Group (in $ Thousands)
20	20	100	2,000
20–40	30	50	1,500
40–60	50	50	2,500
60–80	70	220	15,400
80–100	90	310	27,900
100–120	110	220	24,200
120–140	130	40	5,200
140–160	150	9	1,350
over 160	300	1	300
Total		1,000	80,350

families, the average personal income is $80,350, a little below the actual figure in the United States in recent years and well within the range of average incomes in most advanced capitalist countries. The median income is close to the average, a result of the facts that families are bunched near the center of the distribution and that incomes are not severely skewed at either end. The bottom 20 percent of the population earn 7.5 percent of the income while the top 20 percent earn 29 percent of the income, both figures indicating a more egalitarian distribution than currently exists in the United States.

This is not the only array of incomes consistent with justice — for example, the portion of the population just at the poverty line might be lower. It is, however, a fair array, allowing as it does considerable differences in personal incomes to reflect differences in accomplishments and incentives, while responding to the fact of moral equality by restricting most incomes within a narrow 2:1 band.

Optimal Income Distribution in Capitalism

Could a capitalist economic system achieve an income distribution in the neighborhood of the one specified in Table 3.1? Could an 8:1 ratio be approached? Could most families be clustered within a 2:1 ratio? Could the income share of the highest 20 percent of families be kept to 29 percent? It is unlikely. Chapter 2 identified a large gap between the rich and the poor as one of the defining characteristics of capitalism.

We need to explore, however, how a capitalist system might move in the direction of an equitable income distribution.

One of the characteristics of capitalism posited in chapter 2 was the active participation of governments, at all levels, in the economic life of the society. Chapters 4, 5, and 6 will discuss ways in which governments can alter the income distribution to make it more just. This section deals with the private market in the absence of government intervention. It demonstrates why little if any progress can be made by the market toward a just income distribution, even in the unlikely circumstance in which a significant number of people with private economic power would like it to.

Let us return to the question of why capitalist employers are sometimes willing to pay exceptionally high salaries. In his most lucrative year playing basketball, Michael Jordan's salary was $33 million. This was far higher than would have been needed to persuade him to play basketball and do his best at it. If he would have been willing to play basketball for $20,000, then $32,980,000 of his income was strictly unnecessary. Economists give the name "economic rent" to payments that are unnecessary in this sense: that the person receiving them would have performed his job just the same without them. Most of Jordan's salary was rent. The exercise conducted above, trying to figure out the incomes needed to induce people to do their jobs to the best of their abilities, can be thought of as eliminating the economic rents in their incomes.

Can the capitalist market system eliminate economic rents? One would think that capitalist employers would have a strong interest in doing so. If their goal is to maximize their profits, why would they not eliminate the economic rents and simply pay people the minimum necessary to get them to do their jobs? The answer is that in a competitive market system, what is economic rent to the system as a whole may well be a necessary payment to a particular employer. Why does a tenant farmer pay rent for the land he uses, when the land would still be there in the absence of the payment? Because that particular tenant would not be able to use the land if he paid no rent. If he paid no rent, the landowner would provide the use of the land to someone else who was willing to pay. Why would the other farmer be willing to pay? Because the land is sufficiently fertile that he could still make a living from farming it after paying the rent. Why did the Chicago Bulls pay so many millions to Jordan when he would have been willing to play basketball for much less? Because he would not have been willing to play for the

Bulls for less; he would have taken his talents instead to the Hornets or the Knicks. The organization that actually paid him was the Bulls, and to the Bulls the payment was needed if they were to have the services of the great star. To the Bulls, Jordan's salary was not economic rent; it was a necessary payment.

So we can turn the question around and ask why the Bulls thought it worth their while to pay Jordan such a huge sum. The answer: by securing the services of Jordan, the Bulls' management believed they could increase their revenues by more than $33 million a year. Of course they would have preferred to pay less, but other teams had the same belief as the Bulls and would have been willing to pay roughly the same amount for him.

This story is not the only explanation of wages in the capitalist system. Some wages are set by collective bargaining agreements, by long-standing custom, by the power of senior managers to set their own salaries, or by outright discrimination. Whatever the underlying causes of wage differences in the market, individual firms often find that they have to match the wages being paid by other firms if they wish to secure a competent labor force. Capitalist firms will do this, even if their managers begin with a commitment to keep the wage differentials in their organization narrow. They will not be able to hold out against the fact that the people they wish to employ have alternative opportunities. I have personal experience with this issue that may cast light on the problem that ethical employers face.

For many years I have been a volunteer board member of the Santa Cruz Community Credit Union, a small, nonprofit cooperative financial institution dedicated to improving the economic prospects of low- and moderate-income people in my home community.[21] The credit union first opened in a storefront in 1977, and the few employees earned low, equal incomes. By 1980 the institution had grown, and with it the staffing needs. With some trepidation, we decided to name two of the paid staff people "managers" and the others tellers, the former to receive a modest monthly salary and the latter to be paid an hourly wage rate that summed, over the course of a month, to less than the managers' salaries. The difference in incomes seemed fair to us because of the added responsibilities of management. As the years went on, the tasks became more varied, and the levels of responsibility in the institution increased. By 1985 we feared we were losing our moral bearings in terms of employment policies, so we instituted a maximum 4:1 ratio between the highest and lowest paid person in the credit union. The

4:1 ratio was actually a huge change from our earliest days of equal pay, and we did not think that we would bump up against its limits. We put it in place out of a sense of justice; we thought that no one in our community should earn more than four times the wages of anyone else.

As the institution grew, however, the ratio became confining, and we eventually had to abandon it. We wanted to compensate our manager fairly for her years of skill-building and for her responsibilities. We did not want her to suffer a severe income loss below what she could have earned in another similar institution. We also worried that if she were not paid adequately we would not be able to hire a competent successor when she left. We could not solve the problem by raising the lowest wages in the credit union because — given the relationship of all the wage levels in the hierarchy — that would have required raising everyone's wages, and the institution, already quite marginal financially, would have lost too much money to be viable. So after a good deal of soul searching and even acrimony, we abandoned the ratio and adopted a new rule that all compensation levels in the credit union, including the manager's, would be set in light of the compensation levels for comparable jobs in credit unions of the same size, a little higher than comparable wages for the low-level positions in our institution and a little lower for the high-level positions. We had instituted the earnings ratio in the first place because of our sense of fairness, but without understanding that different conceptions of fairness could conflict. We needed to be fair to our entry-level people, but we needed to be fair to our top person too, and in particular we needed to be fair to the institution, its members, and its mission by attracting the best people we could to our staff. Without having read Plato at the time, we had set an ancient standard of just income differentials, and we found that we could not maintain it if we were going to be true to our principal responsibility, which was to provide for a strong and healthy credit union that could work for social change in the community.

This story reveals quite a lot about the possibility of achieving justice in incomes. It is impossible to accomplish at the level of the individual firm, if the firm wishes to remain competitive by keeping its overall costs in check and attracting effective workers who have other opportunities. Thought of in overall terms — in terms of what was necessary to induce our staff to do their best in their profession — some of the salary we paid was no doubt economic rent. It was not economic rent to our institution, however; it was completely necessary.

It goes without saying that most firms in the capitalist system have different motivations from our little community credit union. They are committed primarily to doing well, not doing good. They have no reason to adopt a goal of keeping to a limited ratio between the highest and lowest earnings in their organization. The goal of the managers may well be to maximize their earnings, not to limit them. So there is no reason to think that a capitalist market will achieve any kind of limit on the distribution of labor incomes. Still less will it achieve any limit on incomes deriving from capital or rental property. The gap in incomes is fundamental to capitalism.

There are many things the private market cannot do on its own, including protect the environment, build highways, enforce workplace safety standards, and avoid severe business cycles. For these and many other purposes we turn to governments to constrain, guide, and supplement the market. If we are to have any chance of moving in the direction of a just income distribution, government intervention is the main tool we have.

It is not the only tool; we have labor unions as well. Over the decades, unions have had a big impact on workplace justice in capitalist economies, helping workers to join forces with each other in order to bargain collectively with employers on terms more favorable than would exist if each worker were dealt with individually. Unions have been in retreat in the lifetimes of most current workers, however, and now represent a small minority of employees in capitalist economies. Everyone is subject to the jurisdiction of governments, and to that subject we now turn.

Notes

1. World Bank, *World Development Report 1999/2000* (New York: Oxford University Press, 1999).

2. Frank Levy, *The New Dollars and Dreams* (New York: Russell Sage Foundation, 1998).

3. Jeff Madrick, "How New Is the New Economy?" *New York Review of Books* 46 (September 23, 1999): 42–50.

4. Edward N. Wolff, *Top Heavy: The Increasing Inequality of Wealth in America and What Can Be Done about It* (New York: New Press, 1996).

5. David Leonhardt, "Executive Pay Drops Off the Political Radar," *New York Times*, April 16, 2000, Week in Review, 5.

6. Louis Uchitelle, "Devising New Math to Define Poverty," *New York Times*, October 18, 1999, A1.

7. See, among many others, Joel Slemrod, "Do We Know How Progressive the Income Tax System Should Be?" *National Tax Journal* 36 (September 1983): 361–70; Richard A. Musgrave and Peggy B. Musgrave, *Public Finance in Theory and Practice,* 5th ed. (New York: McGraw-Hill, 1989); and Harvey S. Rosen, *Public Finance,* 5th ed. (Boston: McGraw-Hill, 1999). The most precise answer from a modern economist that I have found is Ray C. Fair, "The Optimal Distribution of Income," *Quarterly Journal of Economics* 85 (1971): 551–79.

8. Plato, *The Laws,* trans. A. E. Taylor (London: J. M. Dent and Sons, 1934), 126.

9. In his concern that too much inequality will disrupt connections within the community, Plato anticipates modern communitarian philosophers. On communitarianism, see J. Donald Moon, "Communitarianism," in *The Encyclopedia of Applied Ethics* (San Diego: Academic Press, 1998), 1:551–61.

10. D. Gale Johnson and Karen McConnell Brooks, *Prospects for Soviet Agriculture in the 1980s* (Bloomington: Indiana University Press, 1983), 199. There is an extensive literature on agricultural communes, incentives, and reforms in both the Soviet Union and China. See, for example, Kenneth R. Gray, ed., *Soviet Agriculture: Comparative Perspectives* (Ames: Iowa State University Press, 1990), and Kali Kalirajan and Yanrui Wu, eds., *Productivity and Growth in Chinese Agriculture* (New York: St. Martin's Press, 1999).

11. For a survey of the literature on incentives, see Donald O. Parsons, "The Employment Relationship: Job Attachment, Work Effort, and the Nature of Contracts," in *Handbook of Labor Economics,* ed. Orley Ashenfelter and Richard Layer (Amsterdam: North Holland, 1986), 2:789–848.

12. For example, Edward P. Lazear, *Performance Pay and Productivity,* Working Paper 5672 (Washington, D.C.: National Bureau of Economic Research, 1996).

13. For example, David Marsden and Ray Richardson, *Motivation and Performance Related Pay in the Public Sector: A Case Study of the Inland Revenue,* Discussion Paper 75 (London: London School of Economics, Center for Economic Performance, 1992).

14. Other ways exist of linking performance to compensation, including piece work, group profit-sharing systems, and group performance assessment.

15. Frederic W. Cook, "Merit Pay and Performance Appraisal," in *The Compensation Handbook: A State-of-the-Art Guide to Compensation Strategy and Design,* ed. Milton L. Rock and Lance A. Berger (New York: McGraw-Hill, 1991), 542–66.

16. The literature on organizational hierarchies is surveyed in Robert Gibbons and Michael Waldman, "Careers in Organizations: Theory and Evidence," in *Handbook of Labor Economics,* ed. Orley Ashenfelter and David Card (Amsterdam: Elsevier, 1999), 3B:2373–437.

17. Alan Wolfe, "The Pursuit of Autonomy," *New York Times Magazine,* May 7, 2000, 53–56.

18. Reed Abelson, "A Leader's-Eye View of Leadership," *New York Times,* October 10, 1999, sec. 3, 1.

19. Robert Nozick, *Anarchy, State, and Utopia* (New York: Basic Books, 1974).

20. The figures in this paragraph may be found in or calculated from United States Census Bureau, *Statistical Abstract of the United States: 1999,* 119th ed. (Washington, D.C.: 1999), Tables 70, 732, and 750.

21. John Isbister, *Thin Cats: The Community Development Credit Union Movement in the United States* (Davis: University of California Center for Cooperatives, 1994).

Chapter 4

TAXATION OF INCOME

THE CAPITALIST market follows its own logic of financial compensation, a logic that has no relationship to the equality component of justice. Even if their owners and managers wished to, firms could not unilaterally adopt compensation schemes that accorded with their ideas of distributive justice if those schemes differed substantially from the practices of other firms, because they would not be able to attract and retain people to whom they gave relatively low pay packages. Competitive pressures in almost every market preclude any firm from moving very far out of step. If capitalist societies are to focus upon justice in the distribution of incomes, therefore, it must be through the aegis of governments. Governments can impose rules that apply to every firm; an employee cannot avoid dealing with the hand of government simply by switching to another firm.

Governments intervene to change the distribution of incomes in capitalist societies in three main ways. They regulate some wages that are paid by private firms, they impose taxes, and they make transfer payments to people (that is, payments not in return for work or other services rendered).[1] In terms of regulation, national governments, including the US government, set minimum wages below which it is illegal for firms to pay workers. They also often prohibit discrimination based on such factors as race, gender, religious preference, and age. These regulations are important, but it is through the fiscal tax and transfer mechanism that governments can have their principal effect on incomes. This chapter and the next two explore the extent to which government programs of taxation and transfer payments can convert the distribution of incomes generated by the market into one that accords with justice. Chapter 4 deals with taxes in relationship to income, chapter 5 with taxes on wealth, and chapter 6 with transfer payments.

A few words on terminology: taxes are described as regressive, proportional, or progressive, usually with respect to personal incomes. A proportional tax is one that relieves people of the same proportion of their income, whatever their income is. A regressive tax is one that takes a lower proportion from people with higher incomes, and a progressive tax one that takes a higher proportion from people with higher incomes. Tax rates can be thought of as either average or marginal rates. The average tax rate is one's tax payment divided by one's total income. The marginal rate is the extra tax paid on any extra income one earns. In a progressive tax system, the marginal rates rise: perhaps zero on the first $20,000 of income, 10 percent on the next $20,000, 20 percent on the next $20,000, and so forth.

The Right to Tax

The most basic question is whether the government has the right to tax its citizens. Libertarians, as we will see, say that it does not. The argument in favor of taxation must include at least two parts. It must show that taxation serves a useful social purpose and that people do not have an absolute right to retain all their holdings. We begin with the uses of taxes.

The Uses of Taxes

The narrowest use of taxation is in order to protect individual rights.[2] People may have an individual right to hold private property, but that right would be worthless in an anarchic society. For property to have lasting value, it must be protected by a legal system, by a police department, by a fire department, and perhaps by armed forces. Even a person who believed there was no justification for the provision of public goods would still have to acquiesce in some taxation, in order to protect individual rights. In addition, most of us do want public goods. Some goods cannot be provided by the private market, or, if they can, provision by the market would be inefficient. The market might, for example, be able to provide a system of streets and highways, but only with an onerous system of tolls that would greatly diminish their usefulness. Imagine the bother if you had to pay a fee to a corporation every time you took your car out of the garage to go to the grocery store.

A libertarian might object to these uses of taxes. He might say that if some of us want a fire department to protect our private property and a system of accessible roads, we should pay for them. We should not, however, be required to pay for them if we do not want them. Those who want a fire department are perfectly free to contribute as much as they think the fire department is worth to them, but they should not be compelled to pay taxes for its support.

A moment's reflection will reveal that this argument cannot stand. A central feature of public safety and of most public goods is that, once they exist, people cannot be excluded from their benefits. If the armed forces defend one of us against invasion, they defend all. That being the case, and if we are going to be taxed for the support of public goods and services in proportion to how much we say we value them, we will have an incentive to say that we do not value them. If the fire department is going to exist anyway, and if it is going to protect everyone's property (since if it lets one house burn, the fire could spread to other houses), everyone has an incentive to pretend not to value it and therefore be relieved of the burden of paying for it. The consequence will be that the state will not accumulate much if any revenue and we will not get the public goods and services that we want. Fire departments and other public goods and services cannot be supported by voluntary donations if people cannot be excluded from their benefits.[3]

The first two uses of taxes — the protection of rights and the provision of public goods — are valid but limited. A person who accepted the distribution of incomes generated by the private market as being fair could support taxation on these two grounds. Taxation for these purposes does not necessarily change the distribution of incomes, at least not very much. It simply increases the efficiency with which rights are protected and goods and services are provided. A more controversial use of taxes is to change the market distribution of incomes. It is a valid use of taxes because, as we have seen, the market distribution is unjust. Most of chapter 4 concentrates on this use of taxes.

Why People May Be Relieved of Their Holdings

We may grant that the state has legitimate uses for our tax money without conceding that it necessarily has the right to take the money from us without our individual consent. After all, I could make good use of more money, but I do not have the right to steal it from you. Why should the state be in a privileged position? The libertarians have made the case that it should not, and among the libertarian documents there is no more influential statement than Robert Nozick's *Anarchy, State, and Utopia.*

Nozick holds to what he calls an "entitlement theory" of justice. He claims that if a piece of property was not privately owned and you acquired it justly, or if it did not exist and you created it in a just manner, you are entitled to it and no one has the right to take it from you. What does "justly" mean in this context? Nozick does not commit himself to any particular answer, but he argues that there are neutral rules governing acquisition, rules that apply to everyone. You are not permitted to violate these rules, obtaining your resources by fraud, for example, or by robbery. He says further that you are entitled to transfer your resources. You can give them away if you wish, or you can spend them in legitimate markets. Assuming that you transfer them in a just manner, the person who receives them is entitled to them. Again in this context, "just" means according to obvious, neutral social rules. You are entitled to pay money to a producer of shoes, for example, in return for obtaining the shoes, and the shoemaker is entitled to receive that money, but you are not entitled to pay money to a murderer in exchange for killing your spouse. Nozick writes:

> If the world were wholly just, the following inductive definition would exhaustively cover the subject of justice in holdings:
>
> 1. A person who acquires a holding in accordance with the principle of justice in acquisition is entitled to that holding.
>
> 2. A person who acquires a holding in accordance with the principle of justice in transfer, from someone else entitled to the holding, is entitled to the holding.
>
> 3. No one is entitled to a holding except by (repeated) applications of 1 and 2.

It follows that "if each person's holdings are just, then the total set (distribution) of holdings is just."[4]

What could be a possible moral justification for redistribution, for asserting that it is the duty of some people to divest themselves of resources and transfer them to other people, or for saying that the state has the right to change the distribution of income or wealth by lowering some people's holdings and raising others? According to Nozick: only when an injustice has occurred. If I have stolen money from you, for example, I must give it back. The state is not permitted to redistribute holdings for any other reasons, certainly not if those losing their holdings are entitled to them, according to his description of entitlement.

Nozick argues that no *pattern* of economic distribution is morally justified. A pattern could be based on the idea that everyone should have an equal income, or that people's incomes should be in proportion to their productivity, or anything else. The problem with all such patterns, Nozick believes, is that in order to achieve them, the state must take from some people and give to others, and this is an unjust violation of rights. If by some strange circumstance a justly patterned distribution arose at some point, it would be unstable and would disappear immediately. To show this, Nozick tells what has become the well-known parable of Wilt Chamberlain, one of the dominant basketball players of the 1960s. Suppose, says Nozick, that incomes are distributed to people according to the pattern that you prefer: say, equal shares to everyone. Call this distribution D_1. Now Wilt Chamberlain and the owner of his basketball team voluntarily sign a contract. For every person attending a home game, Chamberlain will receive twenty-five cents. When the fans enter the building, they will deposit most of the ticket price in one box, and twenty-five cents in another box with Chamberlain's name. He is such a draw that in the course of the season, 1 million fans attend the home games, and he consequently ends the year with $250,000, much more than anyone else.

The initial distribution, D_1, which you favored, has disappeared. Now we have distribution D_2, in which Chamberlain has more than you think he should have. But where is the injustice? The owner accomplished what he wanted, as did Chamberlain. Both acted ethically. The fans also did what they wanted. No one forced them to attend the games; they did so voluntarily, in order to see the great man play, and they willingly deposited their quarters in the box. So the new distribution of income, D_2, the distribution in which Chamberlain has $250,000, is just, even though it is different from D_1, which you favor. Would the state be justified in taking away Chamberlain's gains in order to restore D_1? Of course not, answers Nozick, because no one — not the owner, not Chamberlain, and not the fans — did anything wrong.

What is wrong with Nozick's libertarianism, the view that people have an absolute right to all the property they have accumulated? One of its failings is that it does not make the distinction advanced in chapter 1 between attributes and willpower. To the extent that our holdings are the result of personal attributes for which we bear no responsibility, we cannot be said to deserve them. We deserve to be compensated only for the autonomous use of our will. Another failing is that while Nozick defends freedom, he neglects the interactive nature of freedom in the way we have developed it: that one person's freedom necessarily impinges on another's.[5] If you have all the resources and I have none, you are freer to pursue your goals than I am; my freedom would be enhanced by getting some of your resources. This relationship is critical to freedom as it really exists in the world.

The most basic problem with Nozick's position is that it does not acknowledge the cooperative nature of social and economic relationships. We are not merely individual units; we are connected to each other in such fundamental ways that without each other we could not survive. He fails to deal with the fact that many people are involved in the production of just about everything. An automobile is the product of countless inventors, engineers, miners, technicians, laborers, financiers, salespeople, advertisers, and entrepreneurs in different countries and over a period of time. All the participants are essential to the production of the automobile; any one of them could reasonably say, "Without me, the automobile would not have been produced, so I deserve a lot of the income."

Not only production but distribution is a social process, resulting from the interaction of millions of people. I earn my income, for example, from teaching — from being productive at something — but exactly what I earn depends on many factors for which I can claim no credit. My earnings depend partly upon my good fortune in living in a rich country, the quality of the schools I went to, population growth in my state, political decisions made by the legislature, the investment successes of my institution's treasurer, the popularity of my particular field, and much more. Wilt Chamberlain was a great basketball player, but the fact that he earned more than the world's greatest canoeist is a reflection not of his superiority or desert but of the fact that more of his fellow citizens would pay to watch basketball than to watch paddling.

The interdependence of our holdings was recognized as long ago as 1795 by Thomas Paine in his pamphlet *Agrarian Justice:*

> Land ... is the free gift of the Creator in common to the human race. Personal property is the *effect of society:* and it is as impossible for an individual to acquire personal property without the aid of society, as it is for him to make land originally. Separate an individual from society, and give him an island or a continent to possess, and he cannot acquire personal property. He cannot be rich. ... All accumulation, therefore, of personal property, beyond what a man's own hands produce, is derived to him by living in society; and he owes on every principle of justice, of gratitude, and of civilization, a part of that accumulation back again to society from whence the whole came.[6]

Nozick's position is that if you act legally, according to the standard rules, you may keep everything you have. To overstate his view only a little, as long as you stay out of jail you are in the clear. This is a misunderstanding of social justice. Social justice is not a subcategory of criminal justice. It consists in getting what you deserve, not just obeying the laws. How can I say that I deserve every cent of my income when I have no control over so many of the factors that are responsible for it? I earn perhaps twenty times the salary of a professor in Russia, not because I am twenty times as meritorious but because of the accident of location.[7]

I am, of course, partly responsible for my income and my assets. I have worked for them. I am not completely responsible, however, because so many other people and factors — besides my own efforts — have contributed to my holdings. It follows, therefore, contrary to what Nozick asserts, that society — acting through the agency of the democratic state — may change my holdings, in order to bring them closer to what I really deserve, that is, in order to improve the quality of social justice. It may not, however, completely confiscate my holdings, because I am *partly* responsible for them. A state that egregiously violated the Fourth Amendment to the US Constitution, "the right of the people to be secure in their persons, houses, papers and effects, against unreasonable searches and seizures," would be unfree and hence unjust.

Protection of our freedom requires that we be able to keep some of what we have, but our society has a claim on some. Because our holdings are the result of complex social processes, we do not have an absolute right to them. A democratic state — a state that legitimately represents the people as a whole — has the right to tax. It may tax in order to protect our rights, in order to provide public goods and services, and in order to improve the distribution of incomes.

Just Taxes and Just Income Distributions

The libertarians are not alone in thinking it illegitimate to use taxes to change the distribution of incomes. Almost everyone — members of the public as well as economists and theorists — thinks that such a use of taxes is wrong. I am going to argue against this view and in favor of the position that taxes should be used to help us approach a just distribution of disposable or after-tax incomes.

Curiously, mainstream opinion is not reluctant to see government transfer payments — social security, unemployment insurance, welfare payments, and so forth — used to improve the distribution of incomes that come from the market. People are averse, however, to seeing taxes used for this purpose. This is not to say that people think taxation is divorced from concepts of fairness or justice. Not at all. Almost unanimously, however, they believe that taxes should be fair, not that taxes should be used to create a fair income distribution. The distance between these two views is substantial. Call the first *just taxation* and the second *just income distribution*.[8] People who hold the first view — that it is taxes that should be fair — implicitly accept the underlying income distribution, the incomes generated by the market, as fair. If the income distribution is already pretty close to fair, and if taxes must be imposed in order to provide for public goods and services and for transfer payments, the question relating to justice is simply how best to allocate the pain of taxation. This is the just-taxation position. Sometimes it is characterized by the phrase that taxes should be "distributionally neutral." That is, people's posttax incomes should be in the same relationship to each other as their pre-tax incomes were. A person who begins, on the other hand, with the view that the market distribution of incomes is fundamentally unjust may be willing to think of taxation as a tool to move incomes in a more just direction.

Public opinion of taxation has often been surveyed; the results are sensitive to the wording of the questions posed.[9] Some surveys show broad support for a proportional tax, others for progressive taxation with graduated rates as incomes rise. One of the most careful studies, by Peggy A. Hite and Michael L. Roberts, shows public support for modestly progressive taxation.[10] Respondents believed that even the poorest people should pay taxes amounting to about 3 percent of their incomes and that the highest-income people should be assessed an amount equivalent to about 20 percent. A tax system such as this, with modestly rising rates, would do little to alter the basic distribution of incomes in the market. It is consistent with what is described below as the ability-to-pay principle, one of the variants of the just-taxation view.

Economists have developed three ways of assessing tax equity, all of them falling within the just-taxation framework: the benefit principle, efficiency, and ability to pay.[11]

Benefit Principle

The benefit principle is that people should pay for what they get from the government. In the private sector, it is usually fair for you to pay the grocer for a bag of food, because the grocer is providing the food and because you, not someone else, are getting it. A similar standard of fairness can hold in the public sector. An example of the benefit principle in action is the excise tax on gasoline. People who drive automobiles pay the tax, the proceeds of which are earmarked for maintaining the highway system. If you do not drive you do not pay, and the more you drive the more you pay for the highways. It is a just tax according to the benefit principle.

The benefit principle cannot, however, define just taxation for many government activities. It is impossible to say, for example, who benefits and by how much from national defense or from macroeconomic stability. So the benefit principle can be used in a few well-defined cases — perhaps the gasoline tax, postage stamps, sewage connection charges, and entrance fees at public parks — but it is inadequate for most activities of the government.

Efficiency Principle

The efficiency principle is that taxes should be assessed in such a way as to maximize production, the rate of economic growth, and/or the level of personal welfare. Economists typically begin with the completely free market as the standard of efficiency and then try to identify taxes that result in the fewest changes in economic behavior away from that standard. The problem addressed by the efficiency principle is that taxes generally have side effects; they induce people to change their behavior as they try to avoid or minimize the tax.[12]

Inefficiencies caused by taxation include the possibility that income taxes will cause people to reduce their working hours and that taxes on savings will cause people to reduce their savings. The empirical studies tend to show that such effects, while they exist, are relatively small.[13] The main way that the current American tax system could be made more efficient is by closing the numerous loopholes in the personal and corporate income taxes that induce people to engage in tax-avoiding rather than productive activity.

Both the benefit and the efficiency principles of taxation accept the market-generated income distribution as just and contain no provisions for changing it. The benefit principle simply says that the standard of justice in taxation is that people should pay for what they get from the government, while the efficiency principle says that taxes should change people's behavior as little as possible.

Ability-to-Pay Principle

The ability-to-pay principle goes a step in the direction of altering the distribution of personal incomes, but only a small step. This principle states that we should pay taxes according to our abilities. How are our abilities to be identified? This is a contentious issue, but for many purposes the best choice is income.[14] The income we earn each year determines our ability to pay taxes.

A long tradition in the field of public finance defines ability to pay by two criteria, horizontal and vertical equity.[15] Horizontal equity means that people who are situated equally should be impacted equally by the tax system, while vertical equity means that people who are situated unequally should be impacted differently. Horizontal equity is precise — equal treatment of equals[16] — while vertical equity is vague, since one can grant that people who are economically unequal should be treated unequally without thereby answering the question of how unequally. Nevertheless, the basic idea of vertical equity within the ability-to-pay framework is that people who are able to pay more taxes should do so.

Most taxes are based roughly on the principle of ability to pay. The more income you earn, or purchases you make, or property you own, the greater your tax liability. An exception to this is the head tax or poll tax, a tax of the same amount imposed on each person without regard to her income or assets. Under a poll tax, for example, each person, whether homeless or a millionaire, might be assessed $100. We no longer have poll taxes because, since they bear no relationship to one's ability to pay, they seem to us to be unfair. When Prime Minister Thatcher's government tried to impose one in Britain in 1990, riots broke out and the tax was withdrawn. All current taxes pass a gross test of vertical equity, therefore. When we try to get more specific than this, we land in difficulty. How unequally should unequals be treated?

We might ask the question in terms of the distinction between regressive, proportional, and progressive taxes. The best justification for a regressive tax system has nothing to do with vertical equity but rather is based on the argument for the benefit principle. According to the benefit principle, taxes are understood as the payment for public goods. In the free market for private goods and services, prices are more or less the same for rich and poor. Some exceptions exist — higher grocery prices in poor central cities, for example, or higher cost of credit for the poor — but these are relatively minor compared to most prices. When you buy a new Chevrolet, you pay roughly the same price regardless of your income. It could be argued that we all consume more or less the same public goods, so we should be presented with the same tax bill for them. This would be the head tax, certainly regressive in structure. A less severe interpretation of the benefit principle would be that people's use of public goods rises as their incomes rise, but less than proportionately. For example, the need for a police force to protect one's property might rise as one's holdings of property rose, but the need for a police force to protect one's personal safety would be independent of one's income. If this were the basis upon which taxes were assessed, tax payments would rise with income but less than proportionately, in a regressive manner.[17]

This justification for regressive taxes collapses for three reasons that we have already seen. First, it is impossible to allocate most government services to individuals in the way envisioned by the benefit principle. Second, regressive taxation does not respect differences in people's ability to pay. Third, the benefit principle begins with the assumption that the market-generated distribution of incomes is just; in a capitalist economy, as we have seen, this assumption is false.

What can justify a proportional tax system? In a way, a proportional tax system seems fair, perhaps even the embodiment of the ability-to-pay principle. If one's ability to pay is measured by income, a person with double the income appears to have double the capacity to pay. Proposals for a "flat tax" appeal to many people for this reason.

The logic in support of a proportional tax system fails as well, however. A person with twice the income has more than twice the ability to pay. This follows from the fact that we each need a minimum of income just to subsist. The subsistence level is no doubt a range rather than a distinct cutoff, and it is certainly influenced by cultural factors. It is higher in the United States than in India. Still it is quite real. In the United States, it is represented by something like the poverty line. People with only poverty-level income actually have no ability to pay taxes; they need all their income just to subsist. In 1999, according to the Indiana Economic Development Council, a family of four in Indiana with about $20,000 a year was able to spend $506 a month on food, $481 on housing, $245 on health care, $249 on transportation, and $199 on personal expenses, for a total of $1,680, with nothing left over.[18] Such a family was unable to pay taxes.

People with twice the poverty-level income have some ability to pay taxes, but nevertheless most of their resources are needed for their own uses. People with four times the poverty-level income have well more than twice the ability of those with just two times, because they are easily able to cover their essential costs and still have significant discretionary income. And so on as incomes rise.

The logic of vertical equity within the ability-to-pay framework calls, therefore, for progressive taxation. As people's incomes rise, the portion of their income that is not required for basic needs rises more quickly. People with higher incomes should pay not only higher taxes but a higher proportion of their income in taxes, if taxes are based on ability to pay. The ability-to-pay principle also calls for a well-thought-out series of deductions from taxable income. For example, two people with different incomes may not have different abilities to pay if the one with the higher income has, say, more children, more medical bills, or more necessary expenses for earning a living. Taxation should be based on income net of deductions based on these sorts of factors.

The ability-to-pay principle gives more attention to income distribution than does either the benefit principle or the efficiency principle. It is important to see, however, that the idea of vertical equity, within the ability-to-pay principle, does not justify the redistribution of personal incomes. Ability to pay lies squarely within the just-taxation framework, not the just-income-distribution framework. Its entire focus is one of spreading the tax burden fairly, so that those who are more able to bear the burden do so. It contains no insight into the fairness or lack thereof of the original market-generated income distribution, and it does not envision the tax system as a tool for changing that distribution.

Redistributive Taxation

The redistribution of people's incomes through the use of the tax system is valid, since the distribution of incomes that is created by an unrestricted market is in many respects unjust. The market cannot provide for the unemployed, for the disabled, for the elderly, for the sick, or for those like mothers of dependent children whose responsibilities keep them out of the labor market. The market allocates incomes to some people that are insufficient to provide a decent life, and it allocates incomes to others that are so lavish as to far exceed any reasonable need or desert. These are injustices, not just regrettable occurrences.

The tax system should redistribute incomes so that the after-tax distribution is more just than the pre-tax distribution, if not completely just. Taxation is the only tool we have for changing the entire distribution. Transfer payments can correct the worst injustices at the bottom of the distribution, but they are powerless to adjust the excesses at the top. The principle that should inform taxation is not ability to pay but justice. Taxation should bring more equality to the incomes that we receive, it should do this while respecting people's liberties, and it should not create disincentives that make the economy inefficient.[19]

Chapter 3 concluded that a just income distribution would confine most of us within a fairly narrow range of incomes, perhaps a 2:1 ratio. It would constrain almost all of us within a broader range, say 8:1. It would permit a few incomes above this range, on grounds of freedom and efficiency. Progressive taxation could help to move us in this direction, although not the full distance.

We can see the problem by returning to Plato, who recommended a progressive tax with a vengeance. To keep the ratio of incomes at a maximum of 4:1, he wanted zero taxation on income or wealth up to the level of four times the value of a lot, followed by 100 percent taxation on all earnings above that limit. This was the way to eliminate incomes above a fixed level: tax them all away. Translating Plato into the language of modern economics, the marginal tax rate (the ratio of additional tax to additional income earned) jumps precipitously from zero to 100 percent at the cutoff income, and this causes the average tax rate to begin rising at that point. One could imagine a tax system so progressive, and perhaps it would have worked in Plato's colony, but it would be wrong to recommend it in a capitalist system. As I argued in chapter 3, if a confiscatory tax led people not to employ their resources productively, because they could get no posttax gain from doing so, it would be inefficient, while if it did not have this effect but simply took away all the extra earned income, it would violate people's freedom.

It is possible to imagine a completely just distribution of incomes, as we did in chapter 3. It is possible as well to invent a social system whose purpose it is to achieve this distribution of incomes. As chapter 2 noted, the world has known many such systems, from preindustrial noncompetitive societies to socialism and communism in the twentieth century. It is not possible, however, to achieve a completely just distribution under a regime of capitalism. The capitalist free market will not come close to achieving it, and the only tax system that would redistribute market incomes sufficiently would be so confiscatory as to be unjust itself.

We can, however, do a better job of income distribution within capitalism than we have done so far. Certainly the United States can do better, since it has the worst record of any industrialized nation. The share of income going to the top 20 percent of the US population is 45 percent. In descending order, the income shares of the top quintiles in the comparison countries are: Switzerland, 44 percent; Ireland, 43 percent; Australia, 41 percent; Spain, 40 percent; France, 40 percent; Netherlands, 40 percent; United Kingdom, 40 percent; Canada, 39 percent; Italy, 39 percent; Germany, 37 percent; Finland, 36 percent; Norway, 35 percent; Belgium, 35 percent; Sweden, 35 percent.[20]

Sweden, Norway, and Belgium make more use of a progressive tax system than the United States does, and they all keep the share of the top 20 percent of the population down to 35 percent, far below the American figure of 45 percent. Each of those countries also succeeds in allocating 10 percent of its income to the lowest 20 percent of the population, exactly double the American share. They use progressive taxes not to confiscate incomes above a cutoff level but to assess those incomes at increasingly steep rates. People with high incomes in those countries get to keep a portion, although a diminishing portion, of the extra income they earn.

Tax Reform

In order to see how taxes can be used to redistribute incomes, we need to know something about the incidence of different taxes, that is, who bears their burden.[21] This turns out to be difficult because some taxpayers are able to shift the burden of a tax. For example, economists suspect that the property tax, while paid by property owners, is often shifted to renters in the form of higher rents. Economists are divided on whether the corporate profits tax is shifted, and therefore whether it is a burden on the stockholders of corporations or on the consumers of goods produced by corporations. In each case, if the tax is not shifted it is probably somewhat progressive, since property owners and stockholders tend to have higher than average incomes, while if the tax is shifted it is regressive.

The personal income tax is progressive since it is based directly on people's incomes and since the effective rates rise as income rises. Deductions or "loopholes" allow people to avoid the tax to a certain extent, and these deductions become more plentiful as personal incomes rise, so the tax is not as progressive as the published rates make it appear to be. Still, there is little opportunity for people to shift the personal income tax onto the backs of others. According to estimates made by Richard and Peggy Musgrave, the payroll tax — the tax that supports Social Security and Medicare — is progressive at the low end of incomes and regressive at the high end. In other words, it is imposed disproportionately on middle-income people. Its high-end regressivity is a consequence of two factors: that it is imposed only on wage, not investment, income and that it is not imposed on annual wages above a cutoff level, currently $76,200. The sales tax is clearly regressive, since poor people spend a high proportion of their incomes on consumer goods and save little, while higher-income people save a higher proportion of their income and consume a lower proportion. Sales and excise taxes together take about 7 percent of the incomes of the lowest 10 percent of taxpayers, but only 2 percent of the incomes of the upper 10 percent.

Taking all the taxes together, and conceding that there is much we do not know about tax incidence, it appears that the overall tax system in the United States is only barely progressive. Federal taxes — principally the personal and corporate income taxes plus the payroll tax — are probably progressive.[22] State and local taxes — heavily weighted by the sales and property taxes — are regressive. Musgrave and Musgrave estimate that if the corporation and property taxes are substantially shifted, the overall tax system is almost proportional at 25 percent of income for each income group, while if they are not shifted, it is somewhat progressive, rising from 17 percent among the lowest 10 percent of income earners to 28 percent among the highest 10 percent.[23] The personal income tax, assessed federally and also by most states, accounts for 35 percent of the revenue of all governments in the country and is the most progressive tax in the system.[24] Without it, the overall tax system would be sharply regressive.

In view of what we know about tax incidence, two reforms would contribute to a more just income distribution. The first is to expand the income tax and reduce if not eliminate most other taxes. Why not eliminate the regressive sales tax, for example, and replace the lost revenue with an expanded income tax? Sales taxes are assessed primarily at the state level, and they could be replaced by state income taxes. The federal payroll tax is sometimes defended as a tax with a special purpose: it funds the Social Security system. Payroll taxes do not need to have this role, however; Social Security could just as easily be funded by income taxes. At the very least, payroll taxes should be applied to all payrolls, not just those below $76,200. Property taxes — the principal source of local government revenues — are probably regressive, and there are other problems with the property tax that will be explored in chapter 5. Local governments could be funded by an income tax collected at the state level and then remitted. While this would reduce the autonomy of local governments somewhat, it would make the tax system more progressive, and it would put an end to the process of localities bidding for businesses by offering tax breaks (although this problem would remain at the state and national levels). The personal tax might even replace the corporation tax, since if the latter is not shifted it is only slightly progressive, while if it is shifted it is distinctly regressive.

The net effect of expanding the personal income tax and reducing the other taxes would be to make the overall system more progressive, since personal taxes are the most progressive we have. The system could be made even more progressive by means of the second reform, which is to increase the progressivity of the income tax. Earlier I argued that a completely confiscatory income tax, such as Plato's, would be unjust. Americans have nothing to worry about; their income tax is far from confiscatory. The poorest 20 percent of income earners should be relieved of paying any income tax at all, and the burden on the richest should be increased, through a combination of raising marginal rates on income earned above the subsistence level and eliminating some tax shelters.

How high could the top marginal rates be raised before they became confiscatory, thereby creating serious inefficiencies and/or violations of personal freedom? A marginal rate of 100 percent is too high. So are rates of 94 percent or 91 percent, rates that were imposed in the United States, the former toward the end of the Second World War and the latter from 1951 to 1964. The effective top marginal rates were much lower than this at those times, because of tax loopholes available for the rich. My guess is that the top marginal tax rate that is justified lies somewhere between 60 percent and 67 percent. Top income earners would pay in taxes between three-fifths and two-thirds of any extra income they earned. Their average tax rates would be less than this, since the highest rates would not apply to a portion of their incomes. They would still have a financial incentive to work, employ their resources, and earn money, since they would keep an appreciable portion of what they earned. The relatively high tax rate would be justified because income is never earned in isolation: each high-income earner owes his or her good fortune in large measure to many people who have toiled in return for much lower earnings. A relatively high rate at the top end would relieve people at the lower end from paying much in the way of taxes and would generate funds for transfer payments to low-income people, as well as for the provision of public goods and services. An expansion of the income tax in substitution for some of the other taxes and an increase in the progressivity of the marginal rates would make the income distribution more just, although not perfectly just.

The Republican Party has developed a different proposal for tax reform, the "flat tax." Proposed by economists Robert E. Hall and Alvin Rabushka, and endorsed by millionaire presidential candidate Steve Forbes, it has been attractive to a broad range of people in the party.[25] The flat tax would replace the complicated personal and corporate income taxes with a simple rule: pay 17 percent (or in some versions 18 percent, or 20 percent) of your income from work. Companies would pay the same rate on their profits. In some versions of the proposals, not all, an exemption is provided for low-income people. Personal income from investments — capital gains plus dividends from stocks and interest from bonds — would be excluded from the tax base, as would all inheritances. Some proponents of the flat tax want it to generate less revenue than the current income tax does, in order to curtail government spending. The flat tax is marketed as a populist measure, as a way of getting the gargantuan tax collector off our backs and simplifying the tax system. It is, however, a regressive proposal. Since it would exclude personal investment income, it would give a huge windfall tax advantage to the rich. Some rich people would pay no personal tax at all under the proposal. The flat tax would be a disastrous move in the direction of injustice. At best — depending upon the exemption — it would be somewhat progressive at the bottom end of the income distribution, but since it would have only one marginal tax rate, it would substantially reduce the progressivity of the current income tax. Taken together with the other taxes that it would not replace, like the sales, payroll, and property taxes, it would doubtless produce an overall tax system that was regressive.

The Constraints on Tax Reform in Capitalism

The limits imposed by capitalism on the use of progressive taxation to make the distribution of incomes more equal fall in three categories: justice, politics, and international competition. The limits relating to justice have already been described. The existence of the capitalist market ensures a wide dispersion in people's pre-tax earnings. Marginal tax rates at the 100 percent level or close to it, rates that would take away virtually all the earnings a person makes above a certain level, would be unjust for one or both of two reasons, that they would lead people to stop productive economic activity, thus violating the criterion of efficiency, or that they would completely confiscate earnings to which people have some right, violating the criterion of liberty. Tax rates may be high and progressive, but they may not, in justice, be confiscatory.

The political constraint on progressive taxation is that people with money have more than their share of political power, power they can use to defeat what they regard as overly progressive taxation. When the political system simply responds to the needs of capitalism, it loses its ability to constrain capitalism, to mold the market system in directions that would promote social justice. Progressive taxation cannot be instituted in a meaningful way without a fully democratic political process in which everyone is represented, in which the votes of some people do not count more than others, and in which platforms and policies are not distorted by campaign contributions.

The international constraint on progressive taxation is similar in form to the constraint we saw earlier that prevents individual firms from establishing just patterns of compensation in their organizations. Chapter 3 made the argument that people who believed their wages were overly restricted in a firm would simply move to another firm where wages were higher. Hence a firm whose management intended to keep the earnings differential within strict limits would find it difficult if not impossible to hire competent people at the higher level. A similar constraint applies to nations. Two characteristics of capitalism identified in chapter 2 were the high degree of financial capital and the global scope of the system. These two features conspire against a country that attempts to set its tax rates significantly differently from the rest of the world. Financial capital can now be switched from one country to another in seconds. If a country taxes the returns on capital more highly, capital is likely to flee that country and go into a low-tax country. This can create major problems for the high-tax country, including a fall in investment, a decline in the foreign exchange rate, an increase in interest rates, unemployment, and depression.

One should not overstate the practical limits of this problem for the United States. American tax rates are currently low, in all categories, in comparison to taxes in other industrial countries.[26] This is one of the biggest reasons that personal incomes are more skewed in the United States than elsewhere in the developed world. The United States could go a long distance in the direction of higher and more progressive tax rates without fear of becoming uncompetitive internationally.

A progressive tax system is an effective tool that can be used in a capitalist country like the United States to move the disposable incomes of its people into a fairer relationship one with another. A fair-income-distribution philosophy of public finance should replace the fair-taxation approach. The constraints on the use of progressive taxation to make the distribution of posttax incomes more just are real, but the United States is far from pushing up against those constraints.

Notes

1. Indirectly, governments also affect incomes through their expenditures on goods and services. The seminal discussion of the relationship between allocation and distribution in the public sector is Richard A. Musgrave, *The Theory of Public Finance* (New York: McGraw-Hill, 1959).

2. Stephen Holmes and Cass R. Sunstein, *The Cost of Rights: Why Liberty Depends on Taxes* (New York: W. W. Norton, 1999).

3. This understanding of public goods has long been a foundation of the theory of public finance. Its most elegant formulation is in Paul A. Samuelson, "The Pure Theory of Public Expenditure," *Review of Economics and Statistics* 36 (1954): 387–89, and Paul A. Samuelson, "Diagrammatic Exposition of a Theory of Public Expenditure," *Review of Economics and Statistics* 37 (1955): 350–56.

4. Robert Nozick, *Anarchy, State, and Utopia* (New York: Basic Books, 1974), 151, 153.

5. For a variation of this critique, see G. A. Cohen, "Robert Nozick and Wilt Chamberlain: How Patterns Preserve Liberty," *Erkenntnis* 11 (1977): 5–23.

6. Thomas Paine, *Thomas Paine Reader,* ed. Michael Foot and Isaac Kramnick (London: Penguin Books, 1987), 485.

7. For a related argument, see Barbara Fried, "Wilt Chamberlain Revisited: Nozick's 'Justice in Transfer' and the Problem of Market-Based Distribution," *Philosophy and Public Affairs* 24 (1995): 226–45.

8. This distinction is similar to the one made by Leslie Green between "interstitial equity" and "distributive equity." See his "Concepts of Equity in Taxation," in *Fairness in Taxation: Exploring the Principles,* ed. Allan M. Maslove (Toronto: University of Toronto Press, 1993), 87–103.

9. Joel Slemrod and Jon Bakija, *Taxing Ourselves: A Citizen's Guide to the Great Debate over Tax Reform* (Cambridge, Mass.: MIT Press, 1996), 59–62.

10. Peggy A. Hite and Michael L. Roberts, "An Experimental Investigation of Taxpayer Judgments on Rate Structure in the Individual Income Tax System," *Journal of the American Taxation Association* 13 (1991): 47–63.

11. Richard A. Musgrave, "Progressive Taxation, Equity, and Tax Design," in *Tax Progressivity and Income Inequality,* ed. Joel Slemrod (Cambridge: Cambridge University Press, 1994), 341–56. See also Musgrave, *Theory of Public Finance;* Richard A. Musgrave and A. Peacock, eds., *Classics in the Theory of Public Finance* (New York: McGraw-Hill, 1958); and Richard A. Musgrave and Peggy B. Musgrave, *Public Finance in Theory and Practice,* 5th ed. (New York: McGraw-Hill, 1989). Richard A. Musgrave has performed the enormously valuable service of making a wide variety of concepts of tax equity accessible to modern economists.

12. The seminal discussion of the theory of optimal taxation is Peter A. Diamond and James A. Mirrlees, "Optimal Taxation and Public Production I: Production Efficiency," and "II: Tax Rules," *American Economic Review* 61 (1971): 8–27 and 261–78.

13. Slemrod and Bakija, *Taxing Ourselves,* chapter 4. On the problem of estimating the behavioral responses to taxes, see Robert K. Triest, "Econometric

Issues in Estimating the Behavioral Response to Taxation: A Nontechnical Introduction," *National Tax Journal* 51 (1998): 761–72.

14. For discussions, see any good text in public finance, for example, Musgrave and Musgrave, *Public Finance,* or Harvey S. Rosen, *Public Finance*, 5th ed. (Boston: McGraw-Hill, 1999).

15. Musgrave, *Theory of Public Finance.*

16. Nonuniversal taxes — taxes imposed on one source of income and not another — do not create horizontal inequities if the units on which the taxes are imposed are mobile. See John Isbister, "On the Theory of Equitable Taxation," *National Tax Journal* 21 (1968): 332–39.

17. Strictly speaking, if the benefit principle holds, taxation will be regressive, proportional, or progressive depending upon whether the income elasticity of demand for public goods is below, equal to, or above its price elasticity, respectively. My assertion is that the income elasticity is likely to be low. See James M. Buchanan, "Fiscal Institutions and Efficiency in Collective Outlay," *American Economic Review* 54 (1964): 227–35.

18. Louis Uchitelle, "Devising New Math to Define Poverty," *New York Times,* October 18, 1999, A1.

19. Note that this justification is different from the utilitarian case for progressive taxation. According to utilitarianism, if the marginal utility of income declines, and if people's utility schedules are identical, social utility can be maximized by taking money away disproportionately, or perhaps even exclusively, from people with high incomes and redistributing it to people with lower incomes. As chapter 1 argued, however, utilitarianism is a useful foundation only for the efficiency component of justice, not for the equality and liberty components.

20. World Bank, *World Development Report 1999/2000* (New York: Oxford University Press, 1999).

21. On problems of tax incidence, see any good text in public finance, for example, Musgrave and Musgrave, *Public Finance.*

22. Congressional Budget Office, *Preliminary Estimates of Effective Tax Rates* (Washington, D.C., 1999), and Richard Kasten, Frank Sammartino, and Eric Toder, "Trends in Federal Tax Progressivity, 1980–93," in *Tax Progressivity and Income Inequality,* ed. Joel Slemrod (Cambridge: Cambridge University Press, 1994), 9–50.

23. Musgrave and Musgrave, *Public Finance,* Table 14–1.

24. Slemrod and Bakija, *Taxing Ourselves,* Table 2.1.

25. Robert E. Hall and Alvin Rabushka, *The Flat Tax,* 2d ed. (Stanford, Calif.: Hoover Institution Press, 1995). For a debate on the flat tax, see Robert E. Hall et al., *Fairness and Efficiency in the Flat Tax* (Washington, D.C.: AEI Press, 1996).

26. Slemrod and Bakija, *Taxing Ourselves,* Table 2.2.

Chapter 5

TAXATION OF WEALTH AND INHERITANCES

CHAPTERS 3 and 4 dealt with the distribution and taxation of income; chapter 5 turns from income to wealth. Wealth is a stock; it is the value of what one owns minus what one owes. It exists and can be measured at a moment in time; one can say, for example, what one's wealth is at noon on a given day. Income, in contrast, is a flow, the value of what one takes in between two moments. It makes no sense to ask what my income is at noon today, but I can say what it is between January 1 and December 31 of the current year, or even between 8:00 A.M. and 5 P.M. today. Income and wealth, while not the same, are related. Income can lead to the accrual of wealth, if one earns income and spends less than all of it on consumption. Similarly, wealth can produce income. For example, people whose wealth is in corporate stocks may collect income in the form of dividends from those stocks.

Wealth is an important indicator of economic inequality. It represents security, freedom, and power. In terms of security, a person with wealth need not fear the future in the way that a person without wealth does. Wealth provides a cushion against future reverses in income. Wealth leads to freedom — the freedom to buy an airplane ticket and go where one wants to go, for example, or to quit an oppressive job. Wealth creates power because it can be used to induce or force other people into actions on one's behalf.

Wealth is distributed far more unevenly than income in most countries. Chapter 3 showed that in the United States, which has one of the most skewed distributions of income among the developed capitalist countries, the top 20 percent of the population receive 45 percent of the income. At the same time, according to a recent estimate, the top 20 percent of the population own 85 percent of the wealth. In terms of financial wealth — stocks, bonds, and similar pieces of paper, as opposed to real assets like factories and houses — the top 20 percent own fully 94 percent. In fact the share of financial wealth going to the top 1 percent of the population, 48 percent, is greater than the share of income going to the top 20 percent.[1] There is no question but that this inequality conflicts with the norms of justice. Morally equal people should not be subject to the sort of power relationships that exist when 1 percent of the population controls almost half the financial wealth of the society. The huge differentials in wealth violate the precept of equal opportunity and make problematic the ideal of equal liberty.

Reducing the inequality in wealth distribution turns out to be a difficult subject. Some have proposed an annual tax on wealth, but this would create its own problem of injustice. A better way of reducing the inequality in wealth is a one-time tax on estates or inheritances. An inheritance tax should be heavy, although it should not completely confiscate estates. The chapter concludes by considering the relationship between inheritances and capitalism.

The Ethical Problem with a Tax on Wealth

The obvious response to the unjust inequality in wealth is to impose a heavy wealth tax, perhaps a progressive tax, but few countries do this. Twelve developed capitalist countries have a general wealth tax, among them Denmark, Germany, Sweden, and Switzerland, but even in those countries the tax generates a relatively small portion of government revenues.[2] The United States, along with most other countries, taxes the income from wealth — interest, dividends, and capital gains — but it has no general wealth tax. The inheritance tax yields so little revenue as to be hardly noticeable. The only substantial wealth tax in the United States is the property tax, which is imposed on one form of wealth only, real estate.

Edward N. Wolff recommends that the United States adopt something like the Swedish tax on wealth. It is progressive, exempting wealth valued at under $56,000 per taxpayer and then rising from a 1.5 percent rate to a top rate of 3 percent. This sort of tax, he shows, would have a significant equalizing effect on the distribution of wealth in the country, if imposed over a period of years.[3] I am unwilling to endorse Wolff's proposal because of the experience the United States has had with the property tax. When the property tax has been raised to relatively high levels, it has created serious injustices.

The ethical problem with the property tax and with all forms of wealth taxation that are imposed on an annual basis arises from the fact that property is a stock, while the tax is a flow. Property is a stock, existing at a moment in time, and it does not necessarily change in value over time. It may increase or decrease in value, but it is the whole value that is taxed by the property tax, not the change in value. Think about a property that does not change in value over time and does not generate any income for its owner. With a property tax as it exists in the United States, this same piece of unchanging property is taxed, and then taxed again the following year, and then again and again and again. If the property is really of unchanging value, and if it generates no income, the sum of the taxes over time gradually approaches and in time exceeds the value of the property. The value of the property net of the taxes imposed on it diminishes and eventually turns negative. In the case of property that does not increase in value and that does not generate an income, a permanent property tax, levied year after year, is confiscatory. Eventually it takes away all the value. Chapter 4 argued that a 100 percent marginal tax rate was unjust because it violated too much the value of freedom. In the same way, a tax that eventually eats up all or most of the value of a property is unjust.

One may object that this is a rare occurrence with the property tax, since most property and wealth increase in value over time and also generate incomes. Hence the tax assessments can easily be deducted from the increase in value or from the income, leaving the value of the property intact if not growing. One could even object that property always generates an income — some services or at least a psychic income, if not a money income — and that the property tax can be thought of as being paid out of this income, so it is not confiscatory. For example, an owner-occupied house generates the service of housing each year, and one could think of the value of this service as being equal to the rent that the homeowner does not have to pay. In a way, then, an owner-occupied house generates income to the homeowner, just as rental property does to the landlord. One can think this way, but when the property tax rises to a high level, it is not of much comfort to people owning property that does not generate sufficient money income to pay the tax.

This problem was behind the tax revolt that began in California in the late 1970s and spread to much of the rest of the United States. In the 1960s and 1970s, local governments in California raised property tax rates considerably, sometimes reaching between 3 and 4 percent of assessed value per year. A great deal of discontent was expressed, but the state government refused to impose any constraints on the tax-setting powers of localities. As a consequence, in 1979 the voters passed a draconian initiative, Proposition 13, which set the property tax rate at 1 percent and severely limited increases. Proposition 13 passed overwhelmingly with support from all segments of the population. In spite of the fact that it has caused enormous problems for the state over the decades, including among other things a sharp decline in the quality of the public schools, surveys show that it is still supported.

Why was and is Proposition 13 popular? A large part of the reason is that voters identified with the stories they heard of homeowners of modest means losing their houses because they could not pay the assessed taxes. The newspapers and airwaves were filled with stories of widows and elderly people being forced out of the houses they had lived in for many years because they could not pay the tax bills out of their current, often quite modest, incomes. Voters could see themselves in the same situation, and it seemed to them an injustice. It made them angry — and afraid for their own futures.

For the most part, people with a lot of wealth have a lot of income as well — but not in every case. Some of these California homeowners were sitting on substantial wealth, because of the boom in real estate values in the state, but they had low incomes. To have asked them to pay a 3 percent tax once on the value of their home would not have been a great burden, but to ask them to pay it year after year was confiscatory.

An annual tax is a flow, not a stock. A person's ability to pay it should therefore be measured by a flow, income, rather than by a stock such as wealth or property. In the majority of cases in which high wealth goes together with high income, no problem is created by the wealth tax, since the taxpayers have the annual income with which to pay it. Even in these cases, however, it would be more direct and defensible to tax them on their high incomes, not their wealth. And in the minority of cases, when wealth is not backed up by income, a wealth tax is unjust.

I opposed Proposition 13 at the time, and would vote against it today if I had the chance, because it so gutted the state and its localities of needed revenues, starving the schools, welfare programs, and other essential public services. I agree with its supporters, however, that a high property tax is a bad tax, an unjust tax. I would go further and say that any property tax is a bad tax, not only because it is potentially confiscatory but also because it is regressive with respect to income to the extent that it is shifted to renters, as chapter 4 noted. It should be replaced by a higher and more progressive personal income tax.

The Taxation of Estates and Inheritances

If a significant wealth tax is not the best response to the extraordinary inequality in wealth in our society, does this mean that we must accept that inequality? No. We have other taxes that can break down the concentration of wealth in a better way: estate and inheritance taxes. They are imposed just once, when people die, not year after year. They can be thought of, therefore, as transferring a stock, not imposing a flow.

Analysts are uncertain how much of the wealth in the United States is inherited and not accumulated by the living; estimates range from a low of 20 percent to a high of 80 percent.[4] The correct answer is likely somewhere in the middle; roughly half the wealth in the country is probably inherited. For those who are troubled by the huge disparity in wealth, therefore, inheritance is a good subject on which to focus.

Estate and inheritance taxes are not quite the same. An estate tax is imposed on the value of the estate, before it is distributed, while an inheritance tax is imposed on the heirs, the people who receive the inheritance. The distinction matters because of the way in which deductions from the tax are calculated. Suppose, for example, that the tax rate is 50 percent, after the first $100,000 is deducted. A person dies with an estate worth $1,000,000, bequeathed in equal shares to each of five children. With an estate tax, $100,000 is deducted, leaving $900,000 subject to the 50 percent tax. The tax is $450,000, leaving $550,000 to be distributed to the heirs, or $110,000 per heir. With an inheritance tax, each heir receives $200,000 in pre-tax dollars, deducts $100,000, pays 50 percent or $50,000 on the remaining $100,000, and nets $150,000. With an estate tax, the total amount that the heirs will get, net of taxes, is independent of the number of heirs, while with the inheritance tax it depends upon the number of heirs. Some countries, including the United States, have an estate tax while others have an inheritance tax, and still others have neither.

Governments regulate and tax bequests, but never severely. According to one estimate, estate taxes in the United States constitute only 0.1 percent of total personal incomes in any one year. Even among the highest decile of income earners, estate taxes take only 0.3 percent of personal incomes.[5] There are two reasons for these low figures, the low rates and the ease with which the tax can be avoided altogether. Some, with good reason, call the American estate tax a voluntary tax.

Justice calls for a steep inheritance tax, since inheritances of large estates are responsible for so much of the wealth inequality in the society. I argued in chapter 1 that adults may deserve somewhat unequal outcomes in their lives, as a consequence of their own efforts, but that children bear no responsibility for the unequal circumstances into which they are born. The children of the rich have done nothing to merit more opportunities in life than the children of the poor; they deserve equal opportunity, not more. Inheritance taxation can reduce, if not completely prevent, the intergenerational transmission of unequal opportunity.

Choosing between the two types of taxes on bequests, an inheritance tax is fairer than an estate tax. Remember that the main point of these taxes is to reduce inequality of opportunity in the next generation. The tax system can be structured in such a way as to encourage people to do this to a certain extent on their own. Return to the example of the estate worth $1,000,000, with a tax rate of 50 percent after a deduction of $100,000. If the tax is in the form of an estate tax, the government takes $450,000 and the heirs are left with $550,000, no matter how many heirs there are. With an inheritance tax, in contrast, the more heirs, the more total money is left in the hands of the heirs. In the example with five heirs, each heir receives $150,000, for a total of $750,000. With only one heir, that person would receive $550,000. With ten heirs, on the other hand, each person's inheritance would just reach the level of the deductible, the government would take no tax, each heir would net $100,000, and together the heirs would claim the full $1,000,000. In other words, a person writing a will can ensure that more of the money in the estate actually gets to the heirs by including more heirs. An inheritance tax, rather than an estate tax, encourages people making bequests to spread those bequests broadly, and this by itself helps to break down the concentration of wealth in the next generation.

An inheritance tax such as this could make an enormous contribution to equality of opportunity and therefore justice, particularly if the proceeds were used in support of welfare and transfer programs. Moreover, a heavy inheritance tax might not even harm the heirs. One of the best arguments against excessive inheritances is Plato's:

> Excess of all such things, as a rule, breeds public and private feuds and factions, defect, subjection. Let no man covet wealth for his children's sake, that he may leave them in opulence; 'tis not for their own good nor for the State's. For the young an estate that tempts no sycophants and yet

has no lack of things needful is of all others best and most consonant; it works general concord and concert and banishes pains from our lives. We should leave our children rich, not in gold but in reverence.[6]

A significant inheritance tax would have to be accompanied by a tax on gifts. Bequests at the time of death are only one of three ways in which wealth is transferred from one generation to succeeding generations.[7] First, parents provide what might be called cultural capital to their children: habits, attitudes, morals, values, and education. Second are inter vivos transfers, gifts of money or goods between the living. Parents give presents to their adult children, helping them out with the downpayment on their houses and in other ways. Third is the transfer of the entire estate at the time of death. The first is quite separate from the second and third, and we would be rightly averse to permitting the state to interfere in the transfer of cultural capital. It is important to see, though, that the second and third forms of transfer are close substitutes. There is not much difference between transferring resources before death or after death. So if the government imposed a heavy tax on estates and left inter vivos gifts untaxed, people could easily avoid the tax by transferring their wealth, perhaps in the form of a trust, to their children before they died. Consequently a tax on estates must be accompanied by a tax on gifts.

Should Inheritances Be Abolished?

If inheritances are responsible for roughly half the wealth inequality in the society, and if we are going to tax them heavily, why not go all the way and abolish the institution of inheritance altogether? It is a good question, and some have argued that we should do just that.[8] This section makes the contrary argument, that while inheritances may be taxed, they may not be completely confiscated.

The confiscation of inheritances would be unjust for the same reason that 100 percent marginal tax rates on income would be unjust. As chapter 4 argued, a completely confiscatory tax is too great an infringement on individual freedom, in this case the freedom to own and control property. The creation of property is a social process, so the people as a whole have the right to take some portion of it and use it for social purposes. The state does not have the right to take all of it because we have a right to some security in property that we have accumulated through just, legal means. A person with wealth is entitled to leave all his property to the state or to a charity, but it would be a violation of that person's right to a certain degree of security in property to require such an act.

The great English jurist William Blackstone propounded a doctrine that leads in the opposite direction.[9] Blackstone held that inheritance was a civil, as opposed to a natural, right, that is to say, a right created by the state and hence revokable by the state. Inheritance, thought Blackstone, was just a social custom, one that the state could regulate in any way it saw fit without thereby violating anyone's inherent rights. Presumably it could confiscate inheritances entirely. Inheritance is not a natural right because, said Blackstone in 1803, if it were it would amount to conferring rights upon dead people: "For naturally speaking, the instant a man ceases to be, he ceases to have any dominion; else if he had a right to dispose of his acquisitions one moment beyond his life, he would also have a right to direct their disposal for . . . ages after him; which would be highly absurd and inconvenient."[10]

Blackstone said that a person's right to direct bequests is different from, and less than, his right to control property while living because he is, after all, dead when the estate is transferred. It would be absurd to confer rights on the dead, said Blackstone, so it follows that the state is free to do whatever it wishes with inheritances. His argument fails to withstand close scrutiny. First, it is not absurd to confer rights on the dead. We do it all the time. We do not give them the same rights as the living; we give them the rights appropriate to the dead. We regard it as an infringement of the rights of the dead to mutilate their bodies for no good reason, for example. Native Americans have successfully asserted the right of their ancestors to a decent burial according to the customs of their culture, and not to be used as exhibits in an anthropological museum. Children of the dead often consider themselves bound by their dying parents' wishes, even if they themselves see little sense in those wishes. The most important right that many people wish for themselves after their death is the right to direct their inheritance. They often build up wealth for the express purpose of passing it on to others after their death and would be shocked to learn that they have no inherent right to do so.

Second, Blackstone worried that if people had the right to dispose of their estates immediately after death this right would have to continue forever, and that this would be absurd and inconvenient. He may well have been correct that it is absurd and inconvenient to allow a dead person's wishes to control the use of resources for a long period of time.

My favorite example of the silliness of allowing long-term control is the stipulation a widow made in her will that the proceeds from her bequest be used to help the poor people of Marin County, a suburb of San Francisco. Years after her death, the bequest turned out to be far more valuable than she had anticipated, and the people of Marin County turned out to be far wealthier. There were few poor people in Marin County on whom to spend her millions, yet the terms of the will, as upheld by a court, prevented spending the money in nearby counties where the need was great. Blackstone was right to claim that that sort of control over the present and the future by a dead person makes no sense. It does not follow, however, that just because a person has the right to direct her bequest immediately after her death she has the right to maintain control for many years. One can have the right to direct one's estate to a certain person without necessarily having the right to control how that person uses the estate.

Third, the possibility of inter vivos transfers makes it inconsistent to claim that a person has a right to own and dispose of property during his lifetime but not after his death. A person who wished to give a bequest and was told he had no right to do so would simply transfer the property while still living. So if it is to stick, a prohibition against bestowing bequests after death must be extended to a prohibition against giving gifts while living. If one cannot give gifts, however, one has essentially lost control over one's property. So the abolition of inheritance, if it is to have real and not just formal meaning, comes pretty close to abolishing private property. And that is a violation of individual freedom, hence unjust.

There is no real difference, therefore, between the right to control property while living and the right to dispose of property immediately after death. They are both constrained rights. In both cases, a democratic state has the right to tax away a portion of a person's holdings, in order to provide public goods and services and in order to make the distribution of resources more equal and hence more just. A person with property does not have an absolute right to keep all of it, since the process of production and the generation of income is a social process. A person with property, legitimately acquired according to the laws of the land, does, however, have the right, based on freedom, to keep a portion.

The criterion of equality points to the abolition of inheritances. The criterion of freedom points in conflicting directions. Equal freedom is advanced when people have access to equal resources, so on those grounds inheritances should be abolished. On the other hand, freedom also implies security in one's holdings and is therefore incompatible with the abolition of inheritances. The resolution, I think, is that inheritances may be severely restricted but not abolished. We have yet to consider efficiency, however, and the relationship of inheritance to capitalism.

The Place of Inheritance in Capitalism

Would a heavy tax on inheritances be permitted in a capitalist economy? This is a question that has been dealt with in a stimulating way by philosopher D. H. Haslett.[11] I think his argument is wrong, but it is wrong for interesting reasons, so it is worth considering.

Haslett claims that inheritance is inconsistent with the values of capitalism. To learn what those values are he turns to Milton Friedman's *Capitalism and Freedom*.[12] Haslett interprets Friedman as saying that capitalism rests on three main principles, distribution according to productivity, equal opportunity, and freedom. He argues that inheritance violates all three.

According to Friedman as interpreted by Haslett, the point of an economic system is to get people to produce goods and services efficiently. They cannot be forced to do so, if their freedom is to be respected, so they must be persuaded. The best way to persuade them is to compensate them for their productivity, to base their rewards upon their economic contributions, and capitalism does this. Inheritance, however, does not. Inheritances provide people with income and wealth irrespective of their economic contributions.

Friedman's second foundation of capitalism, according to Haslett, is equal opportunity. It is an ideal never completely realized, but it is important to capitalism. To the extent that people have opportunity they can realize their full potential and thereby contribute to the fullest extent possible to production and the well-being of the society. Inheritance obviously violates equal opportunity, since it provides some people with far greater resources than others.

The third foundation of capitalism is freedom. Haslett concedes that Friedman himself sees no inconsistency between freedom and inheritance and would view an attempt by the government to confiscate inheritances as a violation of freedom. He argues, however, in favor of a broader view of freedom, a view similar to that expounded in chapter 1. Freedom in what Haslett calls a "broad" sense is the ability and the opportunity to do what one wants to do. Inequalities in wealth result in inequalities in this sort of broad freedom, and since inheritance is implicated so deeply in the inequitable distribution of wealth, it is inconsistent with freedom.

Haslett's conclusion: inheritance is incompatible with capitalism, so in the name of capitalist values it should be abolished. I think his argument is mistaken: inheritance is essential to capitalism. His error comes from defining capitalism in terms of abstract and idealistic values, rather than describing what it really is. His three values — distribution according to productivity, equal opportunity, and freedom — are completely different from the characteristics used to describe capitalism in chapter 2. None of the three is a unique attribute of capitalism. In fact, capitalism systematically violates all three easily as much as it fulfills them.

Inheritance is a requirement of capitalism principally because of two of capitalism's characteristics, private property and continuous expansion. If capitalism has to be defined by one term alone, that term is private property. In the capitalist system, people own most of the means of production, most of the society's assets, in their private capacity. The previous section showed that the abolition of inheritance would be equivalent to the abolition of private property. If inheritance is to be abolished, inter vivos gifts must be abolished too. If a living person cannot control his property to the extent of making gifts of it to his children and others, he has lost control of the property — and the institution of private property has collapsed. Since private property is the central feature of capitalism, it follows that inheritance, far from being incompatible with capitalism, is essential to it.

Continuous expansion is essential to capitalism because capitalism is driven by new technology and by the growth of capital. Capital is accumulated through a process of saving and investing. If the people and their government consumed everything that was produced, and saved nothing, no resources would be available for capital investment, for producing new plant and equipment, and as a consequence the growth of production would stagnate. Growth requires new capital, and new capital requires savings.

Why do people save? This is a controversial question. One answer — called the life-cycle savings hypothesis — is that people save during their working years for the purpose of drawing down their savings during their retirement and that their goal is to die broke. If they have a little left over at the time of death, this is only because they died earlier than they expected or because they saved a little extra as insurance in case of an unusually long life. Under this interpretation, people do not intend to leave bequests and are not driven to save in order to build up an estate for their heirs. The contrary answer is that people save and build up capital and wealth in large measure, if not exclusively, in order to provide for their heirs. Empirical research has not thus far settled the dispute. It is likely that both motives are important. In light of this uncertainty, we cannot say exactly what effect the abolition of inheritances would have on savings, but it is possible that it would be considerable. There is a good chance that without inheritances the rate of savings would fall and the rate of growth of the economy would fall, perhaps stop. Without growth, as chapter 2 showed, capitalism would collapse. It follows that the institution of inheritance, far from being incompatible with capitalism, is essential to it.

Not only are inheritances essential to capitalism, they promote efficiency insofar as they contribute to economic growth, as just discussed, since economic growth allows us to get more of what we want. In terms of the efficiency criterion, therefore, inheritances affect social justice positively. Looking at inheritances through the lenses of the three components of justice we find that equality calls for their abolition, efficiency calls for their preservation, and freedom points in both directions. In any case, capitalism will not permit their complete abolition. The conclusion: inheritances may be heavily taxed, but not confiscated.

An Inheritance Tax

Private property, capitalism, freedom, and efficiency could survive a considerable increase in inheritance taxes. The tax should be progressive — the greater the inheritance, the higher the tax rate. The rate should rise to a fairly high level, certainly 50 percent and perhaps higher. Such a tax would go a long way toward restoring the balance of opportunity in the society. People with wealth would not like having to turn 50 percent of their accumulations over to the government, but the fact that 50 percent or so was still available to their heirs would likely keep them focused on maintaining the value of their property. They might even push a little harder, in order to provide well for their children.

The inheritance tax should have a fairly generous deduction — say $100,000 — so that small estates, which do not lead to an injustice in the distribution of wealth, could be transferred intact. The deduction should perhaps be adjusted according to the income over the past five years of the heir, so that a low-income person, for whom an inheritance is the only chance of achieving a minimally decent standard of living, could receive a higher tax-free amount. The law might make special provisions for the intact transfer of family farms and small businesses below a certain valuation. In other words, an inheritance tax should be directed to reducing inequalities of opportunity that are created by bequests, not to blocking bequests that will facilitate an equalizing of opportunities.

Bruce Ackerman and Susan Alstott have made an interesting proposal for a "stakeholder society," in which each citizen, upon reaching the age of twenty-one, is given an unconditional grant of $80,000.[13] The purpose of the grant is to help equalize opportunities among people beginning their adult lives. The proposal has some merits, although it would not do as much to equalize opportunities as would the sort of tax and transfer proposals made in this book. Particularly objectionable, though, is their proposal to finance the grants. Initially the grants would be financed through a 2 percent wealth tax, which I argued earlier would be unjust. Eventually they would be financed by estates; before an estate could be inherited, $80,000 plus interest would be paid back to the government. This amounts to an inheritance tax with a distinctly regressive rate: 100 percent for small estates falling asymptotically almost to zero for large estates. The rate structure of an inheritance tax that is designed to make opportunities more equal should be the opposite: strongly progressive with a generous initial deduction.

Notes

1. Edward N. Wolff, *Top Heavy: The Increasing Inequality of Wealth in America and What Can Be Done about It* (New York: New Press, 1996).

2. Wolff, *Top Heavy;* Organization for Economic Cooperation and Development, *Taxation and Household Saving* (Paris: OECD, 1994), Annex 1.

3. Wolff, *Top Heavy.*

4. Paul L. Menchik and Nancy A. Jianakoplos, "Economics of Inheritance," in *Inheritance and Wealth in America,* ed. Robert K. Miller Jr. and Stephen J. McNamee (New York: Plenum Press, 1998), 45–59.

5. Richard A. Musgrave and Peggy B. Musgrave, *Public Finance in Theory and Practice,* 5th ed. (New York: McGraw-Hill, 1989).

6. Plato, *The Laws,* trans. A. E. Taylor (London: J. M. Dent and Sons, 1934), 111.

7. Miller and McNamee, *Inheritance and Wealth.*

8. D. W. Haslett, "Is Inheritance Justified?" *Philosophy and Public Affairs* 15 (1986): 122–55.

9. Ronald Chester, *Inheritance, Wealth, and Society* (Bloomington: Indiana

University Press, 1982), and Ronald Chester, "Inheritance in American Legal Thought," in Miller and McNamee, *Inheritance and Wealth*, 23–43.

10. Quoted in Chester, "Inheritance in American Legal Thought."

11. Haslett, "Is Inheritance Justified?"

12. Milton Friedman, *Capitalism and Freedom* (Chicago: University of Chicago Press, 1962).

13. Bruce A. Ackerman and Susan Alstott, *The Stakeholder Society* (New Haven, Conn.: Yale University Press, 1999).

Chapter 6

WELFARE

THE GREATEST INJUSTICE of unregulated, free-market capitalism is that it provides for only some of the people and excludes others. Some get rich, some do reasonably well, and others are left in poverty by the market. Consequently, governments of advanced capitalist countries intervene — in different ways and to different extents — to rescue those for whom the market system does not provide.[1]

The United States Census Bureau estimates that in 1999, 17 percent of the population fell below the poverty line, set at just under $20,000 for a family of four.[2] The poverty rates in the other advanced capitalist countries are at most half the American rate, and in many countries they are far lower than half.[3] Robert M. Solow, citing studies by L. Kenworthy, has shown that the high poverty rate in the United States is the consequence not of anything unusual about American labor markets but rather of a welfare system that does much less to support poor people than do the welfare systems in comparable countries. "What really distinguishes the U.S.," he writes, "is the equanimity with which the majority contemplates the poverty of a minority."[4]

As we did in chapter 3, let us simplify the discussion that follows by taking $20,000 as the poverty cutoff line for each family, ignoring differences in family size, number of wage earners, and cost of living (especially cost of housing) in different parts of the country. An income of $20,000 — or $1,667 a month — leaves a family in very tight circumstances.

One line of thought holds that capitalist systems have created welfare programs primarily for the purpose of self-preservation, to dissuade the disadvantaged from revolution. As a matter of history, such an interpretation may be correct. This chapter, however, takes a different perspective, that of justice. Leaving aside the question of how the welfare state actually came into being, it asks what system of provision for the otherwise poor and destitute is most just.

112

Any assessment of the welfare system is complicated by the fact that there are many different reasons for poverty. Some adults are poor even though they are working for pay part or full time; their wages are insufficient to pull them above the poverty line. Others are in the labor force but unemployed; they are willing and able to work but they cannot find a job. Still others are unable or unwilling to work. In this latter group are found the elderly, the sick, and the physically and mentally disabled, people who simply cannot work, as well as single parents of young children.

One overwhelming fact stands out among all the descriptive facts about poverty, a fact that can guide us through the conflicts of justice and give us a clue to the best sort of welfare programs: all categories of poor adults, no matter what the reasons for their poverty, have children. Children in the United States are twice as likely to be poor as adults.[5] The children are victims of poverty, not its creators. Their parents may or may not be responsible for the poverty in which they live — no doubt some parents are and some are not, some to a greater extent and some to a lesser extent — but not a single child is responsible for her poverty. We can say with certainty, therefore, that programs that punish parents for their alleged irresponsibility do an injustice to their innocent dependent children, none of whom deserve to be impoverished.

Is Poverty Permissible?

The first question is whether it is permissible to have poor people at all in an affluent country. According to the Gospel of Matthew, Jesus said, "For ye have the poor always with you," but first-century Palestine was not a rich society by today's standards, at least in material terms. Jesus' words may still be applicable in today's poor countries, but in a country like the United States where the average family income is close to $90,000, it is not a requirement of nature that some families subsist on less than $20,000. Poverty could be eliminated simply by taxing those who are better off and transferring enough income to the poor to raise them above the poverty line.

It is difficult to argue against the proposition that since poverty could be eliminated in rich countries, justice requires that it be eliminated. The norms of equality and freedom demand it, and efficiency does not stand in its way. At the very least, as chapter 1 argued, equality means equality of opportunity, and equality of opportunity is not available to children who are born into poverty. They lack the opportunities for intellectual and physical development that more affluent children have, and they find it harder to compete as adults. The true meaning of freedom, as chapter 1 argued, is that people have both the means and the absence of restrictions to pursue their goals. Poverty denies people the means to pursue their goals and therefore restricts their freedom.

Neither is poverty required for efficiency. Earlier I argued that income ratios of 2:1 for most people, and 8:1 for almost everyone, are sufficient to create the incentives to induce people to work hard and creatively. In Table 3.1, the range of family incomes between $20,000 and $160,000, with most people clustered in the middle-income area and no one in poverty, met these criteria. It has long been a contention of some social critics that capitalism required poverty or, in Marx's words, a "reserve army of the unemployed," a group of people whose willingness to take other people's jobs disciplined the labor force and kept workers from demanding sky-high wages. This myth should have been laid to rest in the Great Depression, a period that demonstrated that poverty was a threat, not a boon, to capitalism, because low personal incomes kept the demand for products low and this in turn led to the collapse of profits. No doubt capitalists favor low wages for their own firms, as a way of keeping costs in control, but their firms are more likely to be successful when faced with a prosperous population and growing markets than when faced with poverty. On all three grounds, therefore — equality, freedom, and efficiency — poverty in a rich country is unnecessary and unjust.

There is no excuse for working people being in poverty. The minimum wage should be sufficient to raise a working person to the poverty level, rather than to just half that level, as it is now. Better programs than currently exist should be available to help people upgrade their skills and be more productive. Community development programs of all sorts can bring businesses and jobs to low-income neighborhoods. Similarly, the unemployed should not fall into poverty. They are looking for work, and it is not their fault that jobs are lacking. Neither should people be poor who are out of the labor force through no fault of their own, whether they are elderly or disabled or responsible for the care of young children or for some other reason. They are equally worthy as everyone else and therefore deserve some of society's bounty, and furthermore their children deserve the chance to start life on an even footing. There is no moral case that is even slightly plausible for allowing such people to live in poverty in an affluent country.

The tricky moral question comes with the voluntarily unemployed.

The Voluntarily Unemployed

Philippe Van Parijs asks whether surfers should be fed.[6] Do people who could work and voluntarily choose not to, for any reason at all, perhaps because they have better things to do with their lives or even because they are lazy, have the right to be supported by the income-earning taxpayers?[7] To return to the parable in chapter 1, do the cat, the rat, and the pig deserve the support of the hen?

People who have followed the acrimonious debate over welfare may reasonably object to posing such a question, because it seems to malign poor people as undeserving parasites who have chosen to live off others. My purpose is the opposite. It is well documented that most poor people want to support themselves and get out of poverty.[8] Among those who appear not to want to do so are many who are psychologically incapable of sustained work, so their poverty is not really voluntary. Under the current welfare system, it is not clear that an able-bodied person who voluntarily chose a life of poverty could qualify for any welfare support at all. The current welfare system is, however, terribly unjust; later in this chapter I will propose reforms that would lift every person in the country out of poverty, irrespective of his or her motivations. Even though the proposed new welfare system would contain incentives to work, still I expect that under its provisions some people would choose not to work but to live off a grant that would leave them just at the margin of poverty. Unless this can be morally justified, the case for completely eliminating poverty collapses.

Under a welfare system such as I will propose, the voluntary poor would no doubt be a varied group. They might be Van Parijs's surfers; they might be contemplatives, scholars, artists, or wanderers. They might work hard at tasks that produced no income, or they might take it easy. They might hope to earn an income by their activities — like Vincent Van Gogh, creating a masterpiece every day but finding no market for his work — or they might be consciously disengaged from income-producing work. What they did with their time might be useful to other people, or not. They might move in and out of income-earning work. Would they have the right to an income sufficient to raise them out of poverty? Another way to put the question is this. Since they would need some income in order to survive, would they have the right to pursue their non-income-producing goals, or would they be forced into income-producing work that they preferred not to do?

Many people would argue that if they can work for pay they must and that any exemption from work constitutes exploitation of the taxpayers. Political scientist Jon Elster writes, "People who chose to work for an income... would have to pay higher taxes in order to support those who took the other option. They would think, correctly in my opinion, that they were being exploited by the other group."[9]

Against this is the argument from freedom. We have the right to pursue our goals and to have the means that are necessary to pursue them. If our goal is art or contemplation, we have the right to pursue our goal just as much as does the person whose goal is to be an investment banker. This cannot be an absolute right, and in this respect the right to pursue the goal of not working for pay is the same as most other freedoms, few of which are absolute. This particular freedom depends upon the existence of enough total income that the support of a few non-earners is not overly burdensome. It depends upon the number of voluntary non-earners being relatively small and their demands for subsistence being relatively low. It is a right that can be met more easily in the United States or Switzerland than in India or Zimbabwe. Surely it is a good thing, however, not a bad thing, to allow people to pursue the goals they really wish to pursue and not force them into a cookie-cutter life for which they have neither desire nor perhaps aptitude.

Moreover — as with every other group of poor — the voluntary poor have children, people who have no choice in their family lifestyles. Children have the right to opportunities that would be denied them by starting out in poverty. The case for providing support to the voluntary poor with children is particularly strong, because of the principle of equal opportunity, but I think the case based on freedom is strong enough to include those without children as well.

The poverty cutoff is a good state-supported income for such people. It is low enough to keep the burden on the taxpayers from being onerous and to ensure that people not be attracted to this lifestyle just for the money. It is high enough that people can survive on it and pursue at least some of their goals.

Elster finds this sort of argument unpersuasive. He is less concerned with the freedom of the surfers and the scholars than with the freedom of the taxpayers. Just because people prefer work to nonwork, he says, is no reason to tax them for the support of the nonworkers. "They might well prefer the forty-hour week over the fifty-hour week they had to work because of the high taxes imposed on them by those who chose to live on the grant. Hence the argument from freedom of choice fails, because the workers would be forced by the nonworkers to work harder than they wished."[10]

Elster's is a serious objection. It is not as extreme as the objection to taxation made by libertarians like Robert Nozick, who deny that there is any reason for the state to take away people's legitimately earned income without their individual consent. Elster simply argues that the freedom of people to pursue a life of nonpaid work or leisure conflicts with the freedom of working folk to pursue their goals, and he chooses the latter over the former. He is not alone.

He is wrong in this choice, however. Of course people who work for pay find that their life choices are constrained by the fact that they have to pay taxes. Taxation restricts our individual freedom. Virtually no working person has to change his or her way of life fundamentally because of taxes, however. Taxes limit our choices, but they do not eliminate them. The failure to provide a minimum income to a contemplative, however, is likely to make that entire way of life unattainable. The sorts of restrictions on our freedom imposed by taxes are significantly less severe, it seems obvious to me, than the dictate that one cannot pursue one's life goal. If taxes had to be so high as to be confiscatory, that would be an unacceptable violation of people's freedom to be secure in their property. If the transfer payment were so high as to attract a large number of otherwise working people to the nonworking life, the criterion of efficiency would be violated. Where overall national income is high enough, however, and the transfer payment fairly low, justice requires that even voluntary nonworkers receive financial support from the state.

If even voluntary nonworkers deserve support, there is no question but that the involuntary poor, the great majority, should be rescued from poverty.

Welfare Reform of the 1990s

Prior to the 1990s, most poor people in the United States qualified for some financial support — although usually not enough to raise them above the poverty line — simply because of their low income. Depending upon the category into which they fell, their grant might be higher or lower; for example, people with dependent children typically received more than people without. In either case, however, the welfare support continued for as long as the person remained in poverty. In the 1990s a new philosophy was imposed, first in several states and then nationally with the passage of the Parental Responsibility and Work Opportunity Act in 1996.[11] Among other provisions, the law replaced the old AFDC (Aid to Families with Dependent Children) with the new TANF (Temporary Assistance to Needy Families):

- The entitlement of poor people to support was replaced by block grants, limited to a certain amount of money, to the states. If and when the grants run out, the people who depend upon them may be out of luck, since the states are not required to make additional expenditures.

- Welfare recipients can be required by the states to work for pay or to enroll in a training program, as a condition of support. They must work after two years on assistance.

- Support is limited to a lifetime maximum of five years, and this period may be shortened by the states. A recipient who has not successfully made the transition to self-sufficiency can be cut off.

The federal law is supplemented by welfare-to-work laws in the states, plus individual county plans. Taken together, it has been a controversial shift in policy, reversing decades of movement in the opposite direction. As it happened, it coincided with a significant decline in the number of people receiving welfare payments. The reasons for this decline are not clear. They may include an improving economy that offered more opportunities to the previously unemployed, and they may also include the success of the new approach in encouraging people to make themselves employable. Critics worry, however, that the decline in welfare rolls may partly be an indication of people being denied welfare support without having yet developed the skills to take care of themselves. Administrative data in most states do not reveal whether people who leave welfare are better off or if they are leaving welfare for work.[12] A survey of New York State residents dropped from welfare under the new law found that only 29 percent had found employment — when employment was defined as earning at least $100 over three months.[13] Other studies have found better results,[14] but this may be because they added together people who voluntarily left welfare because they found a job with those who were involuntarily dropped.

The new time-limited welfare philosophy grew out of a concern that the previous approach to welfare had failed. The old approach had created, it was alleged, a dependent class of people who were encouraged to be unproductive because they were supported by the state. The new approach would require them to become productive, and this would have benefits both for the taxpayers and for the poor people themselves. The taxpayers would be relieved of much of their burden, and the previously poor would have the satisfaction of entering mainstream society.

The Injustice of the New Welfare System

The state does not have the moral right to impose the conditions on welfare recipients that it currently does, conditions relating to marital status, work requirements, and time limits.[15]

It might be claimed that a democratically elected government has the right to impose these sorts of conditions, in return for offering financial support. To reason by analogy, if you pay money to the launderer, you have every right to impose conditions on him: you expect him to starch these shirts, leave those shirts unstarched, patch a rip in your jacket, and have everything washed and ironed by Wednesday morning. No one's rights or freedoms are violated by such an understanding. Why then is it not justified for the state to impose any condition a majority of the people want on welfare recipients?

The difference between the two cases is that you have no obligation to give money to the launderer, whereas people with means have an obligation to poor people. No one would criticize you if you washed your own shirts or if you took your laundry to a different establishment. You have a purely voluntary contract with the launderer: if you do not want to take your shirts to him you do not have to, and if he does not want to wash them he does not have to.

The obligation of middle-class and rich people to the poor is not like this commercial relationship. I do not owe the launderer anything unless he washes my shirts, but I owe poor people at least enough support that they not be destitute. The poor are owed support not because of the services they provide to the nonpoor but because they are human beings of equal moral standing with the nonpoor, human beings who share the same social space. The state does not, therefore, have an unconditional moral right to impose conditions on welfare recipients. It may impose some conditions, but the conditions should be defensible in terms of justice.

The conditions imposed on welfare recipients in the 1990s moved away from justice, not toward it. The first thing to say about them is that they severely restrict the freedom of the recipients. Most importantly, single mothers who would prefer to work in the home with even their very young children or babies have lost this right. They must be out of the house, either working for pay or getting trained. Political scientist Gwendolyn Mink argues that they have also lost the freedom to decide upon their marital status and to keep their private lives confidential.[16] The law will allow women to stay at home only if they are living with their husband or the father of their children. Authorities are entitled to the most personal of information pertaining to sexual habits, in order to identify absent fathers and collect child-support payments. These conditions are demeaning, and they violate the norms of privacy.

Liberty is not the only component of justice, however. Can the new approach to welfare be justified on efficiency grounds? This is how it is usually defended, as a kind of tough-love approach that gets recipients off their duffs and into the world of work so that they can be self-sufficient. It may well have this effect for some poor people, but it does not for others. The issue of efficiency is complex. The most obvious rejoinder to people who think the new system is efficient is to point out that it is based on the bizarre assumption that the raising of young children is not work. The truth is that child care is demanding and that it is just about the most valuable work that exists in our society. For the most part it is not paid work, but that is irrelevant to its true value. It is hard to think of anything more important than giving children a good foundation in life, but this is foreclosed by the new laws.

Beyond this obvious point, economic theory provides two conflicting perspectives on the relationship of efficiency to the welfare system. The first is that individuals know best what is best for them; the second is that insurance creates what is called a "moral hazard." The individuals-know-best doctrine leads to an argument against the imposition of any conditions on welfare recipients. Recall the definition of efficiency from chapter 1. It means getting the best out of a given set of resources: not the most, in a crude sense of accumulation, but the best. Who is better situated to decide what is best for a person than that person herself? If she is facing the difficult decision to work outside the home or to stay with her young children, is it likely that a social worker or a bureaucrat or a legislator can make the decision better than she can? This is what the current welfare reform assumes, and it is a patronizing assumption. If the conditions imposed by the state are different from the choices the poor person would have made herself, the doctrine of individuals-know-best tells us that the result will be inefficient.

The doctrine of moral hazard, however, gives one pause. The doctrine asserts that the existence of insurance is likely to induce people to make decisions that may be in their own self-interest but that are harmful to society as a whole, decisions they would not make in the absence of insurance. If you have fire insurance on your house, for example, you may be careless with matches, since you will not bear the cost of a fire. There is a real social cost to your house burning down, however, a cost that will be paid by all the purchasers of fire insurance in the form of higher premiums. If you have health insurance, you may go to the doctor more often than is really necessary, since the visits are free to you. They are not free to society, however, and we all pay for excessive medical use through higher health insurance premiums.

Does the welfare system, which can be thought of as insurance protecting against the possibility of being poor, create a moral hazard? It may. Even though the benefits are very low, some people may be induced into staying dependent, not becoming self-sufficient even though they could. This is the reason that the Congress decided to abandon the old entitlement approach to welfare and replace it with the personally intrusive, time-limited, workfare system. The new system can be thought of as an attempt to eliminate the moral hazard attendant upon welfare payments.

We must be careful though. Just because we are likely safe in thinking that some people fall into the moral-hazard trap, it does not follow that every welfare recipient under the old system became dependent or even that most did. At the time of the debate over welfare reform, a pervasive image existed of the slothful, unmotivated, excessively fecund poor single mother, but no actual evidence existed that the image was accurate for a large number of people. The solution, however, was one-size-fits-all. Mary Jo Bane, former assistant secretary for children and families in the Department of Health and Human Services who resigned to protest the welfare reform, writes, "The political rhetoric supporting the new law, unfortunately, made the concept of a federal entitlement synonymous with irresponsibility and lifelong dependency.... This rhetoric was misleading but powerfully effective."[17]

Some people may be helped by the new system, in the sense of being forced to become self-sufficient when they could have done so all along but were discouraged or demoralized. It is clear, however, that others are hurt, because they are not able to measure up to the demands of the new system and will eventually be dropped from the welfare rolls.

The report card on the new system is therefore this: without question it violates people's freedom to choose their marital arrangements and to choose between caring for children or working outside the home.

In terms of efficiency, it may help some become more efficient, but it hurts others by denying them the ability to make choices that they are competent to make. In terms of equality, it certainly harms those — and their children — who are unable in the long run to get a job. Overall, the welfare reform of the 1990s earns a failing grade: it is unjust.

A Welfare System Based on Justice

A way exists to preserve the positive effect of the new system, namely, encouragement of some people to develop labor market skills, while avoiding the negative effects — the facts that it leaves some people still in poverty and worse off than they were before and that it severely limits the freedom of choice of the recipients. It is a system that has sometimes been called the negative income tax.[18] It can be structured in such a way as to meet the goals of pulling everyone out of poverty, giving people an incentive to work and preserving basic freedoms. The current earned-income tax credit goes a small distance in the direction of the negative income tax.

A normal income tax takes money away from people, the amount of the tax depending upon the person's income. A negative income tax gives money to people, the amount of the grant depending upon the person's income. Just as the normal income tax is adjusted by deductions — for example, people can claim deductions for their children and thereby reduce their tax liability — in the same way the negative income tax can be adjusted according to the number of dependents and perhaps other factors. Given these adjustments, the amount of the grant depends only on the person's adjusted income, not upon such factors as marital status, presence of a man in the house, length of time in poverty, participation in training programs, or success in finding a job. In the same way that taxpayers now file a form documenting their income and paying taxes that are based on that income, under the negative income tax poor people would file a form documenting their income and receiving a grant on that basis.

The first and most obvious advantage of the negative income tax over the current or previous welfare system is that it increases the recipients' freedom. They would be free to marry or not to marry, to stay home with the children or not, to get a job or not, to stay in a grant-receiving status for a long time or not. The amount of their grant would be affected by such choices, because the choices would affect their incomes, but their options would not be foreclosed to them by the law. On grounds of liberty, the negative income tax is easily preferable.

The more difficult questions about the negative income tax have to do with equality and efficiency, and here the devil is in the details. The precise terms of the negative income tax make a big difference. Suppose the tax is structured in such a way as to eliminate poverty and nothing more. With zero earned income over the year, a person receives a grant of $20,000. With $10,000 earned income, the grant is $10,000, and with $20,000 earned income, the grant is zero. Above an earned income of $20,000, people begin to pay positive taxes. The consequence is that poverty is eliminated. People who would otherwise be poor are raised to the poverty line. It sounds good, and from the perspective of equality, it certainly is good. It is bad for efficiency, however, since it contains a strong incentive not to work. A negative income tax structured this way has a 100 percent, confiscatory marginal tax rate. Think about a person earning nothing and contemplating whether to get a job and start earning money. Why should she do such a thing when she knows that, until she reaches an income of $20,000, her grant will be reduced by a dollar for every dollar she earns? Her take-home income will be $20,000, no matter how much she works.

The problem can be solved, although not easily. Suppose the negative income tax is set up in the following way. A person earning nothing receives a grant of $10,000. For every dollar he earns above zero, his grant is cut back by 50 cents. So, for example, if he earns $10,000, his grant is cut back from $10,000 to $5,000, and he nets $15,000. When he earns $20,000, the poverty line, his grant is cut back by the full $10,000, and he breaks even. This system solves the efficiency problem. The marginal tax rate is just 50 percent, not 100 percent. People get to keep 50 cents out of every extra dollar they earn, so they have an incentive to work. The problem with this second scheme is that it is not very good for equality. In fact, it raises no one out of poverty. It puts money in the hands of the poor, but the gap between their earnings and the poverty line is cut only in half, not completely.

So far, it seems, the negative income tax is good for freedom, but it contains an inherent conflict between equality and efficiency. A solution to this conflict exists, a solution that most observers have rejected out of hand, but which I think makes sense. Why not set the base income at $20,000, the poverty line, rather than $10,000, and impose something like a 50 percent marginal tax rate on all earned income? Here is how it would work. A person earning nothing would get a grant of $20,000, sufficient to pull her out of poverty. With $10,000 earned income, the grant would be cut back to $15,000, for a net income of $25,000. With earned income of $20,000, the grant would be cut back to $10,000, for a net income of $30,000, and so forth. At an earned income of $40,000, the grant would be eliminated completely, and beyond that level people would pay positive taxes. This scheme would resolve both our problems. It would be good for equality, because it would raise everyone out of poverty. It would be good for efficiency, because people could keep half of every extra dollar they earned.

One may usefully compare this scheme with the current philosophy of time-limited welfare. Both embody incentives to get people off welfare and into the labor market, but the negative income tax uses the carrot while the time-limited scheme uses the stick. The difference is dramatic for those who do not or cannot respond to the stick. With the negative income tax, they are assured of a basic income that will keep them out of poverty, while in the time-limited scheme they are left penniless.

The third variant of the negative income tax is, however, very expensive, imposing a heavier burden on the taxpayers than the first two. In the first two, all the transfer payments from the government go to poor people, while people earning income at the poverty line receive nothing and people earning more than the poverty-level income begin to pay taxes at a moderate rate. In the third variant, people earning an income up to twice the poverty level receive a subsidy from the taxpayers. The overall distribution of the disbursed funds depends upon the number of people at each income level, but it is easily possible that more money will be transferred to the nonpoor than to the poor. Since so much money would have to be transferred, the positive tax rates on people earning more than $40,000 would have to be significantly higher than in the first two schemes.

One of the ways of understanding why the third variant is so expensive is to see that it is equivalent to what has sometimes been called the unconditional basic income, the basic grant or the demogrant.[19] The basic grant is a flat subsidy, the same amount of money paid to everyone regardless of their earned income. It is untaxed, but all earned income is taxed heavily in order to pay for the grant. The third variant can therefore be thought of as a basic grant of $20,000, with earned income between zero and $40,000 taxed at a 50 percent rate and earned income above that level taxed perhaps at a higher rate.

Neither the negative income tax nor the basic grant is in use in any country, but the structure of both programs reveals the problems and contradictions inherent in most programs of transfers to the poor. The American system of welfare subsidies, while more complex than the negative income tax, faces the same contradictions. If a welfare program is restricted to grants to the poor, it can honor the virtue of equality while violating efficiency (like the first scheme) or it can honor efficiency while violating equality (like the second). If a welfare program is to honor both, in the way that the third scheme does, it will transfer significant resources to the nonpoor and will impose a much higher burden on the taxpayers.

It is important, therefore, to decide whether something like the third plan can be justified. Most analysts of welfare programs have concluded that it is completely out of the question; they think it impossible because it imposes too high a tax burden and unjustified because it transfers resources to the nonpoor. I, on the other hand, think it is exactly what justice calls for. From the perspective of justice, the fact that it does not focus only on the poor is a merit. It narrows the dispersal of take-home incomes in the entire population and hence moves the population closer to a just overall income distribution like the one in Table 3.1 All earning less than $40,000 receive some sort of subsidy, helping to push them toward the middle range of incomes. This particular plan does not push them as far as $60,000, which is the bottom of the 2:1 ratio identified in chapter 3, but goes a long way in that direction. The taxes necessary to finance this transfer are high but not confiscatory. They allow high-income earners to retain some of their incomes, as freedom requires, but they can be structured in such a way as to reduce high incomes significantly and hence reduce the overall dispersion of incomes.

Among these various possibilities, therefore, the third is the best. It eliminates poverty and compresses the range of incomes in the society, while retaining incentives to work and allowing people to keep a portion of their earnings. It is certainly better than the time-limited approach to welfare, an approach that is designed to allow people to fall between the cracks and remain desperately poor.

Public Services for the Poor

Even if poverty were eliminated by a negative income tax, serious inequalities in income would persist. Some families would be just at the poverty cutoff, others far above it. The most harmful consequences of this inequality would fall on the children whose opportunities for a productive life would still be varied. Justice for low-income children requires a series of additional measures, among them public education, universal health care, and direct support of child raising.

The importance of high-quality public education is hard to overstate. The establishment of universal education and a system of public schools has been one of the major achievements of the economically advanced countries. The social value of education is so clear that most poor countries set schooling as one of their highest priorities as well. In the United States, however, and in some other countries, public education is supported mostly by local tax revenues, so its quality varies directly with the wealth of the neighborhood. State subsidies and, in some instances, court decisions have abated to a certain extent the inequalities in public education, but big differences remain. The opportunities to children offered by public education are typically much more restricted in central cities than in affluent suburbs. Equality of opportunity requires improvement in the quality of public schools in poor communities.

Spending on education always represents a transfer of resources from one generation to the next. When the working, earning, taxpaying adults think of this transfer as benefiting their own children, they have a self-interested incentive to make it. When the transfer is thought of as benefiting other people's children, they are often reluctant. This is the problem in providing first-rate education in poor areas. The funding has to come primarily from people who are better off, and it frequently has to cross racial barriers, with white taxpayers bearing part of the burden of educating nonwhite children. Justice in providing equal opportunity through education therefore requires generosity.

Good health is the prerequisite of equal opportunity. Without access to good health care, the other components of equal opportunity fade in importance. It is one of the scandals of American public life that health care is so unequally available to the population. In view of the high price of medical care, adequate treatment requires insurance, and insurance is available only unevenly through the private market. Most economically advanced countries provide universal medical care as a human right. These countries find it difficult to do this, because of the ever-increasing cost of care, and they have to make a number of compromises in terms of the services available. Almost none takes the approach that the United States does, however, in which health insurance is a matter primarily for the private market and in which therefore a high portion of the population is uninsured. The consequences for children who begin their lives without adequate health care are particularly regrettable. If equal opportunity is to be meaningful at all, universal affordable health care is a requirement.

Quality child care is essential for both children and parents. In a society in which women are increasingly expected to work outside the home, while they still have primary responsibility in most families for the nurturing of children, the scarcity of good child care results in seriously unequal treatment by gender. The new welfare system has made the problems worse. Two approaches — different but complementary — are worth exploring. The first is that work in the home, the raising of young children, should be paid work.[20] Parents could make a decision whether to work outside the home or not, but if they decided to stay with their children they would be secure in having at least a subsistence income. This would be accomplished by a negative income tax such as I have recommended.

The second approach is to provide good, low-cost child care for the children of working parents. A template of what can be achieved exists in Quebec, the predominantly French-speaking province of Canada. As of 1997, family policy in Quebec has included the following (all money figures in Canadian dollars):[21]

- Universal $5 daycare. Children over two and a half have access to daycare that costs no more than $5 a day. The program is nonprofit and parent-controlled.

- Kindergarten/after-school care. Kindergartens must last the full day; before and after school care is provided for $5 a day.

- Parental leave. The provincial government pays 75 percent of a working parent's salary for up to 30 weeks after the birth of a child.

- Family allowances. Families earning less than $50,000 receive $131 annually for the first child and $975 for each subsequent child.

- Tax benefits. Parents receive tax credits of about $500 per child and tax exemptions of about $2,500.

If the welfare of children is to be protected, both approaches are needed. A guaranteed income would imply that the state was neutral with respect to a parent's decision to work outside the house or not, as opposed to the present policy of the United States that forces poor single women to leave their children, while allowing middle- and upper-class women to choose. Whatever the stance of the state with respect to working women, however, it is clear that many are going to work outside the home — half the mothers of preschoolers are currently in the labor force[22] — so both they and their children deserve affordable, high-quality child care.

Conclusion

Chapters 4, 5, and 6 have explored ways in which the state could use its tools of taxes, transfers, and expenditures to move the income distribution of an advanced capitalist country in a more just direction, approaching if not reaching the array of incomes recommended in chapter 3. Tax reform in the interest of justice should focus upon reducing or eliminating regressive taxes like the property and sales taxes and replacing them with an expanded and more progressive personal income tax. The extreme maldistribution of wealth should be attacked not by a wealth tax but by a steep and progressive tax on inheritances and inter vivos gifts. Poverty should be addressed by a negative income tax that raises everyone to the poverty cutoff level, reduces the grant gradually as earned incomes rise, and taxes people with higher incomes steeply in order to pay for the subsidies. Taken together, these reforms would eliminate poverty and greatly compress the overall dispersion of incomes, while still permitting significant differences.

It would be possible to combine the income tax and the inheritance tax into a single tax, a progressive income tax that treated inheritance as personal income in the year in which it was received. If this were done, it would be essential that people not be allowed to stretch the receipt of their inheritance out over many years in order to shelter it in a lower tax bracket. It is probably not a good idea to combine the two taxes, though, since the legislature may reasonably want to allow a larger deduction from taxable income for inheritances than for annual income.

Is such an approach, which responds directly to the imperatives of justice, feasible in a capitalist society? Not completely. One of the biggest obstacles to achieving such a system is the international competition between countries. A single country that instituted these reforms would likely suffer from the flight of capital and skilled labor. The best way to proceed, therefore, would be through negotiated international agreements. An even bigger obstacle would be the opposition of upper-income people who would stand to lose from the reforms. Moreover, a public that endorsed the welfare reforms of the 1990s is unlikely to be willing to change direction as radically as chapter 6 has proposed. Still, justice calls for pushing the limits of the capitalist constraints, for taxing away some of the excesses of both income and wealth, for developing as generous and universal a welfare system as possible, and for advancing programs to develop the skills and resources of the poor and improving the quality of public education, public health, and the care of children. We are unlikely ever to reach our goal, but much more progress could be made.

Notes

1. For an introduction to the varieties of welfare systems and to the debate about them, see Norman Berry, "Welfare Policies," in *Encyclopedia of Applied Ethics* (San Diego: Academic Press, 1998), 4:511–23.

2. This figure is the result of a new methodology for measuring poverty. Using the old methodology, the figure would be 12.7 percent. See Louis Uchitelle, "Devising New Math to Define Poverty," *New York Times,* October 18, 1999, A1.

3. Robert M. Solow, "Welfare: The Cheapest Country," *New York Review of Books* 47 (March 23, 2000): 20–23.

4. Solow, "Welfare."

5. Gregory Acs and Megan Gallagher, "Income Inequality among America's Children," *New Federalism: National Survey of America's Families* (Washington, D.C.: Urban Institute, 2000), B-6.

6. Philippe Van Parijs, "Why Surfers Should Be Fed: The Liberal Case for an Unconditional Basic Income," *Philosophy and Public Affairs* 20 (1991): 101–31.

7. I should immediately disassociate myself from the view that most real surfers fall into this category. All the surfers I know support themselves.

8. Robert M. Solow has collected evidence to support this statement in *Work and Welfare* (Princeton, N.J.: Princeton University Press, 1998).

9. Jon Elster, *Solomonic Judgements: Studies in the Limitations of Rationality* (Cambridge: Cambridge University Press, 1989), 215.

10. Elster, *Solomonic Judgements,* 216.

11. For summaries and critiques of the legislation, see Mary Jo Bane, "Welfare as We Might Know It," *American Prospect* 30 (January–February 1997): 47–53, and Gwendolyn Mink, *Welfare's End* (Ithaca, N.Y.: Cornell University Press, 1998). For a more positive interpretation, see US Department of Health and Human Services, "The Personal Responsibility and Work Opportunity Reconciliation Act of 1996," HHS Fact Sheet (Washington, D.C.: December 4, 1999).

12. California Budget Project, "Welfare Reform Update" (Sacramento: April 2000).

13. Katha Pollitt, "Let Them Sell Lemonade," *The Nation* 268 (February 15, 1999): 11.

14. See, for example, Pamela Loprest, "How Families That Left Welfare Are Doing: A National Picture," *New Federalism: National Survey of America's Families* (Washington, D.C.: Urban Institute, 1999), B-1.

15. For the opposite point of view, see Lawrence M. Mead, *Beyond Entitlement: The Social Obligations of Citizenship* (New York: Free Press, 1986) and *The New Politics of Poverty: The Nonworking Poor in America* (New York: Basic Books, 1992). Mead argues that the previous welfare system failed because it was too permissive.

16. Mink, *Welfare's End.*

17. Bane, "Welfare as We Might Know It."

18. The negative income tax was proposed by Milton Friedman in 1962 and has received wide discussion since that time. See Milton Friedman, *Capitalism and Freedom* (Chicago: University of Chicago Press, 1962).

19. Van Parijs, "Why Surfers Should Be Fed," and Philippe Van Parijs, *Real Freedom for All: What (If Anything) Can Justify Capitalism?* (Oxford: Clarendon Press, 1995). For a proposal showing how the basic grant would work in practice, see S. Lerner, C. M. A. Clark, and W. R. Needham, *Basic Income: Economic Security for All Canadians* (Toronto: Between the Lines, 1999).

20. Mink, *Welfare's End.*

21. Andre Picard, "A Working Parent's Paradise," *Globe and Mail* (Toronto), September 14, 1999, A1, A9. For a critical assessment of Quebec's program, see Ruth Rose, "Quebec's Family Policy: The Good, the Bad, and the Ugly," *Interaction* 13 (spring 1999).

22. Children's Defense Fund, *The State of America's Children* (Washington, D.C.: CDF Publications, 2000).

Chapter 7

AFFIRMATIVE ACTION

T HE ENORMOUS GAP in personal incomes is the principal source of unequal opportunity, but it is not the only one. Discrimination based on race, gender, sexual orientation, age, disability, and other personal characteristics affects people's opportunities as well. An adequate investigation of discrimination in all its dimensions would take many chapters and is beyond the scope of this book. This chapter narrows the discussion by focusing on racial discrimination and, within that topic, one strategy for confronting racial discrimination, affirmative action programs.[1]

The United States is steeped in a history of slavery and racism. Within the memories of many people still alive, racial discrimination was the official policy of most public institutions in the country. Jim Crow laws enforced a kind of apartheid in the southern states, and exclusionary policies were applied everywhere. The civil rights movement culminating in the 1960s swept away the official racist policies and resulted in the banning of racial discrimination in the private sector in housing, employment, public accommodations, and other areas. The damage caused by centuries of discrimination cannot be erased in a few decades, however, and racist attitudes still mar American social life. The economic status of African Americans, Latinos, and Native Americans is, on average, much lower than that of non-Hispanic whites (or "Anglos") and Asian Americans. For example, the median incomes of Anglo families are almost double those of African American and Latino families. The gap in wealth is even greater: the typical Anglo family has ten times the wealth of the typical African American or Latino family. Poverty rates for African Americans and Latinos are more than triple those for Anglos. For decades, the black unemployment rate has been double the white rate.[2]

Racial discrimination and the gap in socioeconomic status severely limit opportunities for some ethnic groups in the United States. A child born into an African American family, for example, typically has a more restricted set of life chances than does a child born into a white family. In response, many initiatives have been undertaken to improve the status of minorities, including community development projects, training programs, and early childhood education. Affirmative action has been among the most controversial of these initiatives.

Affirmative action programs increase the participation, in institutions, of members of socially disadvantaged groups that are underrepresented, relative to their proportion in the population. Various measures fall under this rubric, including extra efforts to recruit minorities or simply taking care that recruitment processes are open. It is hard to find fault with programs such as these, so the chapter does not address them. It considers instead the justice of affirmative action programs that actually grant preferences to minorities in terms of admission to colleges and graduate schools, hiring and promotion, or contracting. The preferences may take the form of quotas or perhaps of giving added weight to an applicant's race. Defenders of affirmative action programs see them as important steps toward justice, critics as violations of justice.

The Conflict

Racial preferences in admissions, hiring, and contracting have been instituted and are defended for two separate reasons, reasons that have to do with two of the criteria of justice: efficiency and equality. They are criticized on the same grounds, that they produce inefficiency and inequality.[3]

The case for preferences based on efficiency has to do with the diversity of institutions. Institutions function better, the proponents hold, if they are populated by a diverse group of people, since people from different backgrounds have different attitudes and opinions. For example, a student body and a faculty are likely to be more intellectually stimulating to all involved if they include a significant number of people of different races, because people in different racial groups sometimes have different perspectives on issues. One variant of the diversity argument holds that if minorities have positions of power in institutions, they can transform the racist activities of those institutions. The contrary case based on efficiency is that the effect of racial preferences is to substitute race for qualifications. If a particular person of color is the best qualified for a position, it is held, affirmative action is irrelevant since that person would be hired anyway. Affirmative action only comes into effect when it is used to hire someone who is not the most qualified. According to this argument, racial preferences bring about a lower level of competency, hence inefficiency.

The case for racial preferences based on notions of equality is that people of color are the victims of racism, both historical and current, and as a consequence they are underrepresented in many institutions. Preferences can provide them the access they are denied because of discrimination, restoring equal opportunity. The contrary argument is that racial preferences constitute an extension of racism, a failure to treat people as equal individuals. The way to expunge racism, opponents argue, is to cease assigning any weight to race. They say that giving some people a preference because of an irrelevant characteristic like race automatically gives other people an undeserved disadvantage and hence violates equal opportunity.

I will argue that affirmative action programs with racial preferences are justified on grounds of both efficiency and equality — although in the area of equality they present us with some conflicts of justice. Affirmative action programs are necessarily of limited scope, however, and a commitment to racial justice requires us to go far beyond them.

Efficiency

Affirmative action programs are intended, in part, to create racial diversity within institutions. Diversity is a legitimate goal of institutions because people of different racial backgrounds typically bring different values, attitudes, and experiences with them to the job and because these different attitudes create more breadth and strength than would exist if attitudes were more homogeneous.

It is not true, of course, that everyone in a given ethnic group thinks the same way. Many African Americans, however, to take an example, are united by a sense of a common culture, common linguistic patterns, a common legacy of oppression, and other features. They are sensitive to mistreatment not just of themselves but of other African Americans. They bring to an institution a way of looking at the world that is different from, and not open to, other groups. It follows that an institution that includes people of different racial backgrounds is more likely to have a breadth of points of view than one whose members come from a single race.

Within some institutions, diversity of opinion is likely of no use at all. On a professional basketball team, the players' opinions on subjects other than basketball are close to irrelevant to the success of the team. What matters is their ball-playing skills. As long as basketball teams do not exclude certain races as a matter of policy, it would be silly to criticize them for not having a racial makeup reflective of the population as a whole. Many institutions are not like basketball teams, though. Every university, every governmental organization, and every business must take account of the fact that the people with whom it interacts have different racial identities. If the racial identities outside the organization are reflected inside it as well, the organization will stand a better chance of thriving in its mission. The learning process of students is helped by their being surrounded by faculty members who have different outlooks and who disagree about important matters. Some students do better when they have role models and mentors who share their backgrounds, so if the student body is racially diverse this calls for a diverse faculty and staff. Government policy is likely to be sounder if it is hammered out by people who represent the general population, who have different outlooks, and who are forced to work out compromises.

Race is not the only relevant dimension of diversity. A university faculty benefits from having conservatives and liberals, women and men, theoreticians and practitioners, people from disadvantaged backgrounds and the middle class, foreigners and native-born, old and young, straight and gay. Race is one among these factors. Universities and other institutions historically embraced some of these dimensions, but usually not ones related to diversity of origins.

A second argument about efficiency is that a good way to combat racism is to make sure that significant places of power are occupied by people of color. This is the central point made by Richard Wasserstrom in his thoughtful defense of racial preferences. A system of racial injustice may be allowed to persist in institutions because it is not challenged effectively from within those institutions. Racial preferences change this situation, he writes, by

> bringing members of this historically excluded and oppressed group into relationships of equality of power, authority, and status with members of the dominant group. This is important because when relationships of this kind are nonexistent or extremely infrequent, as they are in the system of racial oppression, the system tends most easily and regularly to sustain itself.[4]

Disadvantaged ethnic groups should be able to depend upon people of their own background in the power structure changing the policies of institutions and eliminating their racist vestiges. Anglos in institutions are likely to change their behavior, and perhaps even their views, if they have to interact on a daily basis with people whose backgrounds are different from theirs.

In sum, for most institutions, racial diversity is an asset, and if programs of preferential treatment are needed to achieve racial diversity, the programs can be defended on that basis.[5] This defense of affirmative action programs, the defense based on efficiency, focuses on the mission of the institutions, not on the benefit to those chosen by the racial preferences. A police force, for example, is better able to protect the safety of the public if it has a racially diverse group of officers.

The argument from efficiency does not go unchallenged. A central critique of racial preferences is that it leads to lower standards. It must lead to lower standards, less competency, and inefficiency, the critics argue, because it substitutes race for competency in making selections. If race is used as a criterion for selection, and if it is decisive, a less competent person must take the place of a more competent person. The more this happens, it is alleged, the lower the quality of service the organization can provide.

The typical rejoinder to this criticism, offered by defenders of affirmative action, is that standards are not lowered by racial preferences because for most openings many people are qualified and all the preferences do is select for the underrepresented minority among the qualified people. This is a persuasive argument in many cases. William G. Bowen and Derek Bok's study of students in elite universities who benefited from affirmative action shows that they did well both in college and afterward, and that the programs of preferential admission therefore led to no decline in the quality of the student body.[6] Still, for some positions it is inaccurate to say that there is a minimum standard of qualifications and that anyone who meets that standard will do as well as anyone else. Many cases exist in which the selectors are looking for the best possible person among all who are qualified. For example, a search committee for a faculty position is not satisfied just with someone who meets the minimum qualifications for the position; it wants to find the most brilliant mind, the best teacher, the person most likely to be a productive scholar. The committee might argue that if it is required to consider the race of the applicants, it is unlikely to select the best person.

If the efficiency argument for affirmative action is correct, the best response to the committee's concern is that race itself is a component of competency. It is not irrelevant to competency like, say, left-handedness or hair color. Other things being equal, an economics department with ethnic diversity will do a better job — that is, a better job teaching economics — than one without.

Still, the critics of preferences have a point. The use of race as a criterion for judgment may result in other relevant criteria being downplayed. What this means, though, is not that race should be excluded as a criterion but that it should be considered among other criteria. Were race not the subject under discussion, hardly anyone would disagree with this. It is obvious that competency is not measured in a single dimension; it is not just a matter of scoring high on a test. It is almost always multidimensional. Recruiters for an executive position in a business, for example, may want to find a person who is smart, who is knowledgeable about the product the business produces, who works well with people, and who can make good strategic decisions. They are likely to find a variety of candidates who look wonderful in some categories and not so good in others. In the end the decision might come down to a person with good strategic skills versus a person with a proven track record in the management of people. If so, the recruiters will have to consider the needs of the firm and the particular ways in which the strengths and weaknesses of the candidates are manifested.

This was the basis for Justice Lewis Powell's opinion in the *Bakke* case, decided by the Supreme Court in 1977,[7] which became the legal foundation of affirmative action programs. Powell held that institutions have a legitimate interest in developing a diverse student body — or a diverse workforce — so they ought to be permitted to use race as one of the selection criteria. Race should not replace the other criteria; rather it should stand beside them, because race is only one of the factors that contributes to the achievement of an institution's mission. Powell's opinion barred quotas; that is, it barred the reservation of a certain number of positions for the preferred racial groups. This is appropriate because the use of quotas would eliminate the possibility of comparing candidates with different qualifications. Selection committees ought to compare all candidates who meet the minimum qualifications but whose areas of strength differ, and such comparisons are not possible if selections are made through the use of quotas. The best selection processes are those in which difficult and sensitive judgments are made, trading off one perceived characteristic of applicants against others. Race is legitimately one of those characteristics.

Equality

Racial preferences are also justified in terms of equality. Many people of color are disadvantaged because of racial discrimination, discrimination that had its roots in the era of slavery and that assumed many pernicious forms in subsequent generations. Racial discrimination bars minorities from equal opportunity. When they have been excluded from employment as police officers, for example, they now deserve to be given preference by the police force. This argument is completely separate from the case based on efficiency, that the police force will be better able to accomplish its mission of public safety if it has minority officers.

Racial preferences are an appropriate response to unequal opportunity only if the disadvantage to which they are a response is grounded in present-day racial discrimination. I emphasize this because it differs from some arguments made with respect to affirmative action. Consider the following three: Political scientist Andrew Valls does not deny the current existence of racial discrimination, but he claims that it is irrelevant to the justification for affirmative action. Affirmative action is justified, he says, as a form of rectification for crimes committed in the past against African Americans, *whether or not* they are suffering at the present time. In 1965, President Lyndon Johnson implied that racial discrimination was fast disappearing but that affirmative action was appropriate because African Americans were socially disadvantaged at the present time as a consequence of past discrimination. To Johnson, what was critical was the current social and economic disadvantage of African Americans, not current racial discrimination. African American writer Shelby Steele claims that racial discrimination no longer prevents minorities from advancing and that racial preferences are therefore unjustified. The three arguments are different, but they all deny that current racial discrimination justifies race-based affirmative action. I think all three are mistaken.

Valls, basing his argument on the libertarian philosophy of Robert Nozick, claims that whether or not African Americans are handicapped by racial discrimination today, they are owed affirmative action preferences in rectification for the crimes of slavery.[8] He says that each African American, even the most fortunate and wealthy, would be better off today in the absence of the history of slavery and is therefore owed rectification from the society that benefited from slaveholding. I think this argument is weak because, as I argued earlier, social justice is distinct from criminal justice and does not rest fundamentally on the concept of restitution. If, in spite of the history of slavery, a particular African American is fortunately situated, has equal opportunity, and does not face restrictions because of racial discrimination, she has no claim, I think, to affirmative action on the basis of equality (although she may on the basis of efficiency) because the objective of the equality criterion of justice is to achieve equal opportunity. Such a person has equal opportunity without affirmative action; preferences would give her more than equal opportunity. As a matter of empirical fact, there may be few such people. Still, I think, the right to preferences based on race must be based on an actual current disadvantage based on race. Nozick, I expect, would support Valls's argument and not my rebuttal of it because he rejects the idea that any particular social pattern — equal opportunity or any other distribution of opportunity — defines social justice, but I think he is wrong. Equality is central to justice.

President Johnson originally outlined the reasons for affirmative action in a speech at Howard University:

> You do not take a person who for years has been hobbled by chains and liberate him, bring him up to the starting line of a race and then say, "you're free to compete with all the others," and still justly believe that you have been completely fair. Thus it is not enough just to open the gates of opportunity. All our citizens must have the ability to walk through those gates.... We seek not ... just equality as a right and a theory but equality as a fact and equality as a result.[9]

Speaking at the time of the passage of the Civil Rights Act and the Voting Rights Act, Johnson seems to have envisioned a country without racial discrimination, a country in which African Americans were no longer hobbled by chains and in which the gates had been opened, but he cautioned that, even so, the racism of the past would create disadvantages for minorities in the present and future. They would be handicapped, he thought, not by present discrimination but by the legacy of past discrimination, including poor education and low skills. Hence, he thought, they deserved affirmative action. The problem with this argument is that a legacy of slavery and racial discrimination in the past is only one reason for socioeconomic disadvantage in the present. Many people who were not the victims of racism in the past suffer currently from low economic status. They are of equal moral worth, and it is hard to see why the state should not give them the same advantages as others who are similarly situated. Moreover, some people who were the victims of racism in the past do not currently lag behind whites in skills or accomplishments. If they face no racial discrimination in the present — if they live in the sort of world that Johnson seems to have imagined — it is hard to see why they deserve preferential treatment. In other words, if the current problem is social and economic disadvantage, but not racism, the solutions should not be racial but should be based directly on those disadvantages and available to all who suffer from them. This, to his credit, is what Johnson tried to do; his principal legacy to the nation, aside from the war in Vietnam, was the war on poverty.

Shelby Steele shares with Johnson the view that racial discrimination has disappeared but draws different conclusions; he argues against racial preferences. People of color may lack equal opportunity because of their poverty, he agrees, but those who are not poor face no particular discrimination and therefore do not deserve preferences. In his influential book on race relations, he says that his own children should not receive preferences when they apply to college. They have been raised in an academic environment and are in no sense disadvantaged, he asserts. They have encountered racist insensitivities from whites, but never racial discrimination. They "have never been stopped by their race on any path they have chosen to follow."[10] Why, he asks, should they be given preference in college admission or hiring over whites? There is nothing in their lives to make them deserve it.

One cannot refute Steele by pointing out that most minority children do not have the advantages of his children. It is true that most do not. Most are poorer, and many live in desperate circumstances. This fact does not support racial preferences, however. It supports massive efforts to alleviate poverty, and it also supports preferences based on economic disadvantage. The question Steele raises is whether affirmative action should give an extra advantage to middle-class minorities, solely because of their race. On grounds of efficiency, as the previous section argued, it should. The Steele children and others in their circumstances can make a valuable contribution to the institutions they join, and they can help expunge the racism from those institutions. On grounds of equality, however, I think Steele is right to say that they do not deserve special treatment if they do not face the special disadvantages of racial discrimination. If the world really were the way Johnson and Steele conceive it to be, Steele's conclusion would be the sounder one.

The problem with the positions of both Johnson and Steele is their empirical foundation. Racism has not disappeared. It has changed in form over the years; the civil rights movement was especially important in combating overt approval of racist policies and sentiments. A great deal of evidence exists, however, that discrimination against racial minorities, whatever their class, is still strong. An exhaustive study of race relations by the National Research Council concludes that while progress has been made, significant discrimination still exists in housing, employment, education, criminal justice, politics, and other areas.[11] In 1999, the federal Justice Department appointed a monitor to oversee the New Jersey State Police because of extensive evidence that officers engage in "racial profiling," harassing and arresting minorities because of their color,[12] and the practice is surely not restricted to New Jersey. The president's US Council of Economic Advisers has gathered evidence of discrimination from different sources.[13] Especially interesting are "audit studies," in which matched pairs of candidates, white and minority, similar in all respects except race, are sent to the same sources to look for jobs, housing, or loans. The Council of Economic Advisers reports that the minority applicant typically gets significantly worse treatment. For example, one national housing study showed that unfavorable treatment was 23 to 30 percentage points higher for the minority applicant. The audit studies show that discrimination is directed against middle-class minorities, not just the poor.

The comfortable assumption made by a few minorities and by many Anglos, that racism is a thing of the past, is not borne out by the evidence. The fact that many Anglos make this assumption is an indicator of what is sometimes called white privilege. White privilege is partly objective: better jobs, better education, better housing, freedom from harassment, what Joe L. Kincheloe calls the "unearned wages of whiteness."[14] It is partly subjective: the privilege to disregard race and think it is of no importance. Race is of no importance only if it does not constrain you.

This is the heart of the equality-based justification for racial preferences. Because racism is still a serious problem and because it restricts people of color from achieving their goals, they deserve preferences in admissions, hiring, and contracting. The preferences do not have to be matched exactly to the source of the discrimination. A Latino, for example, deserves some extra consideration in admission to a graduate school, not necessarily because that particular graduate school has been discriminatory but because he faces racial barriers from many sources in his life, so the preferences help to restore the balance of equal opportunity.

Thinking still in terms of the criterion of equality, however, racial preference programs do present some conflicts of justice. The conflicts arise because some particular white people — not all white people — have to pay the price of affirmative action programs. One can see this by contrasting racial preferences with, say, a hypothetical tax-and-transfer program in which whites were taxed, progressively to be sure, in order to provide subsidies to nonwhites. In such a program, all whites would bear a modest cost, which could be thought of as an income tax on Kincheloe's unearned wages of whiteness, which they all receive. In programs of racial preference, in contrast, a few whites — those who would have been admitted, hired, or contracted with in the absence of the preferences — pay the entire price of the program, while the majority of whites pay nothing and in fact benefit from the efficiency improvements that come with affirmative action. The whites who pay the price are selected randomly, not because of a personal failing on their part.

Some proponents of affirmative action claim no injustice is suffered as a consequence of racial preferences. Two arguments stand out. The first — advanced by philosophers Ronald Dworkin,[15] Thomas Nagel,[16] and Richard Wasserstrom,[17] and also four Supreme Court justices in the *Bakke* decision[18] — is that affirmative action preferences lead to no injustice because they are not enacted for the purpose of entrenching a powerful group still further in its position of power. The Jim Crow laws in the post–Civil War South were completely different because they gave racial preferences to people who were already at the top of the social structure. Affirmative action preferences are just, they say, because they are intended to open the social structure up to previously excluded groups. Justices Blackmun, Brennan, Marshall, and White wrote that only government programs that "stigmatize — because they are drawn on the presumption that one race is inferior to another or because they put the weight of government behind racial hatred and separation — are invalid." Nagel describes the difference between unjustified racial discrimination and justified racial preferences (what he calls "strong affirmative action") this way:

> Racial and sexual discrimination are based on contempt or even loathing for the excluded group, a feeling that certain contacts with them are degrading to members of the dominant group, that they are fit only for subordinate positions or menial work. Strong affirmative action involves none of this; it is simply a means of increasing the social and economic strength of formerly victimized groups, and does not stigmatize others.

The argument of these jurists and philosophers shows the difference between Jim Crow and affirmative action preferences, but it is not completely successful in showing that the latter create no injustice. It is not a sufficient condition of justice that no harm be intended.[19] For example, much of the discrimination against women has been justified not on the grounds that women are morally inferior to men but rather on the idea that they need special protections.[20] It is because they are elevated on a pedestal that they are discriminated against, but the discrimination and the injustice are no less real than if they had been thought to be inferior. Even though affirmative action preferences are enacted for the best of reasons, in order to promote a more equitable society, they may still impose unfair burdens on some people.

The second argument is based on probability. In their study of affirmative action at elite universities, Bowen and Bok point out that most applicants are not admitted.[21] Suppose, they write, that the ratio of admissions to applications in a university is 27 percent. If there were no racial preferences, they claim, each person who applied would have a 27 percent chance of admission. Because of racial preferences, the probability of admission for whites and other nonpreferred groups falls to 25 percent. This change in the probability of admission is hardly perceptible, they imply, and certainly not the occasion for the nonpreferred groups to claim an injustice.

The Bowen-Bok refutation is not persuasive because it misstates the admission procedure. Applicants may believe they have a 27 percent chance of admission, but this is not how the process works. Applicants are not admitted by lottery. Rather, admissions committees array the applicants on a continuous scale. Some applicants rank so highly on the scale that they are easily admitted, while some rank so low that they are easily rejected. Those in a middle range are just on the cusp of admission. Consider two admission regimes both selecting 1,080 people from among 4,000 applicants. The ratio of admissions to applicants is 27 percent. The first regime has no racial preferences, while the second selects 107 minority-group members who would not have been admitted under the first regime. It necessarily follows that 107 people admitted in the first regime are rejected in the second. How are we to characterize their situation? By subtracting 107 from both the numerator and the denominator, we can calculate that they are among a group whose ratio of admissions to applications fell from 27 percent to 25 percent, not a big change. These ratios are irrelevant, however, to all the specific applicants, thought of as individuals. The 973 people admitted under both regimes are unaffected by the preferences, as are the 2,813 people rejected under both. A group of 107 people were, however, admitted in the first regime and rejected in the second. For them, the probability of admission has gone from 100 percent to zero, as big a change as there could be. They may not know that they were next on the list and would have been admitted in the absence of preferences and they may therefore not experience a sense of injustice. Nevertheless, it is a fact that those 107 people paid a high price for the affirmative action program, while the other people in their nonpreferred group paid nothing.

The arguments supporting the assertion that racial preferences can be instituted with no cost at all in terms of equal treatment are not successful. The Dworkin-Nagel-Wasserstrom-justices argument shows that racial preferences in affirmative action programs are far more benevolent than the preferences that existed for the purpose of maintaining white supremacy, but this does not imply that they create no injustice at all. The Bowen-Bok argument is intended to show that the effect of preferences on the probability of admission for the nonpreferred group is trivial; what it actually shows is that the injustice, while nontrivial and substantial, is restricted to a small number of people.

We are left, therefore, with a conflict in terms of the equality criterion. Underrepresented minorities deserve preferential treatment because of pervasive racism that is directed against people of color of every class. The cost of preference programs should be shared by everyone who benefits from white privilege, but this cannot be arranged. Consequently, a few whites pay a high price while the majority emerge untouched. No way exists of avoiding at least some injustice. If preferences are barred, some who suffer from racial discrimination will be condemned to unequal opportunity, while if preferences are permitted, some people in the nonpreferred groups will be unjustly treated. When some injustice is inevitable, we must weigh the options and use our judgment. What tips the balance in this case, I think, is the extraordinary importance that racism has had in the development of the United States. Racism is not merely an unfortunate add-on; it has been fundamental to the culture and society. It is therefore critical to do what can be done to expunge it. I think an impartial observer would conclude that racial preferences should be continued, as long as discrimination lasts, in spite of the price that must be paid by some.

Hence affirmative action is justified on grounds of both efficiency and equality: clearly in the case of efficiency, a little uneasily in the case of equality. The movement to abolish affirmative action is a movement in the direction of injustice.

Beyond Affirmative Action

Racial preferences can help us advance toward a more just society. The main problem with them is not that they are unwarranted but that they can fool us into thinking we are dealing with the main problem. The major social problem in the United States is that millions upon millions of people live lives of poverty, destitution, and even hopelessness. They struggle daily to make ends meet and often do not succeed. Included in their number are more than a proportional number of minorities but not solely minorities; the poor include members of every racial group.

Programs of racial preference benefit a few people, some of whom are poor and some of whom are not poor, but they leave untouched the great majority of poor people. The best course of action is to attack poverty directly. This was the subject of the previous four chapters, which focused mostly on government policy. Governments do not have to carry the full burden, however; nongovernmental institutions can contribute as well.

One possibility is programs of preferential treatment based on class or income, in addition to race. One form of income-based preferences is financial aid at colleges and universities. Students who can demonstrate financial need are often given help in the form of grants, loans at reduced rates of interest, and part-time jobs. Financial aid programs are essential, but colleges and other institutions could go much further in giving preferences in admissions and hiring to low-income people. There is no question but that they have unequal opportunity in terms, for example, of preparing themselves for college.

Some who are otherwise sympathetic to the idea have thrown up their hands at what they think of as the impossibility of administering a preferential treatment program based on income or social disadvantage. The main problem seems to be deciding how long the preference would last. A young person whose parents were poor might receive some preference in college admissions, for example, but how could the preference be maintained as the person grew older and developed his own income-producing capacity? Would the same person have a preference in graduate school admissions, in the first professional job, in later promotions? This may mean that universities, for example, could not use income-based preferences in hiring their faculties. There is no reason, however, why they could not give some weight to the socioeconomic disadvantages of applicants' families when selecting an incoming class of students.

Moreover, one should not think that income is a slippery identifier while race is concrete. Race is difficult to pin down as well. Biologists have long told us that race is not a biological category of human beings at all; it is a social category.[22] The characteristics we think of as distinguishing one race from another shift over time, sometimes over a short period. In addition, the races intermarry, to an increasing extent, and produce children with multiple racial backgrounds. The convention in the United States used to be that any African heritage, no matter how small, made one an African, but that convention has for the most part been abandoned. Now many people identify with several races, some with none.

When economic disadvantage can be readily identified, the case for preferential treatment, on the grounds that it would compensate for inequality of opportunity, is strong. Race-based preferences are defensible, but income-based preferences could make even more of a contribution to justice. With the exception of financial aid programs, however, they hardly exist. Still, preferential treatment, whether based on race or on income, should not be the main thrust of policy toward social justice. The more important task is to eliminate the factors that created the unequal opportunity in the first place.

A cautionary tale from the institution in which I work is revealing. In 1995, the Regents of the University of California abolished racial preferences in admissions and hiring. The Regent who led this change, Ward Connerly, then led the movement for a voter initiative to end preferences in all public institutions in the state. Proposition 209, the so-called California Civil Rights Initiative, passed easily in 1996. Its first clause reads: "The state shall not discriminate against, or grant preferential treatment to, any individual or group on the basis of race, sex, color, ethnicity, or national origin in the operation of public employment, public education, or public contracting."[23]

As a consequence of both measures, the university could no longer employ racial preferences. University administrators understood themselves to be in the dangerous position of seeing their institution become more white at a time when the state's population was becoming more nonwhite. They worried, realistically, that such an institution would lose public support. Deprived of the tool of racial preferences, they turned to an expansion of programs of outreach to schools in poor communities. The Regents' resolution that ended racial preferences included as its last clause:

> Believing California's diversity to be an asset, we adopt this statement:
> Because individual members of all of California's diverse races have the

intelligence and capacity to succeed at the University of California, this policy will achieve a UC population that reflects this state's diversity through the preparation and empowerment of all students in this state to succeed rather than through a system of artificial preferences.[24]

Implementing this resolution, the university poured millions of dollars into outreach programs to schools in the state's poorest communities. By law it could not target areas on the basis of their racial makeup, but it could direct resources to communities that were needy in terms of income. The university developed new relationships with high schools and even with elementary schools. It sent students as interns into the schools and professors as consultants. It invited school teachers to come to the university campuses for enriched training programs. It provided technology to the schools and help with getting the most out of the technology. It is too early to assess the program — the results, if any, will occur over a long period of years — but the participants are optimistic.

Why did it take the abolition of affirmative action to bring about this outreach program to educationally needy children? The university should have done it before, but it was lulled into thinking it could solve its problems by racial preferences in admissions. Now the university is doing something potentially much more valuable than racial preferences; it is actually improving the quality of education for children who need it. While affirmative action programs can be beneficial, part of an overall commitment to reducing social inequities, they should be only a small part of that commitment, secondary to efforts to remove the inequities in the first place.

Capitalism, Affirmative Action, and Racial Justice

So far in this book, we have discovered that completely just solutions to social problems are precluded by the requirements of the capitalist system. The rules of capitalism have some flexibility, but they are not infinitely elastic. A totally just income distribution, a totally just tax system, and a totally just welfare system lie outside capitalism's boundaries. Interestingly, though, capitalism has no difficulty absorbing even the most stringent forms of affirmative action.

Preferences for racial minorities and women have, after all, been part of the American capitalist system for decades. They have always been controversial, but the objections to them have not come primarily from capitalist sources. Many large companies have been among the principal supporters of affirmative action, seeing in it a tool for diversifying their workforces and thereby becoming more competitive in the marketplace. The business-based opposition to racial preferences has come mostly from small companies owned by whites who have protested the preferences in contracting given to some of their competitors. In comparison to the large companies, they represent only a minor component of capitalism. If affirmative action is downgraded or eliminated in the United States, it will be because of judicial decisions and white opposition, not because the corporate power structure has turned against it.

This is not to say that capitalism will permit complete racial justice. The struggle against racial injustice is a great deal more difficult than simply instituting racial preferences. It requires extensive programs to remove the sources of poverty and eliminate the disadvantages that centuries of racial oppression have imposed. Effective programs are expensive and require a long-term commitment. They require tax dollars. They therefore threaten corporate profits and the international competitive position of companies. It is not at all certain that the capitalist system will permit the sort of expenditures and transfers that are needed.

Notes

1. For a succinct history of affirmative action and a summary of the legal and philosophical arguments, see Ellen Frankel Paul, "Affirmative Action," in *Encyclopedia of Applied Ethics* (San Diego: Academic Press, 1998), 1:63–80. A good collection of philosophical arguments is in Steven M. Cahn, ed., *The Affirmative Action Debate* (New York: Routledge, 1995).

2. US Council of Economic Advisers, *Economic Report of the President, Together with the Annual Report of the Council of Economic Advisers* (Washington, D.C.: US Government Printing Office, 1998), chapter 4.

3. The following are examples of the arguments for and against affirmative action made on the grounds outlined in this section. Pro affirmative action, because of equality, Gertrude Ezorsky, *Racism and Justice: The Case for Affirmative Action* (Ithaca, N.Y.: Cornell University Press, 1991). Con, on the grounds that it creates inequality, Clint Bolick, *The Affirmative Action Fraud: Can We Restore the American Civil Rights Vision?* (Washington, D.C.: Cato Institute, 1996). Pro, on grounds of efficiency, Janice Drakich, Marilyn Taylor, and Jennifer Bankier, "Academic Freedom *Is* the Inclusive University," in *Beyond Political Correctness: Toward the Inclusive University*, ed. Stephen Richer and Lorna Weir (Toronto: University of Toronto Press, 1995), 118–35. Pro, to attack racism from within institutions, Richard Wasserstrom, "One Way to Understand and Defend Programs of Preferential Treatment," in *The Moral Foundations of Civil Rights*, ed. Robert K. Fullinwider and Claudia Mills (To-

towa, N.J.: Rowman and Littlefield, 1986), 46–55. Con, on the grounds that it leads to inefficiency, Ann Hartle, "Who 'Counts' on Campus?" and Ellen Frankel Paul, "Careers Open to Talent," both in *Affirmative Action and the University: A Philosophical Inquiry,* ed. Steven M. Cahn (Philadelphia: Temple University Press, 1993), 132–33 and 250–63, respectively.

4. Wasserstrom, "One Way to Understand," 48.

5. For the opposite argument, see George Sher, "Diversity," *Philosophy and Public Affairs* 28 (1999): 85–104.

6. William G. Bowen and Derek Bok, *The Shape of the River: Long Term Consequences of Considering Race in College and University Admissions* (Princeton, N.J.: Princeton University Press, 1998).

7. On the *Bakke* case, see among others Timothy J. O'Neill, *Bakke and the Politics of Equality: Friends and Foes in the Classroom of Litigation* (Middletown, Conn.: Wesleyan University Press, 1985); Bernard Schwartz, *Behind Bakke: Affirmative Action and the Supreme Court* (New York: New York University Press, 1988); and Susan Welch and John Gruhl, *Affirmative Action and Minority Enrollments in Medical and Law Schools* (Ann Arbor: University of Michigan Press, 1998).

8. Andrew Valls, "The Libertarian Case for Affirmative Action," *Social Theory and Practice* 25 (1999): 299–323. For Nozick's position and a critique of it, see chapter 4 above.

9. Quoted in Cahn, *Affirmative Action Debate,* xii.

10. Shelby Steele, *The Content of Our Character: A New Vision of Race in America* (New York: St. Martin's Press, 1990), 111.

11. Gerald David Jaynes and Robin M. Williams Jr., eds., *A Common Destiny: Blacks and American Society,* for the Committee on the Status of Black Americans, Commission on Behavioral and Social Sciences and Education, National Research Council (Washington, D.C.: National Academy Press, 1989).

12. David Kocieniewski, "U.S. Will Monitor New Jersey Police on Race Profiling," *New York Times,* December 23, 1999, A1.

13. U.S. Council of Economic Advisers, *Economic Report of the President,* chapter 4. See also Ezorsky, *Racism and Justice.*

14. Joe L. Kincheloe, "The Struggle to Define and Reinvent Whiteness: A Pedagogical Analysis," *College Literature* 26 (fall 1999): 162–75.

15. Ronald Dworkin, *Taking Rights Seriously* (Cambridge, Mass.: Harvard University Press, 1977), chapter 9.

16. Thomas Nagel, "A Defense of Affirmative Action," in *Ethical Theory and Business,* 5th ed., ed. Tom L. Beauchamp and Norman E. Bowie (Upper Saddle River, N.J.: Prentice Hall, 1997), 370–74.

17. Wasserstrom, "One Way to Understand."

18. O'Neill, *Bakke and the Politics of Equality,* 58.

19. Those versed in the literature of moral philosophy will recognize that this statement is fraught with centuries of disputation. Deontological or Kantian theories typically emphasize a person's ethical motives, while consequentialist theories, among them utilitarianism, emphasize the results of an action. I believe that even most deontological thinkers would agree, however, that good intentions cannot trump bad results if the bad results were actually foreseen. For a

brief introduction to the issue, see Thomas Donaldson, "Kant's Global Rationalism," in *Traditions of International Ethics,* ed. Terry Nardin and David R. Mapel (Cambridge: Cambridge University Press, 1992), 136–57.

20. Robert L. Simon, "Affirmative Action and the University: Faculty Appointment and Preferential Treatment," in *Affirmative Action and the University,* 48–92.

21. Bowen and Bok, *Shape of the River,* 285.

22. On the social construction of race, see Matthew Frye Jacobson, *Whiteness of a Different Color: European Immigrants and the Alchemy of Race* (Cambridge, Mass.: Harvard University Press, 1998).

23. Lydia Chavez, *The Color Bind: California's Battle to End Affirmative Action* (Berkeley: University of California Press, 1998); Paul Ong, ed., *Impacts of Affirmative Action: Policies and Consequences in California* (Walnut Creek, Calif.: AltaMira Press, 1999).

24. Board of Regents of the University of California, *Draft Report of the University of California Outreach Task Force* (Oakland: University of California, May 16, 1997).

Part III

International Dilemmas

Chapter 8

GLOBALIZATION

G LOBALIZATION is fundamental to capitalism, and it is not going to disappear. Nor is it a new phenomenon; it is not the case that until recently our countries were self-sufficient, autonomous, inward-looking entities and that an amazing transformation occurred in the last couple of decades to push the world's economies and peoples into a completely new relationship with each other. Still, the decades after the Second World War witnessed major changes in international capitalist relationships.

The late 1940s and the 1950s saw the reconstruction of international economic institutions, following the severe disruptions of the depression and the Second World War. The 1960s and 1970s were marked by an explosion of multinational corporations, gigantic institutions operating in many countries simultaneously and hence subject to the control of none. In the 1970s, the international trading and financial system was thrown into turmoil by the increase in oil prices engineered by the Organization of Petroleum Exporting Countries. The high oil prices and reckless lending by the international banks produced in turn the great debt crisis of the 1980s, when poor countries found they could not service their financial obligations. Trade and foreign investment in the 1990s led to the rapid growth and then, in some cases, collapse of formerly poor economies in East Asia and elsewhere. Investors sent enormous sums of money across national borders and subsequently, almost on a whim it seemed, pulled them back again, leaving not only financial panics but real economic depressions in their wake. Along with the increase in financial flows, and facilitating that flow, came sophisticated electronic technology that brought efficiencies in production, but also instability, since it is used to switch funds halfway around the world in an instant.

The new globalization has brought with it a new ideological orthodoxy, held by many of the policymakers in both rich and poor countries. It is known sometimes as "the Washington consensus": uncontrolled markets, neoliberalism, and free trade. Governments have backed off

153

from the controls they formerly imposed on private markets. Where
once they saw these controls as necessary to direct capitalism in ways
that served people, not just capital, now they regard them as fetters that
reduce the efficiency of capitalism and make people poorer. Governments cut budgets, reduce taxes, eliminate tariffs and currency controls,
take away subsidies and licenses, and generally make the free market
freer. The changes occur internally, as many countries pare back social
expenditures, and externally as well, as they lift restrictions on trade
and investment. The International Monetary Fund (IMF) has made these
sorts of "reforms" the conditions that countries in distress have to meet
before they can receive financial help from outside.[1] The World Trade
Organization (WTO) has ruled many national subsidies and restrictions
on trade to be illegal in the new world of free, unconstrained trade. The
world seems to be withdrawing its faith in governments and replacing
it with a new faith in unregulated capitalist markets.

Globalization and Justice

The new forms of globalization and the new orthodoxy of unconstrained markets create serious problems for all the components of
justice: efficiency, equality, and freedom.[2] Consider efficiency, the ability
of the international economy to get the best results from its resources
and to grow. The United States and Canada have escaped most of the
turmoil in world markets, but they are virtually alone. Europe has suffered from stagnation and unemployment, Japan has been surprised by
falling production, Russia has descended into economic chaos, many of
the African economies have deteriorated to such an extent that death
rates have risen, and Latin America and Asia have seen a remarkable
series of interconnected financial crises. The causes of each economic
disaster are complex, but one can say about them all that the global
system of financial flows and free markets has not prevented them. It is
a telling verdict. The newly freed markets were supposed to unleash the
potential of the world's economies; in more cases than not, however,
those economies have suffered through roller coasters of advances and
defeats.

Both between and within countries, the new globalization has seen
the gap between rich and poor widen. Globalization is sometimes touted
as the way for poor countries to become prosperous, and for some it
is, but not for all. International markets reward the industrious, the
enterprising, and the lucky, while they punish those who cannot keep

up. Some countries have done well in the international competition, while others have fallen further behind. Within countries, the new globalization almost always makes inequalities greater. As governments of both rich and poor countries have reduced their participation in their economies, they have cut back their social safety nets.

The report card on freedom is mixed. Withdrawal of government controls is equivalent, in a way, to more freedom for people to do as they wish with their resources. On the other hand, people who are impoverished by international processes over which they have no control find themselves with less freedom in the sense that they are less able to achieve their ends. Countries certainly have less freedom in the new globalized system. For example, a country that, through its democratic process, decides to ban the import of certain goods for health and safety, environmental, or cultural reasons finds now that the WTO disallows the ban as constituting interference with free international markets. Countries that run budget deficits to support their welfare programs lose the confidence of international investors and see a run on their currency that in turn causes a devaluation of their currency and an economic crisis. The discipline of global markets leaves little room for individual variation in social policies.

The Control of Globalization

What can be done to restore the scales of justice, while acknowledging the permanence of globalization? Quite a lot. We can restrain and guide the global capitalist system in much the way we have restrained and guided capitalism on a national scale. At the national level in economically advanced countries, businesses are not free to operate in any way the capitalists see fit. During a long period in the development of capitalism, they were much less controlled than they are now. A hundred years ago, the indigent had no social safety net, business practices faced no legal restrictions, and national governments took almost no responsibility for unemployment, inflation, and the rate of economic growth. Labor unions were outlawed as illegal constraints of trade. All that has changed now. Governments take the responsibility for guiding and restricting capitalist enterprises inside their countries, and unions exert countervailing power against employers.

The locus of government control has evolved from the local or state level to the nation. At the time of independence, for example, and in the Articles of Confederation, the individual states that made up the United

States had the power to assess tariffs against imports. In the Constitution of 1789 this power was taken from the states and vested in the federal government. Henceforth, and to this day, the United States is a large free-trade zone; when tariffs are imposed, it is by the federal government. In a later period, the labor movement evolved from local groups and local actions to national federations. As firms became larger and nationwide in scope, it became necessary to regulate the economy on a national, not a local or state, level. Social security, unemployment insurance, fair labor standards, the minimum wage, public works projects, countercyclical fiscal and monetary policy — all these and more are federal policies with a dual purpose: to protect individuals against the excesses of capitalism and to keep the system on a prosperous trajectory. All of these policies were opposed by the captains of industry, who claimed that they were too restrictive and that they would kill the goose that laid the golden egg. As it turned out, the national regulatory policies did nothing of the sort. The long-run profitability of capitalist enterprises is much greater now than it was before these measures were instituted. In the capitalist system at the national level, private enterprises compete against each other for profits but are regulated by national governments and constrained in their labor relations by unions of workers organized on a national basis.

To recount this familiar history is to make clear that nothing like it exists on the international level. Capitalism is global in scope, but the controls it faces at the global level are laughably weak. The following is what we have.

We have the United Nations, an organization that does good works but that is starved for funds. As an international peacekeeper, it depends upon consensus of the great powers that are the permanent members of the Security Council. Its economic policy is controlled by the General Assembly, where each country has a vote and consequently the poor countries dominate. For that reason the rich countries have been un-willing to allow it to claim much power. The United Nations lacks the authority to change the global economic system.

We have human rights resolutions and several regional and inter-national courts to adjudicate them. The problem with the system of international courts is that the verdicts cannot be enforced without the agreement of the countries concerned.

We have the World Bank, the IMF, and the WTO. These institutions are controlled by the rich countries, not the poor, so they are given more authority than the United Nations. The World Bank is, on the whole, a positive influence on global justice, helping to direct international investment funds to the needs of the poor. Its allocations are often controversial, however, especially from an environmental perspective, and in any case the funds it controls are relatively small. The IMF is charged with helping countries deal with temporary financial crises, and it does this often while imposing the Washington consensus; it requires countries to reduce their controls over international economic activities. The purpose of the WTO is to reduce the tariffs and other restrictions that governments impose on trade. The WTO has the authority to rule that certain policies of national governments are inconsistent with international rules and must be rescinded. In other words, the IMF and the WTO have authority at the international level, but the authority is used to constrain national governments, not international corporations.

We have free-trade areas in many parts of the world: in Europe, in Latin America, in Asia, and in North America. The North American Free Trade Agreement (NAFTA) eliminates tariffs and other constraints on trade between the United States, Canada, and Mexico. NAFTA has teeth; administrative bodies can ban policies adopted by any of the three national governments in such areas as the cultural content of media, environmental and health protections, and subsidies for distressed areas. Like the WTO, NAFTA restrains the authority of countries, not companies.

In sum, the international institutions that might possibly control the excesses of international capitalism are relatively weak. The international institutions that are larger and more powerful are directed for the most part to freeing international markets of restrictions imposed by governments. When people concerned with justice on an international scale protest this unevenness, they are frequently given lectures about the virtues of free trade. They are told that they should study a little economics and learn what every freshman learns in the introductory principles course, that restrictions on trade hurt all countries while open, unconstrained trade enriches all countries.

This is not the place to delve into the centuries of controversy over free trade, except to say that the issue is complicated and that economists do not all subscribe to the view that unconstrained free trade is the best of all possible worlds. Rather, I want to make this simple point: Suppose we agree (which we do not, but suspend your disbelief) that free trade is the best regime for the international economy. Suppose that every country will be made better off by the elimination of tariffs and quantitative restrictions that impede the free international flow of goods and services. Even if this is true, it does not follow that the world must refrain from regulating corporations that operate internationally. Free trade exists among the states of the United States accompanied by extensive regulation of corporations. All that free trade means is the absence of tariffs restricting the passage of goods across national boundaries; it does not mean the absence of all regulations.

An Agenda of Global Controls

Could we have an effective regime of international regulations? Something like it was proposed in the 1970s by a coalition of developing countries under the name of the New International Economic Order (NIEO). The NIEO was intended to promote trade, not restrict it, but promote it in such a way that it would do the most good for the developing countries. The core of the program was a large "common fund" to be used for stabilizing the prices of primary commodity exports from third world countries. The NIEO also called for a common money supply, regulated by an international body. It called for a code of conduct to be adhered to by multinational corporations operating in poor countries. The code would have established common standards with respect to working conditions, tax holidays, environmental pollution, bribery, and other corporate issues. The NIEO collapsed as a coherent negotiating position at the end of the 1970s, when many of the developing countries became engulfed in the debt crisis. It was controversial, and quite likely some of its proposals would have been difficult to implement or would have led to unintended harmful consequences. In spite of its imperfections, though, it could have provided a base for the construction of a system of international regulations that would have protected the global capitalist system from its own instabilities and advanced the cause of justice. That opportunity was lost. The twenty-first century could see a revival of the idea that the international operations of large corporations can be regulated at the global level, in the interest of justice. The following is a nonexhaustive list of topics that cry out for regulation:

- Wages. Wage rates cannot be equalized around the world. The attempt to do so would eliminate economic activity in many low-income areas. Still, minimum-wage regulations that are appropriate to different societies and different levels of economic development should be applied to corporations operating in more than one country.

- Hours. Maximum hours should be set, beyond which overtime rates of pay would be mandatory.

- Working conditions. Simple minimum standards should be developed, having to do with cleanliness, toxic chemicals, safety, first aid, and related topics.

- Child labor. Enforceable standards should be agreed to.

- Labor unions. Uniform rights should be established for workers to organize and bargain collectively in good faith about wages, hours, and working conditions.

- Nondiscrimination. Companies operating internationally should be held to standards of nondiscrimination with respect to race, gender, social class, nationality, faith, and political opinion.

- Taxation. Minimum tax levels should be established for corporations operating in foreign countries, in order to end the practice of companies bargaining with countries for "tax holidays."

- Disclosure. Companies operating in foreign countries should be required to disclose the sort of information that is now required of companies in the United States by the Securities and Exchange Commission. This would ensure that people buying the securities and financial obligations of the companies would have a fair chance of understanding what they are buying. Consumers should know the ingredients of the products they buy.

- Banking practices. Since banks hold the people's money, and since people's deposits in banks are typically insured by a government agency, the business practices of international banks should be closely regulated, with an eye to seeing that prudent decisions are made.

- Crime and corruption. International standards should be established, enforceable in international courts, forbidding corruption, bribery, and other crimes.

- Human rights. Corporations operating in foreign countries should be held to all the injunctions contained in the human rights treaties.

- Environmental protection. International standards of environmental protection should be developed.

- Capital flows. Now that capital moves in such huge amounts and so instantaneously, countries have reason to slow it down and make it less volatile. One good idea, proposed by economist James Tobin, is a small tax, say half a percent, on new capital flows into a country.[3] The purpose of the tax would be to curtail the fast movement of billions of dollars into and out of countries in search of tiny advantages in interest rates. If there were a cost of moving capital from one country to another, it would move only when the advantages were substantial.

- International taxation for foreign aid. Rather than leave foreign aid up to whatever charitable inclinations the rich countries have, amounts could be assessed by an international tax agency, imposing predetermined tax rates upon changing levels of national income in the rich countries. This would be analogous to the shift in the responsibility for the welfare of poor people in the rich countries, from private charities to the government and its taxpayers.

- Culture. One of the victims of free trade has been the integrity of national cultures. The power of American movies, pop stars, music, and images of all sorts to submerge local and national cultures around the globe can hardly be exaggerated. Under the rules of free trade, countries often find that they lack the tools to combat the globalization of popular culture. To the extent that local and national cultures disappear the world will be terribly impoverished, so exceptions to the rules of free trade should be made in culturally sensitive areas.

- Enforcement. Infractions of regulations in all these areas should be prosecuted in international courts.

To people familiar with the economy of the United States and other economically advanced countries, none of these proposals should appear in any way radical. Regulations like these are the meat and potatoes of capitalism at the national level in these countries.

One might reasonably ask why national regulations should not suffice, even in an age of globalization. The answer is that countries, particularly but not exclusively poor countries, are under pressure to weaken their regulations, in order to attract the business of international corporations. A low-income country that was serious about enforcing its child labor laws might lose business to a neighboring country that was not so careful. Many of these standards will not be enforced at all unless they are enforced collectively, by many if not all of the world's countries.

The main obstacle to moving toward a regime of uniform controls over international corporations is that we have no international government. At the level of the nation-state, regulations are imposed by passing laws in the legislature. This mechanism is not available internationally, since the United Nations is not a world government. Its officials are not elected by the world's people, and it has no authority independent of the nations that constitute its membership. This is not an oversight; its charter requires it to respect the sovereignty of the member states.

There is no possibility of world government in the future that any of us can foresee. The people in the rich countries are greatly outnumbered by those in the poor countries, and they would never agree to subject themselves to a democratic process in which their interests could be overridden. Even people living in the poor countries are unlikely to think that a global government would serve their long-run interests or would advance the cause of justice. A global government, even if fully democratic, would have to operate at such a distance from people that they would feel virtually no connection to it. We are not going to achieve uniform regulation of global capitalism through the laws of a global government. The only answer, therefore, is the slow and painstaking creation of international treaties, documents to which sovereign nations accede voluntarily and to which they agree to bind themselves.

We already have many international treaties, covering relationships between countries on a wide array of issues. We have treaties on human rights, on the use of the oceans, on standards for the treatment of refugees, on the coordination of national tax systems, on tariffs and trade, on rivers that flow between different countries, on the extradition of criminals, on the nonproliferation of nuclear arms, and on many other matters. Countries sign treaties of their own volition. Once they sign, however, the treaties have the force of law and can be enforced by courts within the different countries. One way to view a treaty, therefore, is that by signing one a country gives away some of its sovereign authority. It is sometimes willing to do so, in order to secure the promise of other countries to cede a certain degree of their sovereign authority in a parallel way.

Sovereign nations could accede to treaties establishing a more robust set of international regulations than currently exist. Canadian scholar Sylvia Ostry has suggested, for example, the creation of a new World

Environmental Organization, to parallel the WTO and to have the responsibility for creating global standards relating to emissions and environmental preservation.[4] She has also suggested that the International Labor Organization be strengthened by having the responsibility for the regulation of global labor standards. Such treaties and institutions will be difficult to create because of the conflicting interests that exist in the world. At the present time, for example, representatives of poor countries tend to be skeptical of environmental and labor standards that are proposed by groups in the rich countries. Corporate interests can be counted upon to resist any new regulations on their activities. In the absence of a world government, however, no alternative exists to the slow, negotiated development of international standards and the mechanisms for enforcing those standards, if globalization is not to be a synonym for injustice.

All the proposals made in this chapter merit extensive analysis. The chapters that follow in part III concentrate on a small subset of global issues: the appropriate geographical boundaries of our moral concerns, foreign aid, immigration, and environmental policies.

Notes

1. For a critique of IMF and US Treasury policies by a former chief economist at the World Bank and member of the President's Council of Economic Advisers, see Joseph Stiglitz, "The Insider," *New Republic,* April 17 and 24, 2000, 56–60.

2. For a comprehensive attack on globalization, see David C. Korten, *When Corporations Rule the World* (West Hartford, Conn.: Kumarian Press, 1995).

3. James Tobin, *Full Employment and Growth: Further Keynesian Essays on Policy* (Cheltenham, England: Edward Elgar, 1996), 222.

4. Sylvia Ostry, "Foggy in Seattle" *National Post* (Toronto), November 26, 1999, A16.

Chapter 9

THE BOUNDARIES OF JUSTICE

NATIONAL BOUNDARIES are breaking down. Capitalism has always been international in scope, increasingly so in recent decades. As the economy becomes more global, so too must the responses to it, if we are to make progress toward a just world. Justice means, among other things, equality. If we are to understand justice on a global scale, we must ask who exactly is equal. Do foreigners have equal moral standing with citizens of our own country? Are we required to provide equal treatment to foreigners?[1] As we will see, those questions are not the same, and they may have different answers.

The Dilemma

Jefferson was clear on the boundaries of moral standing. "All Men are created equal," he wrote. If we understand Jefferson's "men" as "people," we read him as saying that every person born in the world has the same value. That is the straightforward meaning of the sentence, and when one hears it one nods in agreement. Virtually no one treats everyone equally, however.

Almost every one of us gives special treatment to family members. We think about them constantly, worry about them, help them, spend money on them, lavish our time on them. We do not come close to devoting this sort of attention to other people. Does this simply demonstrate how selfish and unjust we are, how far we are from Jefferson's ideal of justice? No, that cannot be. Concern for one's family is so universal, not only among human beings but among virtually all species, that it cannot be unjust. It is likely an evolutionary necessity; if parents did not care inordinately for their young, the young would not survive and the species would disappear.

163

So perhaps it is the case that family members have to be an exception to the norm of equal treatment. Are they the only exception? Not in my life. I devote more attention to my friends than to strangers, more to students in my class than to students in other people's classes, more to the people in my workplace than to people who work elsewhere, more to the people in my country than to people on the other side of the world. The political systems of which I am a member encourage these sorts of distinctions. I vote for members of my city council, whose responsibility is for the welfare of city residents, not people outside the city. I vote for state representatives, whose responsibilities are limited to the people of my state, and for national representatives, whose responsibilities are limited to the people of my country. I do not vote for a world government. Politics and morality seem to reinforce each other in this respect; we have circles of political jurisdictions that correspond roughly to circles of moral consideration.

This is troubling, because it seems so contrary to Jefferson's ideal. We face two conflicting principles, equal moral standing, on the one hand, and unequal circles of standing, on the other. Lest one think that the conflict can be easily resolved, consider some further moral circles. Are future people, yet unborn, as valuable as people now living? Should moral standing be restricted to human beings, or should it be extended to animals, or perhaps to the natural ecology as a whole? These latter issues are at the heart of chapter 12. This chapter considers the standing of all living people in the world.

Two opposite approaches have been proposed. Charles R. Beitz and a group of writers he describes as "cosmopolitan liberals" argue that national borders are of no moral significance. All the world's people are connected with each other in an intricate series of institutions and economic relationships, he says, and we depend upon each other. What matters is our common humanity; we are all one family. Whatever we owe to fellow citizens we owe as well to foreigners.[2] The "realist" school of international relations suggests the opposite answer.[3] Tracing their views back to Thucydides and Machiavelli, the realists, exemplified by such modern writers as E. H. Carr, Hans Morgenthau, Henry Kissinger, and Robert W. Tucker,[4] argue that morality stops at national borders. Beyond those borders, no common government exists, hence no institutions for resolving disputes in an evenhanded way and providing justice. The responsibility of national leaders, say the realists, is not to seek justice or ethics in the international realm but to protect the interests of their own state. If the leaders fail to make this their guiding principle, their states will be defenseless in a hostile world. Intermediate positions exist. John Rawls, for example, claims that states have obligations of justice to other states in the international system, but that neither states nor individuals have obligations to individuals outside their national borders.[5]

I find both the extreme positions unpersuasive and suggest in this chapter a somewhat different intermediate position, hinging on the distinction between equal moral standing and the obligation to provide equal treatment. All people in the world are of equal moral standing and therefore deserve equal opportunity. In terms of the obligation to provide equal treatment, however, boundaries are morally relevant. Those who exercise authority within a valid boundary are strictly required to provide equal treatment to people who are inside the boundary. Moral obligations extend to individuals who are outside the boundaries, but the obligations may be fulfilled by less than equal treatment.[6] We will sometimes face conflicts between obligations to those who are inside a boundary and those who are outside, conflicts that cannot be resolved by formula but only by serious moral thinking with all the facts at hand.

Equal Standing

The first question is whether people outside boundaries have equal moral standing with those inside, whether, for example, foreigners have equal moral standing with citizens. We often act as if they do not, but we are seldom willing to put that inequality into plain words. So let us try it: "Americans are better than Mexicans." "British are better than Chinese." Or, if you prefer, "whites are better than blacks"; "Christians are better than Muslims"; "Hutus are better than Tutsis"; "straights are better than gays"; "my children are better than your children."

As we can see immediately, there are good reasons why we are unwilling to say such things aloud. They are monstrous things to say. They are the ideology of Nazis and racists; they lead to slavery and genocide. They are exactly what we mean, however, if we think that some of us have greater moral standing than others. We cannot retreat, therefore, from the commitment to the equal standing of all.

Since people have equal standing, it follows that within boundaries, the requirement of equal treatment holds. I must treat each of my children as an equal, for example; I cannot favor the prettiest or the smartest over the others. The federal government must treat each citizen as an equal; it cannot favor whites over blacks, or men over women, or northerners over southerners. This does not mean, of course, that each person will get exactly the same things. I will buy medicine for my son who is sick and not for my daughter who is well, without thereby being unjust. The government may provide financial aid to students and not to nonstudents without violating anyone's right to equal treatment. Justice requires, however, equal treatment of people, within moral boundaries, when they are in similar situations.

The difficult question is whether morally relevant boundaries exist, beyond which people who have the authority to act are not obliged to provide equal treatment. Am I justified in giving more favored treatment to my own children than to other people's children? Is the federal government justified in treating citizens better than foreigners? I am going to conclude that the answer is yes, that we may favor people inside some boundaries over people outside, but that nevertheless we have obligations of justice to outsiders.

Personal Boundaries

Let us start with the boundaries that are closest to us, that set one's family off from the rest of the world. Must we treat our family members the same as other people, or are we justified in treating them better? One answer to this question has already been given. We must devote extraordinary attention to our own dependent children or the children will not survive. This is certainly true, but it cannot be the only argument. If it were, it would justify providing only for the survival of our children, nothing more, and it would not justify preferred treatment of other family members: parents, spouses, lovers, adult children, grandparents, and the rest. If we are to defend the care that we actually give to our family as being compatible with justice and not merely selfish, we must go beyond the purely evolutionary argument. The way to do so, I think, is by drawing the familiar distinction between the personal and the political. It is a distinction that matters intensely to most of us.

In some ways, it is true, "the personal is political," as the women's movement has often asserted. For example, family and other close relationships can be marked by exploitation, subordination, and the unjustified use of power. When they are, it is important for all involved to understand the system in which they are enmeshed, how that system relates to the wider society, and how it can be reformulated.

Even so, most people think of their family relationships quite differently from their connections outside the family. We defend our personal lives and our personal associations, sometimes fiercely. If we were told that we had to reduce our personal commitments, because they were incompatible with equal treatment or some other broadly political goal, most of us would recoil and fight back. We regard political systems that violate the boundaries of personal family life as suspect at best, and typically as tyrannous. We are sometimes willing to allow the state to intervene in a family by placing dependent children in a foster home, for example, but only when the children are in the most serious danger and always with considerable fear that we may be violating a boundary that should not be violated. One of the worst injustices we have condemned in some totalitarian states has been their encouragement of children to spy against their parents and turn them in for subversive thoughts or actions. Family relationships have, and should have, a certain sanctity.

Philosopher Peter Singer claims that, once we have ensured that our family does not have to live in absolute poverty, the surplus income above that level is used for "stylish clothes, expensive dinners, a so-phisticated stereo system, overseas holidays, a (second?) car, a larger house, private schools for our children, and so on,"[7] in other words, for luxuries that we do not need. I have no doubt that many families, including at times my own, spend money on unnecessary luxuries, but Singer's account is distant from the actual obligations I perceive in my personal life.

The bonds that my family and I have formed with each other over our lifetimes are much stronger than the bonds we have with most other people, and they create special obligations. Out of my middle-class income, I am obliged, I believe, to provide a decent home for my family in a safe neighborhood with good schools. I should provide educational opportunities for my children, both in and out of school, as well as athletic programs and recreation, so that they can grow in mind and body. I should help them to travel, so that they can learn something of their country and the world. I have a particular obligation to their moral development. At the time of my marriage, I made a deep and public commitment to my wife to help her achieve her goals in every way I could, as she did to me. When my family members are sick, they need special help from me. Family members who are not dependent children sometimes find themselves in difficulty of one sort or another, and they should be able to come to me for help, as I sometimes go to them. My obligation is not just to ensure that my family survives but to help its members flourish. I have obligations outside the family as well, but none of them compares with the depth of my personal obligations. Moreover, family life is more than just sacrifice and obligations. My family and I have the right, I think, to some fun: some time for ourselves, some activities we get a kick out of, some entertainment and culture, among other things. We have had and will have plenty of tragedies to face together — they are unavoidable — and we deserve to balance them with happy times.

I do not believe I am unusual in thinking of my family life this way. As far as I can tell, everyone I know has roughly similar priorities in life. We simply cannot be held to a standard that requires us to treat everyone the same.

It would be wonderful if everyone had a nurturing family, if everyone could depend upon the close and loving support of a few other people. Unfortunately, it is not the case. Many children, for example, live in dysfunctional families or perhaps no families at all. The rest of us have obligations to those children. Our public agencies, supported by our tax money, need to step in and do the best they can for them, on our behalf. As individuals we can sometimes help as well, by befriending the children, perhaps by welcoming them into our homes and providing them things they need. We cannot, however, replace their families. Even if we could, we should not be required to, because to require us would represent an unjustified violation of our freedom to conduct our personal, family lives as we see fit.

We cannot always favor our family members over others. As Joseph H. Carens points out, favoritism toward one's children is inappropriate when calling balls and strikes in a baseball game.[8] Almost no one would disagree, however, that in many circumstances we are justified in providing for our family first, and others only secondarily — even if we do not believe that our family members are morally superior to other people. I think that families are not the only groupings about which this can be said: under some circumstances, state and institutional boundaries have moral significance as well.

Arguments for No Obligations to Individuals across National Borders

In order to defend the position that citizens of a country have some obligations to foreigners but not equal obligations, I first attempt to refute four arguments that have been made in support of the claim that morally equal people have no obligation at all to provide justice to each other across national borders.

Realism

As noted, realists like Morgenthau and Kissinger hold that the duty of national statesmen is to protect their states, not to provide justice. Realists proceed from the assumption of international anarchy. Within states we have governments that bind people together, but outside states no government exists and no rule of law prevails. To be sure we have treaties, conferences, and international organizations, but these are all voluntary institutions. States comply with their rules as long as it is in their interest to comply, but when it is not they reject the rules. This is the way the world is, the realists claim: it's a jungle out there. A country's leaders would neglect their duty by trying to behave morally in the international sphere, because they would necessarily endanger the survival of their state.

Realism fails, I think, because its proponents misrepresent the nature of international relations. The world is not predominantly anarchic. Examples of anarchism can be found, but they are more than balanced by examples of cooperation and the obeying of international rules. In all aspects of international life we have norms and institutions, to which our countries have voluntarily acceded, that constrain the power of countries to act unilaterally. Countries can act "realistically" and selfishly if their leaders wish, of course, but they do not need to since — with some noteworthy exceptions — they do not have to fear for their survival. With the end of the Cold War, the exceptions are mostly among the world's poorer countries. The prosperous countries of Europe, North America, and a few other places, the countries whose favored positions impose the greatest obligations of justice upon them, are able to act on those obligations without courting national disaster.

Communitarianism

Communitarians regard the entire attempt to find abstract and universal principles of ethics as a fool's journey.[9] We are not isolated units, they tell us. Each of us is born into an ongoing community, and we grow up, learning right from wrong, in the context of the culture of that community. One of our responsibilities is to protect and develop our communities. Communitarian Michael Walzer argues that countries are communities like clubs, which are organizations that are allowed to control their membership, or like families, which are entitled to keep strangers out of their homes but which have to accept even long-lost relatives when they show up.[10] Walzer claims that the very existence of clubs, families, and countries depends upon their making a distinction between members and outsiders. To require them to have obligations to outsiders would be to force them to dissolve. They can accept new members if they choose, and presumably they do so only when the new members can be expected to enhance rather than diminish the community. If a community is to survive and thrive, its members' obligations must be to each other, not to outsiders.

One problem with the communitarian argument is that the communities we experience are not in fact limited by national boundaries. In an age of mass migration and instant communication, we have many community connections that cut across borders. Even if our obligations to provide justice are limited by our communities, therefore, we are not precluded from providing justice to foreigners. The more basic problem with the communitarian position is that it contains no independent standard of justice. Communitarianism is really a variant of ethical relativism, which is an inadequate basis for justice. According to the communitarians, moral standards come naturally out of the interactions of members of communities. Justice cannot, however, be only what the people of a community think it to be, still less can it be defined as what is needed to protect a community. The white communities of the nineteenth-century American South and twentieth-century South Africa knew what was needed to preserve their communities — slavery and apartheid — and they were morally wrong. Community members may value insiders more than outsiders, and they may regard the preservation of their community values as of central importance. Those community values need to be arrayed, however, against other values with which they come in conflict, if we are to approach justice.

Justice as Reciprocity

Some theorists argue that justice is relevant only under conditions of reciprocity. I have obligations of justice to you if you have obligations to me, and not if you do not. Those who think of justice in this way sometimes go on to say that the institutions and cultures that permit reciprocity exist within national borders but not across them.[11] The most important difference between the two spheres is the political system. Within countries we participate in governing institutions that embody our collective commitment to justice. Such institutions are lacking internationally, so we are not connected to each other by a relationship of justice across borders. John Rawls argues that an international system of states exists, the consequence being that states have obligations of justice to one another, including the obligations to respect each other's sovereignty and to refrain from intervening in domestic affairs. He claims, however, that neither states nor individuals within states have obligations to individuals outside their national borders, because individuals lack connections across borders.

My rejection of the reciprocity argument is parallel to my rejection of the communitarians; it is based partly on empirical grounds and partly on moral grounds. On empirical grounds, as I have just argued, many connections exist across borders, so if justice is to be based upon reciprocity, it can be provided internationally as well as nationally. The more fundamental problem with this argument is that justice does not really depend upon reciprocity. It is true that I cannot provide justice to someone whose life I cannot affect; I have no way of doing it. That is quite different, however, from saying that I cannot provide justice to someone who cannot affect my life. Suppose I am a billionaire and you are impoverished. I have enormous power, which I can use for good or ill to affect your life, while you have no power at all to affect my life. We have no reciprocity between us. Still, if justice is marked by equality, freedom, and efficiency, I can provide justice to you. A parent has obligations to her child, even if the child does not reciprocate. So too do people in rich countries have obligations to people in poor countries. Reciprocity is not a prerequisite of justice.

Impossibility

Philosopher John Rawls, economist Walt W. Rostow, and others have argued that only national societies are capable of providing justice.[12] Foreigners might like to, but they are unable. Whether the poor are provided for, whether people's liberties are respected, whether a society's resources are used effectively to meet the legitimate needs of its people: these are all issues that must be decided, one way or the other, internally. Foreign intervention is powerless. If the government or people of a rich country try to provide justice to the individuals of a poor country, so the argument goes, they will fail unless the government and people of the poor country take the initiative. Since foreigners can have no impact on the quality of justice enjoyed by individuals, they surely have no obligation to provide it.

The impossibility argument is just wrong.[13] The entire world has been shaped by the international capitalist system. Capitalism has brought technology to every country, along with trade and investment. It has subjected the people of every country to the discipline of international markets. It has brought economic advances in some cases and terrible exploitation in others. One can dispute whether domestic or international forces have been stronger in influencing a particular economy and its income distribution, but it has almost never been the case that the international forces have been negligible. Since international capitalism has been so potent in shaping each of the world's societies, it makes no sense to say that everything is completely different now and that foreigners can no longer have an impact.

The weakness common to all four arguments is that they fail to come to grips with globalization, with the interconnectedness of the world's peoples. The idea that each country is a separate island, separate from all other countries, has been mistaken for as long as capitalism has existed. From its earliest days, capitalism brought with it trade, foreign investment, and imperialism. People were pulled, often against their will and even violently, out of their previous isolation and into the world marketplace. Today the age of formal imperialism has passed, but the economic, political, and cultural connections are stronger than ever. Electronic media provide instant communication to and from every part of the globe. Money is switched instantaneously around the world. Pop music, pop art, and advertising know no boundaries. International travel is ever cheaper, and with each passing decade states become less able to control the migratory movement of people. Actions taken in one country fundamentally affect the natural environment of other countries. Philippe Van Parijs writes, "we are bound, for better and worse, by an ever tighter interdependence from which there is no escape but through further involvement."[14]

One might object that these international connections, strong though they are, are weaker than the connections that exist within countries. No doubt this is true, since countries do, after all, have national governments, national courts of law, national currencies, and national media, among other features. Within large countries like the United States, however, the institutional and emotional connections among people are uneven. Mexican Americans living in the Southwest, for example, typically have stronger personal and cultural connections with people living in Mexico than they do with the forestry and fishery folk of Maine, who in turn have stronger ties to Canadians. If the obligation to provide justice is based upon our connections with people, it cannot be the case that we have no international obligations of justice, since we are closely connected to foreigners.

The arguments denying an obligation to provide any justice at all across national boundaries do not hold up. We may often have difficulty, it is true, deciding exactly how strong our obligations are to foreigners. If we have any obligations at all, however — and we do — one thing is clear. We must not leave outsiders in a less-just situation than they would be in if they had no contact with us. We must not make them less equal, with each other or with us. We must not make them less free, and we must not take actions that leave them less able to achieve their goals. We may be required to do more, but this is a minimum. It is unjust, for example, to permit the toxic emissions from factories in our country to create acid rain over a neighboring country's forests. It is unjust to permit foreign investment from our country to create workplace hazards in another country. One could easily multiply these examples and see thereby that the requirement to do no harm outside one's borders is a stringent one.

Must We Provide Equal Treatment across National Boundaries?

Let us approach the question from the opposite side. Is it possible that our obligations to foreigners are so strong that our government must treat them the same as it treats its own citizens? We have already established that people outside our borders are as valuable as people inside. A destitute man in Delhi deserves, therefore, the same sort of opportunities as are available to people living in the United States. Although this is true, I do not think it implies that the government and people of the United States must provide equal treatment. That is a separate question.

No government in the world takes on the obligation of treating foreigners the same as citizens. A destitute man in Chicago gets better support from the US government than does the destitute man in Delhi. Is this fact compatible with justice, or does justice call for the US government to treat both men the same? At least four arguments have been advanced to show that the US government has unequal responsibilities, that it is justified in treating its own citizen better than the Indian, even though the two are of equal moral value. Some of the arguments are less persuasive than others, but, taken together, they add up to an adequate defense of unequal treatment.[15]

Relative Efficiency

It would be silly to have an undifferentiated world welfare system. Peter Singer argues that people can be helped more effectively by those who are closest to them and who understand their situation better, and furthermore that we are likely to be more generous to those with whom we have a more personal connection.[16] A world welfare system would likely be unwieldy and wasteful. It is more efficient to assign each person to the care of a different government: the Delhi man to the Indian government and the Chicago man to the US government.

This argument is valid as far as it goes — it is certainly more efficient for each government to pay attention to the needs of its own citizens — but by itself, as Singer certainly agrees, it does not relieve the governments of the rich countries of responsibility for seeing that the two are made equal. India is poorer than the United States, and it can afford to do much less for its destitute citizens. Once the Indian government has helped the Delhi man and the US government has helped the Chicago man, the former will be much worse off than the latter. If relative efficiency is the only argument supporting unequal treatment, the US government would still be required to make up the difference. It would end up giving a little less to the Delhi man than to the Chicago man, because the Indian government would have contributed something to its own citizen, but it would still be responsible for seeing that the two are made equal. While correct, therefore, the argument from relative efficiency is the weakest of the four justifications of unequal treatment.

Incapacity

Rich countries can have an impact on the lives of individuals in poor countries, but they are incapable of treating them equally. As I will show in chapter 10, if the rich countries transferred enough of their income to the poor countries to equalize the average posttransfer incomes in all countries, they would have to give up about 80 percent of their own income. They could not do this without fundamentally altering their economies in such a way that the income would probably not be generated in the first place.

The incapacity argument is correct. Still, it is not a strong enough argument to relieve the rich countries of an extraordinary obligation to the world's poor. If it is impossible for them to transfer enough money to equalize the world's incomes, and if this is the only argument against equal treatment, they should transfer as much as they possibly can. The incapacity argument is akin to Rawls's difference principle, but on a global scale. According to this argument, some inequality in treatment may be justified, but only if complete equality would make the most disadvantaged countries worse off. The only inequality permitted would be inequality that allows the total incomes generated in the rich countries to be high enough to maximize the transfer to the poor. The incapacity argument only marginally constrains the obligation of the rich countries to treat people in the poor countries equally.

Moral Saints

If the only reasons not to treat foreigners equally were the relative efficiency and the incapacity arguments, the rich countries would still have an exceptional obligation to the world's poor. They would have to give up a very high portion of their incomes, and the lives of their citizens would be fundamentally changed. To do this would be remarkably generous, but generosity is by its nature voluntary. The question before us is not what actions we might voluntarily take but rather what the actual obligations are of rich countries toward people living in poor countries. Most people would agree that we are not obliged to be what Susan Wolf calls "moral saints," people whose entire lives are devoted singlemindedly to doing the right thing for others, with no thought for our own pleasures and preferences and for the people who are closest to us.[17] A few among us choose to live this way, but most do not, and it defies common sense to think that we are immoral because of this choice. A standard of justice that routinely requires us to be saints flies in the face of the fact that we are not saints and condemns us to lives of injustice. It resembles the doctrine of original sin. It makes injustice inevitable, and it therefore devalues the very idea of justice. If we cannot come anywhere close to being just, we may conclude, why bother with justice at all? The moral saints argument leads us to conclude that people with good fortune are obliged to be reasonably generous to those less fortunate, but not to be saints.

The moral saints argument can be abused, since some cases certainly exist in which justice requires exceptional sacrifices from people. Slavery is unjust, for example, and when slavery is abolished the slaveholders justly lose a substantial portion of their wealth. The king of France and the tsar of Russia were justly deposed in the French and Russian Revolutions — although whether they were justly executed is another question. Under some circumstances, wars are just;[18] when they are, some people are justly required to make the ultimate sacrifice. If the argument always prevails that people cannot be required to inconvenience themselves seriously in the cause of justice, justice will be unattainable. This means that we must use our judgment. People who think that the inequality in the world's wealth is overwhelmingly the consequence of unjust exploitation, that it is akin to slavery and apartheid, must conclude, I think, that justice requires an extraordinary transfer of resources to the world's poor. Those who think that the two situations are morally separate may conclude that people in the rich countries must be generous to people in the poor but that they are not obliged to treat them equally and thereby behave as saints. The moral saints argument requires moral thinking, not easy acquiescence.

Stronger Domestic Connections

Americans have some obligations of justice to the destitute man in Delhi because he is a fellow human being, but they have more obligations to the destitute man in Chicago because they are closer to him, because their lives are more connected to his, because they share the same space and institutions more intensely, and because in all likelihood they are more responsible for his predicament. The two men are in a state of some conflict. If the US government is required to treat the two people equally, it will have no option but to reduce significantly the help it can provide to the American. This would not be justified. The United States is a community of a certain sort, a community that has an obligation to take care of its members.

Most of the arguments against any obligation of justice to people outside one's national boundaries are based, as we saw earlier, on the assertion that international institutional and emotional connections sufficient to support a relationship of justice do not exist. This assertion is factually wrong, or so I argued. It is correct to say, however, that those connections are typically — not always — stronger within a country than across its borders. If the US government treated the Chicago man the same as the Delhi man, it would do an injustice to the former because it has a stronger obligation to him, an obligation that follows from the institutional connections that people within a country have to each other. Our international obligations are real, but they must not be exercised in such a way as to penalize the disadvantaged at home.

The conclusion thus far is that boundaries matter, but they do not cut us off from obligations to people who are outside the boundaries. At the very least our governments and other institutions, acting on our behalf, must not make the situation of outsiders less just, and in many circumstances they must help those who suffer from unequal opportunity, wherever in the world they are. Within each valid moral boundary we are required to provide equal treatment, but we are permitted — even required, in many cases — to provide better treatment to people inside the boundaries than to those outside. We should take care that our global responsibilities not be so open-ended as to harm the disadvantaged among the people for whom we have more responsibility.

What Boundaries Are Valid?

The hardest question is saved for the end. How are we to know which boundaries have moral significance and which do not? We certainly cannot say that all boundaries that mark particularly strong institutional and emotional connections between people also mark the limits of their obligations to provide equal treatment. This is obvious when the boundaries are racial. White South Africans doubtless had stronger connections with each other than with nonwhite South Africans, but their regime of apartheid violated all the canons of justice. So too with all other forms of racial discrimination, of which the United States has known many.

One approach to an answer is to say that within political, legal, and institutional jurisdictions, and only within them, must authorities provide equal treatment. The government of the United States must treat all Americans equally, the government of South Dakota must treat all South Dakotans equally, the government of Philadelphia must treat all Philadelphians equally — and parents must treat their children equally. The Boy Scouts of America must treat all scouts (whether gay or straight) equally, and the Roman Catholic Church must treat all Catholics (whether male or female) equally. They are not required to provide the same treatment to people outside those jurisdictions, since their prior obligation is to provide equal justice inside. This approach is helpful, if not definitive. In some cases, the core meaning of the state is that it includes all people who must be given equal treatment. For example, when Germany was divided into two states, the West German government was not required to provide equal treatment to East Germans. The explicit meaning of reunification was that henceforth the united German government would owe equal treatment to all Germans; what this meant in fact was that the former West Germans undertook the huge fiscal burden of pulling up the standard of living of the former East Germans. Absent a unified German state, they would not have had this burden.

The reason this is not a definitive answer is that jurisdictions sometimes restrict membership for the precise purpose of withholding equal treatment from a disfavored group. The South African government took away the citizenship of Africans and substituted for it citizenship in a separate "homeland," as a way of denying rights. The Nazis treated the Jews as noncitizens, without rights. If we are to stick with the idea that political, legal, and institutional jurisdictions represent valid moral boundaries, we must insist that those jurisdictions be legitimate, where legitimacy means at least that the jurisdiction is inclusive of all who reasonably have a claim to membership, that membership not be manipulated for the purpose of withholding equal treatment.[19] Within a family, for example, it is unjust for a parent to disown a son or daughter, to expel him or her from the family as a way of expressing disapproval; our children are our children, and we owe them equal treatment.

Moral boundaries are not permanent. The German state changed its borders; so too have many other states. As they have changed, the nature of moral obligations among people has changed with them. Families change continuously, and even the meaning of the word "family" changes, as our societies become more accepting of the variety of ways people have of living with and making a commitment to each other. Moreover, the precise boundaries are often ill defined and unclear. In some families, for example, cousins are members of the core group, while in others they are so distant as to be almost strangers. Countries have more obligations to their own citizens than to foreigners, but when foreigners turn up on their soil, they often automatically acquire new rights. In sum, the identification of valid moral boundaries is a moral problem, sometimes not easily resolved. It cannot, however, be wished away. While everyone in the world is of equal value and therefore deserves equal opportunity, and while we have some obligations of justice to individuals who live on the other side of boundaries, nevertheless people, institutions, and states may place some limits around their obligations to others.

Notes

1. An interesting symposium on these questions is contained in *Ethics* 98 (July 1988). See also Onora O'Neill, "Distant Strangers, Moral Standing, and State Boundaries," in *Current Issues in Political Philosophy: Justice in Society and World Order*, ed. Peter Koller and Klaus Paul (Vienna: Verlag Holder-Pichler-Tempsky, 1997), 119–32.

2. Charles R. Beitz, "Social and Cosmopolitan Liberalism," *International Affairs* 75 (1999): 515–29. See also his "International Liberalism and Dis-

tributive Justice: A Survey of Recent Thought," *World Politics* 51 (1999): 269–96; and *Political Theory and International Relations,* 2d ed. (Princeton, N.J.: Princeton University Press, 1999).

3. For surveys, see Steven Forde, "Classical Realism," and Jack Donnelly, "Twentieth Century Realism," both in *Traditions of International Ethics,* ed. Terry Nardin and David R. Marpel (Cambridge: Cambridge University Press, 1992), 62–84 and 85–111, respectively.

4. Edward Hallett Carr, *The Twenty Years' Crisis, 1919–1939: An Introduction to the Study of International Relations* (New York: Harper and Row, 1946); Hans J. Morgenthau, *Politics among Nations: The Struggle for Power and Peace,* 2d ed. (New York: Alfred A. Knopf, 1954); Henry A. Kissinger, *American Foreign Policy,* 3d ed. (New York: W. W. Norton, 1977); Robert W. Tucker, *The Inequality of Nations* (New York: Basic Books, 1977).

5. John Rawls, *The Law of Peoples* (Cambridge, Mass.: Harvard University Press, 1999).

6. My argument is influenced by Stanley Hoffman, who argues that people in rich countries have some obligations to people in poor countries but that those obligations are limited by their obligations closer to home. See his *Duties beyond Borders: On the Limits and Possibilities of Ethical International Relations* (Syracuse, N.Y.: Syracuse University Press: 1981), chapter 4.

7. Peter Singer, *Practical Ethics,* 2d ed. (Cambridge: Cambridge University Press, 1993), 232.

8. Joseph H. Carens, "Open Borders and Liberal Limits: A Response to Isbister," *International Migration Review* 34 (2000): 636–43.

9. For a comprehensive survey, see J. Donald Moon, "Communitarianism," in *The Encyclopedia of Applied Ethics* (San Diego: Academic Press, 1998), 1:551–61.

10. Michael Walzer, *Spheres of Justice: A Defense of Pluralism and Equality* (New York: Basic Books, 1983), chapter 2. See also Michael Walzer, "The Moral Standing of States: A Response to Four Critics," *Philosophy and Public Affairs* 9 (1980): 209–29.

11. Variations of this argument — in both cases with much more complexity — are made in Rawls, *Law of Peoples,* and in Brian Barry, *Democracy, Power, and Justice: Essays in Political Theory* (Oxford: Clarendon Press, 1989), chapters 16 and 17.

12. Rawls, *Law of Peoples;* Walt W. Rostow, *The Stages of Economic Growth: A Non-Communist Manifesto,* 2d ed. (Cambridge: Cambridge University Press, 1971). See also Brian R. Opeskin, "The Moral Foundations of Foreign Aid," *World Development* 24 (1996): 21–44.

13. For an elaboration of this rebuttal, see Beitz's "Social and Cosmopolitan Liberalism" and *Political Theory and International Relations.*

14. Philippe Van Parijs, "Justice and Democracy: Are They Incompatible?" *Journal of Political Philosophy* 4 (1996): 101–17.

15. The four arguments are outlined in John Isbister, "A Liberal Argument for Border Controls: Reply to Carens," *International Migration Review* 34 (2000): 629–35.

16. Singer, *Practical Ethics,* 233.

17. Susan Wolf, "Moral Saints," *Journal of Philosophy* 79 (1982): 419–39.

18. Michael Walzer, *Just and Unjust Wars: A Moral Argument with Historical Illustrations* (New York: Basic Books, 1977).

19. On the legitimacy of states, see David Copp, "The Idea of a Legitimate State," *Philosophy and Public Affairs* 28 (1999): 2–45; and Allen Buchanan, "Recognitional Legitimacy and the State System," *Philosophy and Public Affairs* 28 (1999): 46–78.

Chapter 10

FOREIGN AID

THE GAP between the rich and the poor countries is enormous. Dividing the world somewhat arbitrarily into two blocs, the developing countries and the industrialized countries, we find that in 1998 the developing countries, with 85 percent of the world's population, had an average annual personal income, when converted into US dollars, of $1,250, while the industrialized countries had an average income of $25,510. The ratio of average incomes in the two areas of the world was 20:1. Those are simply averages; some of the developing countries — particularly in Africa but not confined to Africa — had incomes very much lower than $1,250, while some industrialized countries had incomes much higher than $25,510. In Switzerland the average income was $40,080, and in the United States $29,340. Moreover, income was not distributed equally within any country; everywhere there was a substantial gap between rich and poor people.[1]

The United Nations Development Programme estimates that about a third of the population of the developing countries — 1.6 billion people, or twice the total population of the industrialized countries — subsist on the equivalent of less than a dollar a day. Half of them are children.[2] They suffer from a high incidence of malnutrition and disease and have lower life expectancies than do people with higher incomes. They are less educated and less literate. The World Bank calls the phenomenon "absolute poverty," poverty so stark that it prevents people from reaching their physical and mental potential as human beings. Most people in poor countries have nothing like the opportunities of most people in rich countries, and the absolutely poor in the poor countries seem to have no opportunities at all. They are all people of equal moral worth, yet they are not receiving, cannot receive, the help they need from their own relatively impoverished countries.

The Obligation to Give Foreign Aid

People who enjoy good fortune must provide justice to those who do not because we are all human beings of equal worth who deserve equal opportunity. Obligations do not stop at national borders, although they may be weaker across borders than within them. The connections that we share across boundaries — historical, economic, political, cultural, and other kinds of connections — are sufficient to establish a bond of mutual aid between us. Two other sources of the obligation exist, rectification and self-interest. Neither is as fundamental a source of the obligation to help, but both are relevant when thinking about the relationship between people in rich and poor countries.[3]

The obligation to aid people in poor countries can be understood in part as a response to the exploitation of the poor by the rich. Even the libertarian Robert Nozick, who can find almost no obligation of people to divest themselves of any of their holdings, concedes that when a crime has been committed, resulting in the improper or illegal accumulation of property, the property must be given back.[4] It is not fanciful to interpret the huge gap in living standards between rich and poor countries as partly the result of massive criminal acts. This is not how the rich usually understand it. Their ideology typically is this: we and our forefathers worked hard and creatively for what we have, and we are therefore entitled to it. If other people are poor, it is because they and their ancestors did not follow our example of hard work. If they want to better themselves, they should get to work now. The poor, however, tend to see it differently: we are poor, they often say, because we have been exploited by the rich; in fact, the way they became rich was by impoverishing us. The only way we can improve our situation now is for them to take their feet off our necks.[5]

The credo of the poor, that they are victims of a kind of criminal act, is plausible in many cases. For the most part, poor people in the world today are not living in any form of "traditional" culture, since precapitalist social formations have almost completely disappeared. Today's poor people in poor countries do menial jobs, they work in mines and on plantations, they produce goods for export, they are unemployed or underemployed, they live in massive urban slums or in rural areas where the fertility of the land has been sapped by monoculture, they sell chewing gum and lottery tickets on street corners, and on and on. In all these roles, they are part of the world capitalist system. For centuries, the growth of the world's industrial core depended upon cheap inputs produced by poor people. The capitalist empires forced people out of their traditional cultures and into these modern impoverished roles. To some extent, the prosperity of the core states created and depended upon the poverty of the periphery.

In 1944, Eric Eustace Williams, a West Indian historian and later prime minister of Trinidad and Tobago, showed how the slave trade devastated the economies of West Africa, led to the development of a sugar economy in the Caribbean islands that was marked by intense poverty and exploitation, and at the same time generated the profits that were used to fuel the industrial revolution in Britain.[6] Williams's account is an example of how the prosperity of the core capitalist countries depended upon the impoverishment of outlying areas.

Some imperialists were individually guilty of severe crimes. King Leopold of the Belgians made the Congo his personal fiefdom at the end of the nineteenth century and was responsible for deaths and destitution on a mammoth scale.[7] He was joined by many others who enslaved, killed, and plundered.[8] The damage, though, was much greater than any individuals or even groups of individuals can be held accountable for. It was the growth of the entire Western capitalist system that imposed penalties upon what became the third world. If the damage in the past was caused by an entire civilization, and if the people who initiated the damage are for the most part long dead, can we find anyone today to hold responsible? Perhaps not.

Still, the citizens of the rich countries may need to rectify their unjust advantage. The best that can be said about them in this situation is that they are like unknowing recipients of stolen property. If a thief steals property and then bequeaths, gives, or even sells it to you, and it is later proven that the property was stolen, you have to give it back. You have to give it back because you benefited from wrongdoing, even if you yourself did nothing wrong. Those of us in the rich countries are in this situation. Justice requires that we help the poor people of the world improve their lot in life, because we owe our riches in part to a social and economic process that destroyed their traditional cultures and substituted poverty.

The unfair relationships continue. The connections between rich and poor countries are complex, and they are not entirely exploitative. Enough exploitation exists, however, to give rise to a continuing obligation to compensate. When rich countries impose tariff barriers against imports from poor countries, in order to protect jobs and industries at home, they cut off access to markets that could help people in poor countries. When they impose immigration restrictions, to protect the standard of living at home, they eliminate opportunities that would otherwise be available to people living in poor countries. When rich countries consume far more than their share of the world's scarce natural resources, and do so at a rate that is nonsustainable over time, they foreclose opportunities to the world's poor. All these connections and more that could be listed represent large disadvantages imposed on the poor by the rich, and they give rise to an obligation to compensate.

When opportunities are unequal because of exploitation and crimes, the duty to provide rectification is a valid reason to give foreign aid. We should be careful, however, not to identify rectification completely with social justice. As I have argued earlier, social justice should be founded largely on equal opportunity, not on the correction of past improper actions. Opportunities in the world are severely unequal for many different reasons, some of them having nothing to do with past exploitation. Whenever opportunities are unequal, we have work of social justice to do, not merely when crimes have been committed. When poor people in a developing country are suffering because their own leaders have exploited them, or because of a natural disaster, or for any number of other reasons, the obligations of the rich countries are no less binding than when rectification is owed.

The second argument is based on self-interest, and as such it is only dubiously a moral argument. Still, it is a strong argument. It is in the self-interest of people living in the rich countries to pay attention to the needs of the poor countries.[9] In the post–Cold War era we tend to forget this. In the Cold War, it was critical for each side to show to noncommitted or wavering people that their side was worthy of support, and one of the ways to do this was to help the economic development of poor countries. President Kennedy's Alliance for Progress was intended to bring advancement to the poor people of Latin America, for the explicit purpose of keeping them from aligning with the Soviets as the Cubans had done.

The Cold War is now a fading memory, so Americans feel less urgency about buying the allegiance of foreigners by helping them along their economic paths. Disaffected peoples still pose potential threats against the United States and other wealthy countries, however. Terrorism is a continuous danger. Nuclear technology has spread, and the countries of the former Soviet Union still have nuclear capability. The rich have never felt secure when surrounded by a sea of poor people, and there is no reason why they should do so now. Pope Paul VI appealed to this motivation for foreign aid in his 1967 encyclical, *Populorum Progressio:*

> We must repeat once more that the superfluous wealth of rich countries should be placed at the service of poor nations. The rule which up to now held good for the benefit of those nearest to us must today be applied to all the needy of this world. Besides, the rich will be the first to benefit as a result. Otherwise their continued greed will certainly call down upon them the judgement of God and the wrath of the poor, with consequences no one can foretell.[10]

If threats of terrorism, nuclear attack, and the judgment of God seem farfetched, there is a whole series of rather more prosaic but compelling reasons why the self-interest of the rich countries should lead them to extend a helping hand to the poor. Many of them have to do with expanding trade and investment. It was once true, at the height of the European empires, that the profits of the rich countries depended upon the poverty of the poor. When industrialization was getting underway in Europe, the Europeans needed cheap food and raw materials from their empires; the way to keep those goods cheap was to keep the incomes of the producers low. Those days have largely passed, however. In the age of high technology, what industries most need is not cheap labor and cheap inputs but expanding markets. They can produce enormous amounts, but they cannot always sell their goods. So profitability is increased, not threatened, by rising standards of living in foreign countries. The richer the foreigners are, the more of the capitalists' output they can buy. What is true of trade is also true of foreign investment. Once foreign investment was concentrated in extractive industries and plantations, producing goods to be sold back in the core capitalist states. The prosperity of the local people was of no interest to the foreign investors. Today that has changed. Much foreign investment now builds plant and equipment in order to produce goods that are to be sold in the local economy. If the local people have low incomes, the investments fail.

Americans and Europeans are worried about massive immigration from poor countries. These days, most immigrants come because they think the prospects for a decent life are greater in the rich countries than at home. Prosperity at home could help, in the long run, to stem the tide of immigration. Infectious diseases are global in scope. If they are eliminated in only one area, they will reappear again throughout the world. The spread of AIDS from one poor region to the entire world has been devastating in itself and is even more frightening as a precursor of what may happen with other diseases.[11] The greatest environmental problems are global in scope. The increase in average temperatures, the disintegration of the ozone layer, the disappearance of species, the pollution of air and water — none of these are problems that can be adequately addressed by a single country. They require global solutions, and if some parts of the globe are too poor to play their role, the solutions may never be achieved.

This is only a sampling of issues that demonstrate that if the rich take no responsibility for the world's poor people, if they are content to see the disparity in living standards in the world expand rather than contract, they will put themselves in increasing danger. Self-interest constitutes a strong basis for foreign aid and other ways of the rich countries' helping the poor. On the other hand, to the extent that the rich act out of self-interest, they shield themselves from the question of what they owe the poor. What they owe, and what the poor deserve, is the help of the rich in achieving equal opportunity.

Must the rich help through the mechanism of foreign aid, however? Must they actually transfer resources? Many are skeptical. In the several decades following the Second World War, foreign aid was well thought of, even understood as the center of the relationship between the rich countries and the poor. Today, however, the optimism about foreign aid is long gone. It has few defenders in the rich countries. It is attacked from the right as a waste of the taxpayers' money and from the left as supporting a new class of pampered jet setters, going into the pockets of the rich and powerful in the poor countries, and supporting projects that do more harm than good.[12] Michael Harrington once said that foreign aid represents a transfer "from poor people in rich countries to rich people in poor countries."[13] From the developing countries themselves, the aid relationship is often seen as demeaning; it sets up a relationship of dependency of the poor countries upon the rich that diminishes the former's autonomy and restricts their sovereignty. What is common to all the complaints about foreign aid is disappointment that it has not worked as well as was hoped. The world's poor are still poor.

The critics are correct that aid has not worked as well as it should have. Even so, aid from the rich to the poor is a moral imperative, a requirement of justice. One of the reasons that aid has had so little impact is that there has been so little of it. Sometimes we talk as if we had squandered huge amounts, but the opposite is the case. Aid allocations are typically small, as we will see, and often vulnerable to being reduced when overall budgets have to be squeezed, because they have almost no domestic constituencies arguing on their behalf.

The argument against aid from the right, on the grounds that tax-payers in rich countries should not have to support foreigners, is just wrong. They must support poor foreigners, for the reasons outlined above. The argument from the left, that aid is wasted because it goes into the wrong pockets and does more harm than good, is sometimes accurate and sometimes not; aid has often gone to the right places and done a lot of good. To the extent that the argument from the left is correct, the best response is not to abandon aid but to see that it goes where it should go, to the support of the poor. Donors must take care that the projects funded with foreign aid not lead to the deterioration of ecosystems, to the disintegration of rural communities, to the exploitation of women and children in sweatshops, to a widening gap between the rich and the poor in third world countries, to an arms race, and to other evils, but that it is used to make opportunities more equal. The argument from the third world, that the aid relationship is one of dependency and hence incompatible with autonomy, sovereignty, and self-respect, is taken up next.

Conditionality and Sovereignty

Donors seldom give aid to poor countries without attaching conditions to the aid. The conditions restrict the choices of the governments and businesses in the poor countries and hence limit their sovereignty, their ability to make decisions on their own.[14] Representatives of the poor countries often call for the conditions to be relaxed or eliminated, so that they can control their own affairs. Conditions should not be eliminated, however, but rather should be managed sensitively so as to provide the most possible benefit to the poor and the least possible infringement on local initiatives and sovereignty. Provided the conditions are established properly, the aid relationship need not unduly damage the autonomy of the recipients.

Political philosopher Brian Barry argues that certain types of foreign aid should be given by rich countries to poor countries with no conditions attached.[15] He argues that the obligation to give aid comes from two different motives, humanity and justice. What he means by humanity is close to what this book means by equality. Because we are all human beings, those of us who are more fortunate have an obligation to see that the less fortunate have more opportunities, perhaps even equal opportunities. This is the obligation from humanity, and it is completely different, Barry argues, from the obligation deriving from justice. The latter he understands, for the most part, as rectification. The obligation of justice is to compensate for past and present exploitation of the poor by the rich. The relevance of this distinction to Barry is the following. When the justification of aid is humanitarian, to help the poor, the rich countries can and probably should impose conditions on the use of the aid, to ensure that it actually is used for this purpose. If, however, the aid is given for purposes of justice, that is, as rectification, the donors have no right to stipulate how the money is used. The money belongs to the poor countries, and they can do what they want with it. To reason by analogy, suppose you have been the victim of medical malpractice and are awarded damages by the court. The offending doctor simply owes you the money; he has no right to tell you how to spend it. Barry argues that aid given to fulfill the requirements of justice should similarly have no strings attached.

Barry's argument has two weaknesses. The first is that the victims of international exploitation have not been the leaders and the powerful people in the poor countries, but the poor people. If the rich countries have an obligation of rectification, therefore, they should impose suffi-cient conditions to ensure that the aid goes to those who deserve it. The second weakness is that, as we have seen, social justice should not be defined as rectification. Justice should be defined instead as equal op-portunity, freedom, and efficiency. The distinction Barry draws between the motives of humanity and justice does not, I believe, stand up in the end. The two are not separate; rather, the principal foundation of social justice is humanity. If I am correct, the case against the imposition of conditions on foreign aid collapses. The donor countries have not only a right but a duty to ensure that the aid they give is used to reduce poverty and expand opportunities among the world's least fortunate.

Conditions upon the use of aid are both inevitable and desirable, but the nature of the conditions is critical. Too often, they are unrelated to the welfare of poor people, as when aid is tied to the donor country's exports. When aid can be used to import goods only from the donor country and no other, it becomes a subsidy to the donor country's export industries, and it is thereby transformed from a moral act in support of equal opportunity into a domestic industrial policy. This sort of condi-tion should simply be eliminated. There is no excuse for donor countries using foreign aid to support their own economic interests rather than the welfare of the world's poor.

Donor countries also sometimes insist that recipient countries com-pletely change their economic policies — cutting tariffs, eliminating industrial and agricultural subsidies, selling state-owned enterprises to the private sector, and so forth — as a condition of receiving aid. Such conditions may or may not be in the long-run interests of the recipient countries and their poor people, but they represent an extraordinary infringement upon the autonomy of an independent country. This kind of infringement of sovereignty imposes costs that are real, not just symbolic, if it induces national leaders to take less responsibility than they otherwise would for their own economic policies.

One way to approach the sovereignty problem is through the distinction between project aid and program aid. Project aid is in support of specific economic development projects: perhaps an irrigation project, a public health network, an industrial complex, or urban infrastructure. Program aid goes directly to the recipient government, in support of its overall economic strategy. Program aid might be designed to help a country with its balance-of-payments crisis, for example, or its budget deficit.

The conditions appropriate to the two types of aid are different. The conditions attached to project aid always include the requirement that the money be spent on the project, and they may go beyond, perhaps to include stipulations about fair labor practices, environmental impacts, and other relevant factors. The conditions can all be restricted, however, to the particular project being funded. Since they are so limited, they do not pose much of a threat to the sovereignty of the recipient country. Program aid — which increased substantially during the debt-crisis years of the 1980s — is given in order to help solve a fundamental imbalance in the economic structure of the country. Program aid lends itself naturally to the most expansive of conditions. If, for example, the problem being addressed is the overall government budget deficit, the donors may offer to fill the gap for a few years, on condition that the government reform its public finances during that period in order to eliminate the deficit. In effect, then, foreigners rather than local elected officials determine basic government policies.

A way to avoid this sort of infringement of sovereignty is to emphasize project aid over program aid. A second way of managing the conflict is to direct as much aid as possible through international agencies in which representatives of the poor countries have a voice, rather than directly from a single donor country to a single recipient. Multilateral aid can eliminate the most self-serving types of conditions, and it can give the poor countries a voice in the structure of the conditions. The argument typically made against multilateral aid is that a donor country is likely to give more aid if it can control its use directly. This may be true, but it is not an argument about justice. What justice calls for is that the transfer of foreign aid be controlled only by conditions that increase the likelihood of its being used to relieve poverty. Provided that is done, the legitimate arguments against foreign aid from recipient countries disappear.

How Much Foreign Aid?

How much aid are the rich countries required to give? Earlier I concluded that while well-off people in the rich countries are not obliged to treat disadvantaged foreigners equally with fellow citizens, they must contribute to their well-being. This section puts some rough numbers on the obligation, showing that the rich countries can make a substantial contribution to the economic development of the world's poor.

Table 10.1 shows some possible options. The first column contains eight different purposes of a foreign aid program. The eight figures in the second column are the total amount of aid that would be given by all the rich countries, taken together, if they were to fulfill each of the eight purposes. The third column shows this amount as a percentage of the total output, or Gross Domestic Product (GDP), in the recipient, developing countries, while the fourth column shows the amount of aid as a percentage of total incomes generated in the rich, donor countries.[16]

The first row, labeled (a), shows the amount of foreign aid, or "official development assistance," given by the industrialized countries to the developing countries, as calculated by the World Bank, in 1997. While the absolute numbers become somewhat higher in subsequent years, the percentages stay roughly the same. The total was $48 billion, amounting to 0.9 percent of the total production (or GDP) of the developing countries, and 0.2 percent of the total income of the industrialized countries. The United States gives the smallest proportion of its income of any of the donor countries, less than 0.1 percent.[17]

Consider the possibility that the purpose of foreign aid is to transfer income from the rich to the poor in order to equalize, or at least make less unequal, the purchasing power of people in each country. Rows (b), (c), and (d) show that this is impossible to achieve. Row (b) shows how much money would have to be transferred if the goal is to equalize average incomes among all the world's countries. Recall that the average income in the poor countries is $1,250 while the average income in the rich countries is $25,510. If enough aid were given to equalize the

Table 10.1
Possible Levels of Foreign Aid
(Based on 1997 figures)

The Purpose of Aid	Amount of Aid ($Billion)	Aid as a Percentage	
		of GDP in Developing Countries	of Income in Industrial Countries
(a) current aid amount	48	0.9	0.2
(b) to equalize world incomes	18,267	292	81
(c) to make countries' income ratio 2:1	14,800	236	66
(d) to make countries' income ratio 8:1	5,700	91	25
(e) to relieve worst poverty	2,477	40	11
(f) to make aid 10 percent recipients' GDP	626	10	2.5
(g) to make aid 5 percent of recipients' GDP	313	5	1.3
(h) to make aid 0.7 percent of donors' income	158	2.5	0.7

average incomes, at $4,894 in every country, the total amount of aid would be $18,267 billion, amounting to almost three times the current output of the poor countries and 81 percent of the incomes in the rich countries. A transfer of this magnitude is impossible. The rich countries would never agree to give away four-fifths of their income. Even if, in some counterfactual world, they did agree, their economies would be completely changed, and they would not produce as much as they do now. People would probably not continue to work if the great majority of their income were confiscated. Such a transfer is certainly incompatible with the structure of capitalism, which requires a circular flow of income, from producers to consumers and other spenders and then back again to producers in an unending stream, and it is probably incompatible with any economic system. Row (b) should disabuse anyone of the fantasy that foreign aid by itself could remove the global inequalities in income.

Perhaps, though, justice does not require equality, just a substantial movement in the direction of equality. In chapter 3, I developed arguments in favor of a 2:1 gap in personal incomes, or perhaps, for some, an

8:1 gap. To be sure, those arguments related to individuals and had to do with such factors as incentives for hard work and rewards for successful work; they are not transferable to relationships between countries. Just to speculate, though, rows (c) and (d) calculate the aid that would be required to bring the ratios of the rich and poor countries' average incomes to those two levels, 2:1 and 8:1.

Row (c) shows the transfer that would be needed to bring the average incomes into a 2:1 ratio. The poor countries would have an average income per person of $4,246 and the rich countries $8,512 (not shown in the table). The transfer in this case would be $14,800 billion, still more than twice the level of GDP in the poor countries, requiring the rich countries to give up two-thirds of their income. This is still out of the question. Row (d) shows that relaxing the ratio to 8:1 (the poor would have an average income of $2,399 and the rich $19,193) would ease the problem, but still not enough. The transfer, $5,700 billion, would almost equal the GDP of the developing countries and would be a quarter of the GDP of the rich countries. Even if the poor countries could find a way to absorb such a large transfer productively, the rich countries would never agree to give it, nor would their economies be at all recognizable if they did.[18]

There is not much point going to a ratio higher than 8:1, because even 8:1 is a huge gap between rich and poor countries. Remember that we are discussing countries here, not individuals, and that within each country a substantial gap between rich and poor would remain. It is hard to see how a gap any greater than 8:1 could be compatible with justice.

What about the goal of eliminating poverty in the third world? Could foreign aid be thought of as a uniform, global welfare system? Our information on income distribution in poor countries is too scattered to make a precise calculation of the transfer that would be needed. As a first approximation, however, we can calculate how large a transfer would be needed to raise the average income in the lowest-income countries up to the average of incomes in all the low-income countries, $1,250 a year. There is no guarantee that this money would actually be allocated to the poor, but it is a ballpark estimate of the total needed. Row (e) shows that the amount is $2,477 billion, amounting to 40 percent of the poor countries' GDPs and 11 percent of the rich countries'.

Such a transfer is perhaps more feasible than the transfers in the first three rows, but it is still very unlikely. It is fifty-two times greater than the current amount of aid, and it would amount to about a third of total government expenditures in the rich countries. Taxes might be raised to pay for the foreign aid, but it would be hard to reconcile this increase with the tax increases recommended earlier as needed for welfare payments at home and to improve the domestic income distribution. If the funds were raised by public borrowing, they could decimate the rich countries' investment in new equipment and technology, something that would be inconsistent with the capitalist imperative to grow. If no new government revenues were raised, the foreign aid would have to substitute for current public expenditures, and this would be hard to do without diminishing the quality of justice at home. Education, welfare, and/or health care might have to be drastically cut. The best place to turn, to find the resources for foreign aid, would be a reduction in military budgets, but this will likely have to happen anyway in support of domestic priorities.

We should not think of foreign aid, therefore, as a direct means of equalizing world incomes, or making them more equal, or providing welfare-type grants to poor people in the third world. Transfers from the rich cannot raise the net incomes of the poor — consisting of the income they create for themselves plus the income they get in the form of aid — up to a level anywhere close to what justice requires. Foreign aid cannot do this, and it probably should not, even if it could. The autonomy and sovereignty of the poor countries would be damaged if they depended, year after year, upon foreign largesse to meet their basic needs. Aid has its limits. The limits can lead to a sense of despair or futility about aid. A correspondent to the *New York Times* denounced "this country's wasteful policy of sending billions of dollars abroad in a doomed attempt to help the indigent population of the world. This country cannot afford to solve this international problem."[19]

If the purpose of foreign aid were to redistribute the world's income, then indeed it would be "a doomed attempt to help the indigent population of the world," and the letter writer would have a point. There is no justice in wasting money, even if one's intentions are beyond reproach. This is not the purpose of foreign aid, however. What aid can actually succeed at is helping the people in poor countries develop their own production, their own economies, so that they can generate their own income without depending on charity. This goal for foreign aid is more modest, but it has the merit of being achievable. No doubt some foreign aid is properly used to increase directly the consumption levels of poor foreigners. When people are starving they need food immediately, not seeds and irrigation canals that may help them sometime in the future. Absent immediate catastrophes like famines, however, aid should be directed toward helping the people in poor countries to help themselves.

Foreign aid can help countries develop their own productive abilities by providing funds for investment in infrastructure, plant, and equipment, as well as for investment in human capital through education and health. Investment is often a bottleneck in poor countries. In the early postwar years, most development economists thought that investment was the only constraint on economic growth: the more investment there was, the more growth there would be. We now know better. Real economic development requires much more than investment. It requires technology; fair markets; respect for the rights of women, oppressed minorities, and the poor; education; and much more. The need for investment has not disappeared, however. Economic growth still requires new capital stock of all kinds. Investment in capital is difficult for poor countries because it requires cutting back already low consumption levels. So help from the outside, whether from the public or the private sector, can be critical.

According to World Bank surveys, developing countries typically save and invest about 15 percent of their GDP. Row (f) of Table 10.1 shows what would be required to supplement this in a major way, by providing aid in the amount of another 10 percent of the poor countries' incomes. The amount of foreign aid would be $626 billion, or 2.5 percent of the rich countries' incomes. It is a huge amount, a thirteenfold increase over today's foreign aid, but one could imagine such a transfer actually happening. To supplement the poor countries' investment resources by half this amount, or 5 percent of their GDPs, would require a transfer of $313 billion, or 1.3 percent of the industrial countries' income, as shown in row (g), certainly an amount within the limits of possibility.

Economists have studied countries' "absorptive capacity" for foreign aid, their ability to make productive use of outside funds. Absorptive capacity may be limited by the skills of the labor force, by the quality of the infrastructure, or by the ability of the country's producers to break into new markets. Absorptive capacity appears to be quite limited in some cases, so some countries, perhaps most, might not make good use of a sudden vast increase in foreign aid. If the increase were gradual, however, and if it were accompanied by policies designed to relax the constraints on absorption, a substantial increase in aid could probably be put to good use, raising investment in poor countries.

In 1970, the United Nations set a goal for the industrialized countries of transferring 0.7 percent of their national income to the developing world. The industrialized countries agreed to the goal, although (with the exception of a few countries) they never met it. It would amount to $158 billion, or 2.5 percent of the poor countries' GDP, as shown in row (h).

Rows (f) through (h) are demanding but possible. The industrialized countries could make a major contribution to the development programs of the poor countries by increasing the level of foreign aid substantially. Even a commitment to meet the UN goal of 0.7 percent would be a huge improvement over the current level of aid, and increases beyond that are well justified. Foreign aid in these amounts would help to achieve distributional justice on a global scale not by redistributing output but by helping the poor countries to grow rapidly. Of course they may grow without aid from the rich countries. Economic development is a consequence of many factors, not just aid. Aid could help, though, and it would be an expression of the commitment of the rich to help transform the economies of the poor. To date, it has hardly been tried.

The Obligations of Individuals

What are the obligations of individuals living in rich countries, if their governments do not adequately represent them by giving the amount of foreign aid they believe to be required? Table 10.1 shows that aid from the governments of the rich countries currently is far below even the level that the governments once voluntarily agreed to, let alone a level that would make a major contribution to the investment resources of poor countries. The first obligation of people living in the rich countries is to lobby their governments to increase foreign aid. What are we to do as individuals, if this lobbying is not totally successful?

We have three choices. The first is to do nothing. The need is so great, we could say, that only governments drawing on the resources of entire nations can collect enough money to make a real difference. Faced with the imperative of raising total aid from $48 billion a year to, say, $626 billion, anything that you or I or almost any individual could do would be a drop in the bucket, without appreciable impact. This is not, however, a satisfactory answer. Of course no individual can prevent world poverty, but this is irrelevant. An individual in a rich country can help one or perhaps many individuals in a poor country, and each life helped is a net gain in the balance. Moreover, we have by now a lot of experience of nongovernmental organizations (NGOs), funded by private contributions, mostly from individuals in the rich countries. The NGOs, both individually and collectively, have made a big difference to societies where they have operated.

The second choice, recommended by philosopher Robert N. Van Wyk, has much more to recommend it; it is that each of us should give our "fair share."[20] For example, if one is persuaded that foreign aid should amount to 10 percent of the output of developing countries, or, as the table shows, 2.5 percent of income in the rich countries, individuals should calculate what percentage is currently being paid by their governments out of tax receipts, and make up the difference. Thus a resident of the United States, a country that contributes about 0.1 percent of its GDP to foreign aid, should contribute an additional 2.4 percent of his personal income.

The third answer, also plausible, is that each of us should give until it hurts seriously. Peter Singer argues that when people are dying of conditions related to poverty, each of us should prevent what poverty we can "without sacrificing anything of comparable moral significance."[21] Not a great deal is of comparable moral significance with life itself, so this standard calls for us to reduce our personal expenditures to the bare minimum needed for survival and give the rest away in aid. He suggests that minimum needs in the United States can be met for about $30,000, so a person with an income of $50,000 should donate 40 percent of her income, while a person with $100,000 should donate 70 percent.[22]

The serious dilemma lies in the tension between the second and third answers. The "fair share" represents the minimum baseline. Since our country should be giving 2.5 percent of its income in foreign aid, if it is not doing so, we are obliged to make up our share of the difference. It is not a big share of our personal income, less than 2.5 percent. Once we have given this amount, though, we are faced with the uncontradicted fact that the need is just as great. Millions of people are still malnourished, they are still dying prematurely, they are still barred from the sort of life options we regard as essential. The third answer is compelling, that we reduce our personal expenditures to a minimum. To do so, however, would be to put ourselves in the position of moral saints, a position I argued earlier is commendable as a voluntary action, but not morally obligatory.

This sort of reasoning leads me to think that our obligations come down somewhere close to the "fair share" or a little above. We must give at least our fair share. In recognition of the fact that even after we have done so the need will be enormous, we should give more than our fair share. Most people — not all — living in rich countries can do this without giving up anything they really value. Instead of giving 2.4 percent of one's income, perhaps 4 percent is a better goal, or even more. Singer himself apparently gives 20 percent. Probably the percentage should rise with people's incomes, as the progressive income tax does, since people with higher incomes have a higher proportion of discretionary income.

Foreign Aid and Capitalism

By giving 0.2 percent of their national incomes to foreign aid — less than 0.1 percent in the case of the United States — the world's rich countries do not come close to the limits on aid imposed by the capitalist system. Those constraints are, indeed, real. If the rich countries gave 50 to 80 percent of their incomes in foreign aid, the circular flow of spending that sustains any economy, including the capitalist variant, would be disrupted. If tax rates were so high that people could keep only the amount needed for subsistence, they would likely produce only their subsistence, and the dividend available for aid would disappear. There is nothing to worry about, though; those limits are far away.

Not only could the advanced capitalist countries increase foreign aid greatly — they would be stronger if they did so. As I argued earlier, what capitalism needs most is expanding markets, not a destitute global labor force. Almost anything that can be done to stimulate economic growth and development in the poor countries, including a substantial increase in foreign aid, will rebound to the advantage of capitalism.

Notes

1. The data in this paragraph are from United Nations Development Programme, *Human Development Report 1999* (New York: Oxford University Press, 1999), and World Bank, *World Development Report 1999/2000* (New York: Oxford University Press, 1999).

2. UNICEF (United Nations Children's Fund), *State of the World's Children, 2000* (New York: United Nations, 1999).

3. For a comprehensive survey of this topic, see Brian R. Opeskin, "The Moral Foundations of Foreign Aid," *World Development* 24 (1996): 21–44.

4. Robert Nozick, *Anarchy, State, and Utopia* (New York: Basic Books, 1974).

5. For an introduction to these ideologies, see John Isbister, *Promises Not*

Kept: The Betrayal of Social Change in the Third World, 4th ed. (West Hartford, Conn.: Kumarian Press, 1998), chapter 3.

6. Eric Eustace Williams, *Capitalism and Slavery* (Chapel Hill: University of North Carolina Press, 1944).

7. Adam Hochschild, *King Leopold's Ghost: A Story of Greed, Terror, and Heroism in Colonial Africa* (Boston: Houghton Mifflin, 1998).

8. Sven Lundqvist, *Exterminate All the Brutes,* trans. Joan Tate (New York: New Press, 1996).

9. For a survey of self-interested and political reasons for giving aid, see Sarah J. Tisch and Michael B. Wallace, *Dilemmas of Development Assistance: The What, Why, and Who of Foreign Aid* (Boulder, Colo.: Westview Press, 1994), chapter 3.

10. Pope Paul VI, *Populorum Progressio* (Vatican City: Polyglot Press, 1967).

11. Laurie Garrett, *The Coming Plague: Newly Emerging Diseases in a World Out of Balance* (New York: Farrar, Straus and Giroux, 1994).

12. For a blistering attack on aid by a former aid worker, see Graham Hancock, *Lords of Poverty: The Power, Prestige, and Corruption of the International Aid Business* (New York: Atlantic Monthly Press, 1989).

13. Quoted in Jeff Faux, "Debt: Just Forget It," *The Nation,* November 22, 1999, 6–7.

14. On the conflict between aid and sovereignty, see Bartram S. Brown, *The United States and the Politicization of the World Bank: Issues of International Law and Policy* (London: Kegan Paul International, 1992); Joan M. Nelson, "Promoting Policy Reforms: The Twilight of Conditionality?" *World Development* 24 (1996): 1551–59; and Christopher Kilby, "Aid and Sovereignty," *Social Theory and Practice* 25 (1999): 79–92.

15. Brian Barry, *Democracy, Power, and Justice: Essays in Political Theory* (Oxford: Clarendon Press: 1989), chapter 16.

16. Those who have studied introductory macroeconomics will know that, by the conventions of national-income accounting systems, output is identically equal to income. This is so because the value of all output, measured at market prices, goes into people's pockets. Columns 3 and 4 could equally be labeled "GDP" or "Income," therefore. The argument advanced in this section is a little clearer, however, if we think of aid in relationship to the output of the recipient countries and in relationship to the income of the donor countries.

17. United Nations Development Programme, *Human Development Report 1999,* Tables 14, 15.

18. Theodore A. Sumberg recommended a transfer from rich to poor that would fall somewhere between rows (c) and (d). The amount should consist, he said, of the entire increment in GDP in the rich countries over a decade; by his calculations this would amount to 156 percent of the GDPs in the poor countries. He failed to show, however, how the rich countries' economies would be able to produce so much if they gave it away, nor did he consider the constraining rule of capitalism, that it must grow or die. See his *Foreign Aid as Moral Obligation?* Washington Papers 1 (Beverly Hills, Calif.: Sage Publications, 1973).

19. Robert W. Corcoran, "Help Indigenous Poor," *New York Times,* November 23, 1999, A30.

20. Robert N. Van Wyk, "World Hunger and the Extent of Our Positive Duties," in *Social and Personal Ethics,* 3d ed., ed. William H. Shaw (Belmont, Calif.: Wadsworth Publishing Co., 1999), 472–80.

21. Peter Singer, *Practical Ethics,* 2d ed. (Cambridge: Cambridge University Press, 1993), 229.

22. Peter Singer, "The Singer Solution to World Poverty," *New York Times Magazine,* September 5, 1999, 60–63.

Chapter 11

IMMIGRATION

T HE MOVEMENT of people is one of the most important global connections. Immigration responds to the uneven expansion of global capitalism, and it creates problems of justice that are not completely soluble. Here I focus on immigration to the United States, but the dilemmas that beset Americans in the formulation of their immigration policy confront other countries as well.

Immigration has fluctuated widely in numbers and in countries of origin throughout American history.[1] In the last years of the twentieth century and the beginning of the twenty-first, the population grew by about 1 million immigrants each year — three-quarters of them legally admitted, one-quarter in undocumented status. The totals match the numbers in the last great wave of immigration at the end of the nineteenth century. The overall American population now is greater, however, so the ratio of immigrants to population is currently lower than at its peak. Today's immigrants come principally from the countries of the third world, from Asia and Latin America, while those of a century ago came from Europe. The previous wave was largely uncontrolled — any white person who could find passage was entitled to enter — while today's immigration is regulated, although with uneven success.

Capitalism, Immigration, and Justice

International migration would have occurred, no doubt, in a global system of almost any type. Still, the migration the world has experienced in the last several centuries has been instigated and shaped by capitalism, which produced both the demand for and the supply of migrants. The growth of international capitalist markets created the demand for immigrants in many parts of the world. Industrialization in Europe led to a growing demand for food and raw materials from abroad. Hence European emigrants were able to find opportunities in North and South

200

America, Australia, and parts of Africa. At the same time, slaves were transported from Africa to the Americas, and indentured workers from China to many parts of the world, to build the new global labor force.

On the supply side, migrants have come largely from areas of the world that have suffered major social dislocations. One theory of migration posits that migrants come primarily from the poorest areas of the world to the richest, but this is not typically verified by the historical evidence.[2] The first transatlantic immigrants came largely from Britain, France, Spain, and Portugal, which were the leaders in European capitalist development, not the laggards. Not until the end of the nineteenth century did many migrants move to the United States from southern and eastern Europe, and not until the end of the twentieth century did many come from Latin America and Asia. In some cases, the flows were from poor countries to a rich country, to be sure, but the source areas had typically been poor for centuries prior to the migration. What caused the emigration was not just poverty but the dislocation and sometimes destruction of traditional societies. When eastern Europe was isolated and largely self-sufficient at a subsistence standard of living, people did not move, but when transportation improvements, commercial agriculture, and export-oriented industries appeared at the end of the nineteenth century, the old ways of life to which people had been accustomed collapsed, and they had to look for new homes. Sometimes the new homes were in the nearby towns or cities, and sometimes they were in the United States. Capitalism always produces uneven change, and the change often creates havoc. Capitalism is not the only socially destructive force — the emigration from Vietnam in the last decades of the twentieth century was the result of military, not capitalist, destruction — but it is the most important one.

Countries like the United States that receive immigrants are faced with serious policy problems. Almost always, policymakers consider the problems from the perspective of the national interest or perhaps particular interests associated with employers or ethnic groups. Here we consider immigration instead from the perspective of justice, the criteria of which are not the national interest but equality, freedom, and efficiency. Among the many questions of justice, three stand out. How many immigrants should be allowed into the country? What categories of potential immigrants should have priority? How should immigrants be treated?

How we view justice in immigration depends heavily upon how we view the moral significance of national borders. If we believe not only that each person in the world is of equal worth but in addition that each person deserves equal treatment from the US government, we will have a hard time justifying any restrictions on immigration. If, on the other hand, we believe that the US government is entitled to give some degree of preferential treatment to US citizens, we will find ourselves facing a series of conflicts.

How Many to Admit?

If everyone is to be given equal treatment by the US government, the case for open borders is strong, because immigration laws restrict access to wealth and privilege.[3] The United States is one of the richest countries in the world with one of the most dynamic economies. Some people — native-born Americans — have access to those riches through the accident of birth. One of the ways Americans maintain an island of privilege in a sea of economic misery is by restricting the flow of people who want to come to the country. If the doors were thrown open, millions of additional people could benefit from taking part in the American economy. If equal treatment is required, immigration laws violate the norm of equality, because they treat morally equal people unequally. They violate the norm of freedom, because they restrict freedom of movement. In all likelihood they also violate the norm of efficiency, because they prevent people from working where their productivity is highest.

I think, however, that justice does not require the US government to treat everyone in the world equally. As I argued in chapter 9, the government may justly give prior attention to the needs of its own citizens. If this is so, the US government — along with other national governments — has the moral authority to impose some restrictions upon immigration if those restrictions make a contribution to alleviating injustices among Americans.[4] The principal problem of justice that would likely be exacerbated by unlimited immigration is the gap between the rich and the poor. Analysts are not agreed about this, since careful econometric research has so far found no impact of the current level of immigration upon the wages or unemployment of low-income Americans.[5] It is quite likely, however, that a doubling, tripling, or even greater increase in immigration, such as would probably occur if all restrictions were lifted, would lead to a reduction in wages and an increase in profits in the United States, and therefore a substantial movement of the income distribution in the direction of injustice.

This is, I think, the only reason why the US government is justified in controlling the overall flow of immigration. Immigration restrictions are not justified because the newcomers bring unfamiliar languages and cultures with them; the genius of US society almost from its beginning has been the ability to absorb many of the world's cultures and mold them into a functional mosaic. Restrictions are not justified merely on the grounds that immigration might lower Americans' average standard of living. It would probably not have this effect, since the increase in profits would balance the reduction in wages, and in any case Americans already have one of the world's highest average standards of living. Neither are restrictions justified on the grounds that immigrants exploit American taxpayers by absorbing more in government services than they contribute in taxes; the weight of the evidence is that they do not.[6] The problem of justice that would result from unlimited immigration is that in all likelihood rich Americans would become richer and poor American poorer, and this is the opposite of what they both deserve. Looking at the question from the perspective of justice, therefore, the US government may control the number of immigrants entering the country.

It may not, however, eliminate immigration. In a world characterized by a wide gap between rich and poor, Americans are required to provide justice in some degree to foreigners. They may not simply ignore their needs. One may ask, of course, whether Americans must meet foreigners' needs by allowing them to immigrate. Is foreign aid not sufficient? Foreign aid, even if substantially greater than it currently is, does not relieve rich countries from the obligation of permitting some immigration from poor countries. If successful, foreign aid and other types of development assistance typically facilitate small improvements in the lives of a large number of people, while immigration permits a small number of people to transform their lives. The two types of policies do not substitute one for another; they are complements.

What guidance do these conflicting criteria give us to the number of immigrants who should be admitted? No precise answer exists, but the current number is in the acceptable range. For several decades, the United States has been able to absorb about 1 million immigrants a year. In the 1990s it did so while sustaining the longest economic expansion on record, an expansion that drove the unemployment rate down to relatively low levels. If past history is any guide, we can be reasonably sure that when the economic downturn occurs, as it inevitably will, immigrants will be made the scapegoat and the calls for reducing immigration will intensify. We have no convincing evidence, however, that the existing level of immigration negatively affects the distribution of incomes among Americans. So no reason exists to cut the numbers drastically. An increase in immigration might be tolerated, but a major expansion would be dangerous. Low-income Americans might begin to suffer from the competition of huge numbers of newcomers. Obviously the numbers can change somewhat without raising serious issues of justice, but big changes are not called for.

Considerations of social justice permit countries to restrict the number of immigrants, but when they do so they necessarily create a series of new injustices. Foremost among them are discrimination between applicants for immigration and unequal treatment of immigrants. Some injustices in these areas are inevitable, as long as immigration is restricted, but much can be done to alleviate them

Who Is to Be Admitted?

A country that restricts immigration must choose among the applicants, and it should do so as fairly as possible. Fairness might call for using the principle of first-come-first-served or perhaps a lottery. Both these mechanisms are employed by the US Immigration and Naturalization Service (INS), but only in limited ways. Within each of the standard immigrant categories, people are often admitted in the order in which they apply. A lottery is used to select among applicants who do not fit into one of the standard categories. For the most part, however, the government eschews these rather neutral procedures and instead assigns immigrants to categories that are given different priorities.[7] The three principal categories of immigrants are those admitted for the purpose of reunifying families, those admitted to meet labor market needs, and refugees. The family reunification category is easily the largest, comprising two-thirds of legally admitted immigrants in most years. Employment-based immigration accounts for about 10 percent of the legal inflow each year, and refugees about 15 percent, with the remainder going to a variety of other small categories.

Do these priorities correspond to the requirements of justice? I think not. The first priority, with the largest number of allocated slots, should be refugees. They are people without a country, in extreme need. According to the 1980 US Refugee Act, as well as to the UN protocol on the subject, a refugee is a "person who is unable or unwilling to return to his country of nationality or habitual residence because of persecution or a well-founded fear of persecution on account of race, religion, nationality, membership in a particular social group or political opinion." Refugees are the victims of civil and international warfare and persecution, almost always innocent victims. Michael Walzer describes the precarious situation of people who are members of no state:

> [They] are vulnerable and unprotected in the marketplace. Although they participate freely in the exchange of goods, they have no part in those goods that are shared. They are cut off from the communal provision of security and welfare. Even those aspects of security and welfare that are, like public health, collectively distributed are not guaranteed to non-members: for they have no guaranteed place in the collectivity and are always liable to expulsion. Statelessness is a condition of infinite danger.[8]

"Statelessness is a condition of infinite danger," and think how refugees become stateless. They are persecuted and sometimes tortured, their homes are destroyed, and their relatives are killed. They are told that they are useless, or if not useless, a threat to the state and to the state's legitimate citizens. Sometimes they are attacked for their political views, sometimes simply for their ethnicity or other characteristic over which they have no control. For one who has not been a refugee, it is hard to imagine the terror. They are the victims of warfare and oppression in the former Yugoslavia, in Somalia, in Rwanda, in Vietnam, in East Timor, in Afghanistan, in Chechnya, and in many other parts of the world. In some of the former Nazi concentration camps a simple marker has been erected saying the same thing in different languages — "*nie wieder,*" "never again," "*plus jamais*" — yet the dislocations and exterminations go on.

No one knows with certainty how many refugees there are. The estimates made by the UN high commissioner for refugees are over 20 million in most years. Those numbers are certainly undercounts, however, because the definition of a refugee with which the high commissioner must work is a restrictive one. It does not include "internal refugees," people who have been driven from their homes but are still within the boundaries of their own country. It also does not include "economic refugees," people who have had to flee not because of persecution or warfare but because of economic catastrophe. Whatever these other groups are called, some of them are just as needy and just as desperate as the people who fall within the official definition of refugees. Taken together, the number of refugees, broadly defined, is certainly greater than the total number of immigrants who are going to be admitted by the United States or even by all the rich, developed countries taken together. Still, they are among the neediest people in the world, and they are surely the neediest of the applicants for immigration. The norm of equality cries out for the world to come to their aid.

If the United States were required to give equal treatment to everyone in the world, and yet still restricted the number of immigrants, it would likely have to allocate every available slot to refugees, so great is their need. It does not, however, have to go this far, since it can give at least some preferential treatment to Americans without being guilty of an injustice. We need to consider, therefore, the other two categories, both of which relate more strongly to the interests of Americans — family and employment-based immigration.

Family reunification is a worthy goal. It is painful to be separated from one's family, and the pain can be overwhelming if the separation is thought to be permanent. The American immigration system responds to the needs of families; sometimes the entire purpose of immigration is described as being the unification of families. In chapter 9, I defended the extraordinary attention, moral and otherwise, that most of us devote to our families. In a conflict between obligations to our families and wider social obligations, we usually do, and should, choose our families. The state should not, however, favor a few of our families to the exclusion of meeting other justifiable social goals, as it does when it reserves two-thirds of the immigration slots for family reunification. The problem with family reunification is not that it is an unworthy goal but that it squeezes out other worthy goals. Each immigrant who arrives leaves behind many relatives in the home country, and when some of them arrive, they too leave different family members behind. We are enmeshed in intricate family networks that can overwhelm the immigration system in a kind of chain reaction.

While family reunification is a just goal of immigration policy, it should predominate only if one takes a perspective on justice that excludes obligations to foreigners. Taken as a group, refugees are far more needy of the help that American residence could provide than are the typical relatives of US residents. The latter are separated from some of their loved ones, and that is a serious matter, but their lives are not in danger if they stay home. Even if we are not required to provide absolutely equal treatment to everyone in the world, it would be more just to restrict the number of family slots to very close relatives: spouses and minor children. With no increase in the overall level of immigration, this one change would reduce family immigration by about one-third and release almost 200,000 slots a year to refugees.[9]

What about the employment slots, usually between 10 and 15 percent of the overall number? Of course the great majority of adult immigrants, whatever their category, come to the United States expecting to work. What distinguishes the people in the special employment categories is not that they expect to work but that they are sponsored by an employer. They enter because they will fit a particular employer's need. Sometimes they are people with technical skills, perhaps electronic engineers brought in to fill a vacancy in a quickly expanding sector of the economy. Sometimes they are people with low skills, brought in to do jobs it is alleged Americans will not do.

Even if we grant that US immigration policy can give a degree of preference to American residents over foreigners, it is hard to justify employment-based immigration. For the most part, not always, this category of immigration speaks to narrow, special interests, not to the national interest, and it has the potential to harm Americans. To begin, immigrants sponsored by an employer are typically the least needy of the applicants. From the point of view of a country's obligations to disadvantaged foreigners, they should rank last.

Even from a national perspective, a compelling case for their services seldom really exists. This is not, of course, how employers see it. They face expanding markets, on the one hand, and a labor shortage, on the other; if they cannot fill their labor needs, they will not be able to meet the market demand. In order to sponsor immigrant workers, they have to certify to the INS that they cannot find a qualified resident for the job. From a broader perspective, though, a labor shortage is almost always a positive phenomenon. Faced with a shortage of labor, employers have alternatives to using immigrants, alternatives that will benefit Americans. They can raise wages, in order to attract people to the jobs; they can provide on-the-job training so that people not presently qualified for the job can acquire the needed competency; and they can develop productivity-enhancing technology. Without the incentive of labor shortages, they are unlikely to take these measures.

What about the argument that immigrants are needed to fill jobs that Americans will not fill? One hears the statement all the time, but it is seldom valid. If immigrants were not available to fill those jobs, employers would have to improve the working conditions, develop new technology, and raise wages so that Americans were willing to fill them. The jobs of farm laborer and hotel maid could be made attractive to Americans, no doubt at the cost of higher prices for food and hotel rooms. Indeed the reverse of the standard argument is likely more correct: it is because low-wage immigrants are available to do some jobs that the job conditions have deteriorated to such an extent that Americans do not want to perform them.

Sometimes the need for immigrant workers is defended on the grounds that particular foreigners will bring something so valuable to the workplace that they will enhance production, improve its quality, and even generate jobs, in ways that American workers could not. This may sometimes be the case, and when it is a few employer-sponsored slots are justified. It is not typically the case, however, at least with technically skilled immigrants. They normally are paid salaries lower than Americans of comparable training receive, and this would not likely be the case for a person who was the critical link in her production chain. It is hard to avoid the conclusion that the principal reason employers seek an immigrant labor force is to reduce wages and avoid the expenses involved in upgrading and training their current labor force. The employment-based preferences could be reduced by 80 to 90 percent, releasing perhaps 75,000 additional slots for refugees each year.

The greatest good that can be achieved by an immigration policy is to alleviate the catastrophe faced by refugees. Their needs are so overwhelming that they should be given the majority of slots. An argument against refugees is that they often prove more difficult than other immigrants to integrate smoothly into American life. They usually do not have family members in the country who can help them make the transition to a new culture, certainly when the refugee flow from a certain area first begins. They are more likely than other immigrants, therefore, to require public assistance. For a country to accept refugees is to take on a burden for a period of years. This is a burden, however, that people in a rich country can bear. In recognition of a country's greater duties to its own residents, it should reserve some positions for close family members and perhaps even a few for immigrants sponsored by employers.

Civil Rights for Undocumented Immigrants

The treatment of immigrants, once they have arrived, poses many issues of justice. Here I focus on just one, but the most important one, the civil rights of undocumented immigrants.

If immigration is restricted, some who cannot make an adequate living at home will come uninvited. From across the border with Mexico immigrants swim rivers, trek through the desert, climb fences, and even crawl through sewer pipes. From Asia they enter clandestinely in unmarked vessels. They are often escorted by smugglers, or coyotes. The INS and the border-police forces have devoted manpower and technology to stemming the flow of undocumented entrants, and they doubtless have had some effect. They cannot stop the flow, however, any more than the controls on illegal drugs can stop drug smuggling. There is a big payoff to entering the United States illegally, so people are willing to take big risks. If they are arrested at the border and turned back, they frequently try again.

From time to time, the federal government increases the resources devoted to stopping illegal entries, but it never succeeds in reducing the number of undocumented residents in the country (except when it grants retroactive amnesty). The border area between the United States and Mexico has become an integrated area of migrant labor. People move back and forth across the border, sometimes several times a year, sometimes monthly, weekly, or even daily. People have homes, families, and jobs on both sides of the border. For obvious reasons, we do not know exactly how many people enter the country illegally, but demographers have estimated a number in the vicinity of 2 million a year. They have also estimated that the population of undocumented immigrants in the country rises by about 275,000 a year.[10] About 41 percent of these did not enter the country illegally but came in on some sort of temporary status — as a student perhaps, or a tourist — and overstayed the limit of their visa. In other words, probably only 150,000 to 200,000 of the new undocumented immigrants each year entered illegally. How can it be that 2 million border crossings lead to an increase in the population of less than 200,000? It must be that the majority of the illegal entries — perhaps 90 percent — are matched by exits. This is indeed what ethnographic surveys tell us.[11] The illegal labor market is in constant flux, with people moving back and forth across the border frequently.

In the face of such a fluid labor market, what is the consequence of increasing the severity of border controls? Demographer Sherri A. Kossoudji has given us a startling insight. Her studies show that when the INS apprehends more people trying to enter the country illegally, it inadvertently but necessarily reduces the number of exits as well. "INS policy may be backfiring," she writes. "Migrants stay in the United States longer on non-apprehended trips and stay in Mexico for shorter spells between trips to compensate for the cost of a past apprehension."[12] People who have been arrested and sent back across the border are likely to try another crossing soon, and, if successful, they are likely to extend their stay in the United States longer in order to compensate for the earnings lost as a result of their arrest. Furthermore, when it becomes more difficult to enter the country, those who successfully make it across the border are less inclined to go back and have to face the ordeal again when next they attempt to return. No doubt the very existence of border controls reduces the number of immigrants below the number that would exist were the border uncontrolled; beyond this, however, changes in the intensity of surveillance have unknown and perhaps perverse effects. It is possible that the periodic intensifications of effort by the border patrol actually increase the number of people who are illegally in the country.

As long as people want to make a better living than they can in a poor country, and as long as American employers are willing to hire them, they will come. In the war on drugs we have learned that if Americans are willing to pay for illegal drugs, the drugs will come, whatever the risk to the smugglers. So too with labor. The way to win the war on drugs is to eliminate the demand. The way to stop illegal immigration is to stop employers from hiring the immigrants. The government has put a lot of money into border controls, but little into employer sanctions. And for good reason. The employers vote and contribute to the political parties, and they want the labor.

In 1994, the voters of California revealed that they had a different theory of illegal immigration. They presumed that the immigrants were coming to the United States in order to take advantage of the welfare state. Thinking it would reduce illegal immigration, they passed Proposition 187, barring undocumented immigrants from access to all welfare, health, and educational services, with the exception of emergency medical care. Undocumented children were to be barred from the public schools. Fortunately the courts found the proposition to be unconstitutional in most of its provisions. Not only was it inhumane, it would have had little if any impact on illegal immigration since, we know from surveys, immigrants are far more attracted by the prospect of a job than they are by social services.

Undocumented workers present a challenge to justice. They are in the country of their own volition to be sure, but they are in the country also because a significant segment of American society wants them. Employers want to hire them, and consumers want the cheap products that can be obtained through their low-wage labor. One often hears the statement that Americans all agree that illegal immigration should be stopped. This is incorrect. Americans do not agree; many want illegal immigration.

A country that restricts immigration automatically generates two unequal classes of workers, the documented and the undocumented, the former with more rights than the latter. It is for this reason that immigration is an issue of civil rights.[13] The civil rights movement in the United States began in response to the unequal legal status of African Americans; in time it succeeded in expunging those legal inequities. A civil rights movement by and on behalf of undocumented immigrants cannot even hope for such a victory, since by definition they do not have the right to be in the country. The best that can be hoped for is to ensure that undocumented immigrants benefit from the same labor standards and the same public services as do legal residents. They should be covered by the minimum-wage legislation, and they should be subject to the occupational-safety and health regulations. They should be eligible for public health and housing services, for welfare programs, and for unemployment insurance. Their children should go to the public schools.

It is sometimes maintained that they do not have the right to such treatment and such services, precisely because they have entered the country illegally. One reason people hold this view is their belief that undocumented immigrants exploit the American taxpayers, using services for which they have not paid. This belief was one of the motivations behind Proposition 187, but it is incorrect.[14] Undocumented immigrants use public services, but they also pay taxes. Research on the balance between sources and uses of government tax monies is difficult to conduct, but it appears in the case of undocumented immigrants that the two are roughly equal. The undocumented do not exploit American taxpayers, and they should not be denied services for this reason.

Moreover, to deny them the benefit of public programs and of fair labor standards is to exploit not only them but American workers as well. If employers can hire the undocumented for less than the minimum wage, and deny them minimal health and safety provisions, they have a decided incentive to hire them instead of Americans. If the undocumented are ineligible for welfare programs, they are more likely to turn to a life of crime when their incomes fall. If they are denied access to public health programs, they will create a threat of infectious diseases for the entire population. Undocumented children denied an education will grow up without the skills needed to contribute to the American economy and will impose a continuing burden on the country if they decide to stay. As long as the undocumented immigrants are present, therefore, and they will be present as long as immigration restrictions are maintained, justice for them and justice for Americans require that they benefit from the same laws and programs that benefit Americans.

What is needed, not just in the United States but in the entire developed world and perhaps in all countries, is an explicit legal mechanism for the protection of migrant workers. Migrant labor is a phenomenon almost everywhere, sometimes permitted by the laws of the receiving countries and sometimes not. In 1990, the General Assembly of the United Nations adopted the "International Convention on the Protection of the Rights of All Migrant Workers and Members of Their Families."[15] It will come into force when twenty countries sign it, but to date only nine have, all of them poor countries that send migrants elsewhere. Neither the United States nor any other economically developed country has signed it.

If the convention were adopted widely, the civil and human rights of migrants would be protected. Among its ninety-three articles, the convention calls for equal treatment of all workers, whether migrant or not, whether documented or not. According to Article 25:

> Migrant workers shall enjoy treatment not less favorable than that which applies to nationals of the State of employment in respect of remuneration and
>
> (a) Other conditions of work, that is to say, overtime, hours of work, weekly rest, holidays with pay, safety, health, termination of the employment relationship and any other conditions of work....
>
> (b) Other terms of employment, that is to say, minimum age of employment, restriction on home work and any other matters which, according to national law and practice, are considered a term of employment.

Other articles in the convention cover legal protections in the criminal justice system, freedom of religion and expression, collective bargaining, social security, and the access of children to education and health services. The basic stance of the convention is that all workers and members of their families deserve equal treatment. The convention should be adopted widely. Countries that send workers to other countries have an interest in the protection of their citizens, while countries that receive the workers have an interest that their own workers not be undercut by the migrants, and common decency calls for them to have an interest that the rights of the guest workers be sustained as well.

The one freedom that undocumented workers cannot have, though, is freedom from the fear of deportation. To free them from this fear would be, in essence, to abolish the border controls. What the border controls mean is that some people are forbidden to enter and that when they do enter they may be expelled. The central practical question, therefore, is how their rights to fair treatment inside the country can be upheld at the same time that they are subject to deportation. The principal reason that their rights are violated even when those rights exist in law is that they are rightly afraid to assert the rights. If they complain to the authorities that they are being paid less than the minimum wage, for example, or that their working conditions are unsafe, they risk identifying themselves and being deported.

It follows that justice can be approached only if there is a strict separation, a fire wall, between the border enforcement authorities and the authorities responsible for fair labor standards and for public services. Immigrants should be secure in the knowledge that if they register a complaint about unfair treatment, if they enroll their child in a public school, or if they visit a health clinic, they will not thereby be identified as undocumented and deported. Without the fire wall, undocumented immigrants will be afraid to report violations, violators will know this, and the violations will continue. One of the reasons that Proposition 187 was so misguided was that it required health providers and teachers, on pain of criminal penalty, to report undocumented people to the authorities.

Conclusion

When the topic is immigration, we are confronted with any number of conflicts of justice. The fundamental conflict is how much weight to give to the needs of foreigners as opposed to citizens. It is a conflict that can be resolved only by compromise, and it leads inevitably to a restriction in the number of immigrants allowed into the country. This in turn leads to two more conflicts: How shall the available slots be allocated among the contending applicants, and how shall those who enter illegally be treated? Neither conflict can be solved completely, but justice would be advanced if American immigration policy gave a higher priority to refugees and if firm steps were taken to protect the civil rights of undocumented immigrants.

As we have found in many instances before, the structure of capitalism will not permit a completely satisfactory solution to any of these conflicts. The culprit is the uneven expansion of the global capitalist system: always changing, always upsetting the relationship of one area of the world to another, creative in some areas, destructive in others, never completely predictable. It automatically generates instability and dislocation, which in turn send millions of people across national borders, some in desperate circumstances.

One could imagine a world in which immigration created no particular problems of injustice. It would be a stable world, with no major social inequities and no wholesale social dislocations. In such a world, people might want to move across national boundaries for a variety of reasons, but the flows in and out of countries would be roughly equal, and they would create no disruptions. Such a world would require suspension of the law of uneven capitalist expansion, so it is not one we are likely to experience. The best we can do is patch together ad hoc solutions.

Notes

1. For a more extensive discussion of the history, causes, and current problems associated with immigration, see John Isbister, *The Immigration Debate: Remaking America* (West Hartford, Conn.: Kumarian Press, 1996).

2. The most influential statement of the income-gap theory of migration is John R. Harris and Michael P. Todaro, "Migration, Unemployment, and Development: A Two-Sector Analysis," *American Economic Review* 60 (1970): 126–42. Saskia Sassen has developed the social-dislocation theory in a number of publications, among them *The Mobility of Labor and Capital: A Study in International Investment and Labor Flow* (Cambridge: Cambridge University Press, 1988).

3. This case is outlined in more detail in Isbister, *Immigration Debate*, chapter 9. See also Joseph H. Carens, "Aliens and Citizens: The Case for Open Borders," *Review of Politics* 49 (1987): 251–73. Carens's extensive contributions to the argument for open borders are sympathetically but critically reviewed in Peter C. Meilaender, "Liberalism and Open Borders: The Argument of Joseph Carens," *International Migration Review* 33 (1999): 1062–81.

4. For a debate on this question, see John Isbister, "A Liberal Argument for Border Controls: Reply to Carens," and Joseph H. Carens, "Open Borders and Liberal Limits: A Response to Isbister," both in *International Migration Review* 34 (2000): 629–35 and 636–43, respectively.

5. The research is summarized in Isbister, *Immigration Debate*, chapter 4.

6. Isbister, *Immigration Debate*, chapter 6.

7. Michael Fix and Jeffrey S. Passel, *Immigration and Immigrants: Setting the Record Straight* (Washington, D.C.: Urban Institute Press, 1994); Isbister, *Immigration Debate*, chapter 3; US Immigration and Naturalization Service (INS), *Statistical Yearbook of the Immigration and Naturalization Service, 1997* (Washington, D.C.: US Government Printing Office, 1999), 21.

8. Michael Walzer, *Spheres of Justice: A Defense of Pluralism and Equality* (New York: Basic Books, 1983), 31–32.

9. INS, *Statistical Yearbook*, 21.

10. See Robert Warren, *Estimates of the Unauthorized Immigrant Population Residing in the United States, Country of Origin and State of Residence* (Washington, D.C.: Statistics Division, Immigration and Naturalization Service, 1994); and Immigration and Naturalization Service, *News Release*, http://www.ins.usdoj.gov/graphics/publicaffairs/newsrels/illegal.htm.

11. See, for example, Douglas S. Massey, Luin Goldring, and Jorge Durand, "Continuities in Transnational Migration: An Analysis of Nineteen Mexican Communities," *American Journal of Sociology* 99 (1994): 1492–1533.

12. Sherrie A. Kossoudji, "Playing Cat and Mouse at the U.S.-Mexican Border," *Demography* 29 (1992): 159.

13. Susanne Jonas and Suzie Dod Thomas, eds., *Immigration: A Civil Rights Issue for the Americas* (Wilmington, Del.: Scholarly Resources, 1999).

14. Isbister, *Immigration Debate*, chapter 6.

15. United Nations Center for Human Rights, *The Rights of Migrant Workers*, Human Rights Fact Sheet 24 (New York: United Nations, 1995).

Chapter 12

ENVIRONMENT

ALL ECONOMIC ACTIVITY alters the natural environment. Production makes use of natural resources, some of which are renewable and some not, but even the use of renewable resources like trees and farm animals alters the ecology of which the renewable resources are part. Agriculture has transformed much of the earth's land mass irrevocably. Cities and suburbs have paved over the land. Highways, airports, golf courses, ski resorts, and beach spas completely change the landscape. The expansion of human civilization destroys natural habitats and the species that depend upon those habitats. Industrial wastes pollute the land, the waters, and the atmosphere. The production of all goods creates heat as a byproduct.

The transformation of the natural environment became a major problem in the twentieth century because of the explosion of technology and production. Prior to the twentieth century people had much milder effects on the environment, and few imagined that those effects could be permanent and devastating. Now we know we are capable of transforming the earth to such an extent that we may destroy or permanently diminish the material basis of our civilizations. It is possible that through our economic activities we will raise the temperature of the earth, reduce the biological diversity upon which our ability to feed ourselves depends, destroy the ozone layer that protects us and all nature from harmful rays of the sun, and transform the earth's natural resources into forms that are no longer usable. We have already eliminated many species and wilderness areas. In some cases the poisons we leak into the earth have permanent effects. The damage so far and the potential dangers are real.

It is not capitalism specifically that is to blame; environmental degradation in the twentieth century was even worse in socialist countries than in the capitalist world. It is the inexorable demands of a population growing in both numbers and standard of living that put pressure upon the natural world of which we are a part. Still, it is within a capitalist world that we must confront our natural environment.

The Challenge of Environmental Ethics

As the magnitude of the environmental problems facing us became apparent, theorists began to construct a new environmental ethic, an ethic grounded in assumptions different from this book's approach. The criteria of equality, freedom, and efficiency, as I have outlined them, relate to human beings: all human beings and only human beings. So do most conceptions of ethics and justice, certainly the classical systems associated with such thinkers as Aristotle, Mill, Kant, and Rawls. While they conflict in many ways, they all take it for granted that the subject of ethics is people. The new environmentalism is based on a contrary foundation, that while humans matter, so do nonhumans: animals certainly and, for some, the environment as a whole. Nonhuman entities have inherent value, it is asserted, value that is independent of their impact on humans.[1] Environmental ethics therefore challenges the entire structure of ethics in a way that no other applied field has done.

This section discusses two versions of the new environmental ethics, versions that are sometimes called "extensionism" and "ecocentrism." Environmental philosopher J. Baird Callicott defines them this way: extensionism is "the extension of moral standing and/or moral rights from human beings inclusively to wider and wider classes of *individual* nonhuman natural entities," while ecocentrism is "moral consideration for the ecosystem as a whole and for its various subsystems."[2] I try to show in the next few pages that both approaches help to make us sensitive to environmental issues that we might otherwise have overlooked, but if accepted in their totality they lead to unacceptable moral conclusions, so they should not replace the more traditional, human-centered approach to ethics and justice.

The extensionist doctrine comes in two principal variants: animals have interests, or they have rights. The first is propounded by Peter Singer, who claims that the basis of ethics is the equal consideration of interests.[3] People have interests, he says, and so do animals that are sentient beings, that have the capacity to feel, experience pleasure, and, most importantly, suffer. It is unjust for people to impose suffering on animals, unless that suffering is in support of a demonstrably greater interest. So, for example, Singer concludes that we may not eat animals because our interest in doing so is trivial—we can get all the nutrients we need from plants — while the interest animals have in life is substantial. Most experimentation on animals is unjustified as well, because the suffering endured by the animals is not commensurate with the benefit of the experiments to human beings.

To think that only human beings have interests is to be guilty, Singer claims, of "speciesism."[4] White people were once able to impose untold suffering upon nonwhites because they regarded them as having no inherent interests; whites thought that the only purpose to the existence of nonwhites was to provide service to whites. We are guilty in just the same way, he says, if we fail to understand that animals have interests.

Singer's argument is for equal treatment of interests. He does not claim that all animals have equal interests, so he does not argue for equal treatment of all animals. He writes:

> [T]he commonsense view that birds and mammals feel pain is well founded, but more serious doubts arise as we move down the evolutionary scale. Vertebrate animals have nervous systems broadly similar to our own and behave in ways that resemble our own pain behavior when subjected to stimuli that we would find painful; so the inference that vertebrates are capable of feeling pain is a reasonable one, though not as strong as it is if limited to mammals and birds. When we go beyond vertebrates to insects, crustaceans, mollusks and so on, the existence of subjective states becomes more dubious, and with very simple organisms it is difficult to believe that they could be conscious.... The boundary of beings who may be taken as having interests is therefore not an abrupt boundary, but a broad range in which the assumption that the being has interests shifts from being so strong as to be virtually certain to being so weak as to be highly improbable. The principle of equal consideration of interests must be applied with this in mind.[5]

Singer's principle of equal consideration of interests is inconsistent with one of the principles upon which this book is based, that all people have equal moral standing. He is clear about this. In the passage just reproduced, he advances the view that animals have different interests. A chimpanzee, presumably, has a greater interest in avoiding suffering than a mosquito does. It would be difficult to find a competing interest so great as to justify imposing suffering on a chimpanzee, but it would not be too hard to justify swatting a mosquito. What gives them different interests, Singer says, is their different capacities to have feelings, in particular to suffer. This is likely true, but if equal consideration of interests is to be the foundation of ethics, as Singer asserts, one has to admit that not only animals but human beings also have different capacities to feel, different capacities to suffer, and hence different interests.

If it is the interests that deserve equal treatment and not the people, and if the people have different interests, people may be treated unequally. Consider this troubling passage that follows the previous one by a few paragraphs in Singer's text:

> If for some reason a choice has to be made between saving the life of a normal human being and that of a dog, we might well decide to save the human because he, with his greater awareness of what is going to happen, will suffer more before he dies; we may also take into account the likelihood that it is the family and friends of the human who will suffer more; and finally, it would be the human who had the greater potential for future happiness. This decision would be in accordance with the principle of equal consideration of interests, for the interests of the dog get the same consideration as those of the human, and the loss to the dog is not discounted because the dog is not a member of our species. The outcome is as it is because the balance of interests favors the human. In a different situation — say, if the human were grossly mentally defective and without family or anyone else who would grieve for it — the balance of interests might favor the non-human.[6]

The implication of this passage is not just that under some circumstances a dog might have greater moral standing than a person but that one person (a "normal human being") might have greater standing than another person ("a grossly mentally defective" human being "without family or anyone else who would grieve for it").

I think Singer has worked himself into a trap from which there is no reasonable exit. He wants to extend moral standing to nonhuman animals, but he cannot claim that all animals have equal standing; no one would accept the assertion that a mosquito has equal standing with a person. Therefore he must find some characteristic on which to focus, a characteristic that is shared, although necessarily in unequal degrees, by people and by some animals. The characteristic he has chosen is "interest." When he chooses a characteristic, however, rather than the simple fact of being human, he is confronted inevitably by the truth that human beings possess that characteristic in unequal degrees. The problem cannot be solved by choosing a different characteristic: say, consciousness or moral responsibility or preferences. Every characteristic one can think of is possessed unequally by human beings, so if it is a characteristic that is to be given equal consideration, it follows that human beings are to be given unequal consideration. Singer's method of extending moral standing to animals is incompatible, therefore, with the most basic assumption of this book, that all human beings are equally valuable.

Singer is not the only thinker to assign moral standing to animals, but the others have not solved the fundamental problem any better. Philosopher Tom Regan proceeds not from the equal consideration of interests but from the idea that animals have rights.[7] He regards this as a sounder basis for vegetarianism, for example, since equal consideration of interests might permit animals to be eaten provided they were raised in a respectful manner and killed painlessly. If they have rights, however, they surely have the right not to be killed. The doctrine of animal rights solves some of the problems created by Singer's formulation but creates new ones. Most notably, it does not restore the equal standing of human beings. If animals have rights, they cannot have equal rights; again the chimpanzee must have more rights than the mosquito, else we are drawn into an absurdity. Yet if the chimpanzee has more rights than the mosquito, it must be because of some characteristic that it has to a larger degree, perhaps consciousness of one's life. Once that is conceded, it must also be conceded that some human beings have more consciousness than other human beings, and hence more rights.

The achievement of Singer, Regan, and others in their school is that they have helped us to think of animals not only in terms of their contribution to human welfare but as ends in themselves. Looked at through their eyes, the reason to stop polluting a river is not just to allow us to swim in it and drink the water, and not just to preserve the fish so that we can catch and eat them, but to preserve the habitat of the fish because the fish deserve it. The problem with this doctrine, though, is that while it extends the sphere of justice in one way, it narrows it in another. If we follow this route, we have no basis for asserting that people in comas, people with limited imaginations, people with low intelligent quotients, and perhaps even infants have equal moral standing with other people.

The problem can be resolved, I think, only if we abandon the ambition to have a single theory of ethics that applies equally to animals and people. This ambition leads inexorably to the assignment of unequal moral value to different people, and that is too great a cost. Another way of proceeding — messier and less elegant to be sure — is to *assume* the equal moral standing of all people, as I have done throughout this book, and then to say in addition that animals deserve our respect, not just because of the ways they affect our lives but because they are inherently worthy. This way of proceeding has its own costs. If people and animals are not subject to the same ethical principles, we will find it difficult to compare our relative responsibilities to them when they are in conflict. Still, it corresponds with our intuitions better than either of the alternatives does, namely, the conclusion that people are not equal in moral standing or that animals have no inherent value. We can, for example, follow Singer's lead in thinking about animals. Animals have interests, we can agree, interests that differ depending upon the level of consciousness of the animal and that must be given equal consideration. We should part company, however, at the boundary that divides people from animals. Beyond that boundary, Jefferson should replace Singer: all people are created equal.

The second approach, ecocentrism, is the idea that the natural ecology itself has moral standing.[8] Variants exist, some of them deriving from Aldo Leopold's "land ethic," outlined in his seminal *Sand County Almanac*.[9] The most fundamental fact of existence, the ecocentrists argue, is ecology. We as individuals and we as the human species, together with every other entity and species, are embedded in the complex texture of natural life, and it is the entire texture that must be preserved. No individual entity within that texture has privileged status, not even human beings. Callicott writes: "The land ethic directs us to take the welfare of nature — the diversity, stability, and integrity of the biotic community or, to mix metaphors, the health of the land organism — to be the standard of the moral quality, the rightness or wrongness, of our actions."[10]

Some ecocentrists use the term "deep ecology" to describe their position, in contrast to the shallow ecology of those who take a human-centered or even animal-centered approach.[11] Singer and Regan struggle to find a basis for treating some animals like human beings, but their standard is still a human one. The more like a human being an animal is, in their formulations, the more that animal deserves. From the point of view of the ecocentrists, this is just as hopeless as the view that only human beings have moral standing. Other natural entities and species are valuable, they claim, not because they are like human beings but because they are like themselves, because they are part of the ecology of life. Through their eyes, the reason to stop polluting the river is not just to preserve clean water for human use, and not just to preserve a habitat for fish, but to preserve the place of the river in the entire ecology of its region. If the river deteriorates, countless species of flora and fauna will suffer. It is the entire ecosystem that deserves protection.

The ecocentrists are not necessarily vegetarians, and they do not focus upon the prevention of suffering. The natural world is marked by a great deal of suffering, along with a food chain that contains both predators and prey. While Singer argues that we ought to prevent what suffering of animals we can, the ecocentrists claim there is no reason for us to forgo eating animals provided we do not affect their ecology. Through their eyes the domestication of animals and the slaughter of those animals are wrong because the farming of animals transforms the original ecology, but the hunting of animals in their natural state is permissible provided the species is not threatened.

The focus of the ecocentrists is upon species, not individuals. For Singer and Regan the opposite is true; their concern is for each individual sentient animal, irrespective of whether that animal's species is threatened. The understanding of the ecocentrists, however, is that nature is a continuous process of birth and death, of renewal and destruction. Individuals come and individuals go; what must be preserved is not the individuals but the species and the ecosystem within which the species flourish.

Nothing in the ecocentrist position privileges human beings. We are simply part of nature, no more important and no less important than other parts. We are nature's greatest danger, to be sure, and we also have the capacity for self-conscious, moral action, so we can be appealed to to do the proper thing, in a way that other species cannot. We do not, however, have any higher moral standing.

Ecocentrism contains serious problems for human beings. As with the views of Singer and Regan, the problems derive from the ambition of the deep ecologists to develop a single theory of ethics that comprehends all existence. At the risk of oversimplification, we can divide the ecocentrist position into two propositions. First, the natural ecology has its own independent moral value. Second, human beings have no place of privilege in the ecology. The first corresponds to a profound sense many people have of the inherent value of natural life. Try the following test. Somewhere in the world is a large, unspoiled tract, teeming with wildlife and an enormous variety of plant life. It contains snow-capped mountains, rushing streams, dense forests, and broad vistas. No human being has ever seen it, nor will a human being ever see it. Humans do not benefit from it in any way. Must we preserve it, or would it be a good place to drop our garbage? If you think it must be preserved, as I expect most people would, you agree with the ecocentrists that the ecology has its own value, independent of the benefit it provides human beings.

The problem comes with the second proposition, that people are to be thought of simply as part of the ecology, with no privileged status. People are, after all, the main cause of ecological changes. It is for the most part people who have caused the disappearance of species, the removal of forests, the pollution of rivers, the poisoning of the ground, and much else. The best way to stop those changes and restore, to the extent possible, the rich diversity of the natural ecology would be to eliminate a high proportion of the world's people, thereby getting rid of their destructive environmental impacts, taking care to leave only enough people to ensure that the species would survive. This is the implication of the ecocentrist position, and it is incompatible, to put the point mildly, with the idea that the foundation of justice is the equal moral standing of each human being.

The ecocentrist position logically requires the dismantling of most of the achievements of human civilization. Our cities, our farms, our factories, our highways and airports, our suburbs, our mines, our schools and universities, our laboratories — all these human creations and many more have massively changed the natural ecology of the whole world. If the standard of justice is ecology and not the welfare of human beings, all of it is wrong and must go. The criteria of freedom and of efficiency that were advanced in chapter 1 as components of justice would have to be abandoned. People could not experiment, develop, and build. They could not be efficient, in the sense of getting the most and the best out of the world they inhabit.

Some ecocentrists, sensitive to this sort of criticism, respond by pulling back from the most extreme of the doctrine's conclusions.[12] They assert that human beings are entitled to give extra consideration to their own species, since every species behaves in the same way, favoring its own welfare over that of other species. This response helps, but if carried very far it really is inconsistent with the entire ecocentrist position. Human beings differ from other species in that they are capable of more devastating impacts upon the environment, and they are capable of self-conscious moral action. If the ecocentrists concede that human beings do not have to use their moral consciousness to limit their own moral privilege, they have given up the essence of ecocentrism, which is that ecology, not human beings, is the standard of ethics.

As with Singer and Regan, the best response to the dilemma created by the ecocentrists is, I fear, inelegant. We can recognize that the ecology has its own inherent value, a value independent of the benefits it provides to human beings and even to other sentient animals. We must insist, however, that deep ecology is not a valid universal theory of ethics or justice. Human beings have their own individual and equal value. The interests of human beings will frequently come into conflict with those of the ecology, and when they do we must look for compromises. Again, this way of understanding the situation does not give us easy answers to practical problems, but it is preferable to either of the alternatives: that nature has no inherent value or that people's lives must be judged exclusively in terms of their impact upon nature.

One cannot prove in a logical way that the extensionists and the ecocentrists are wrong. The former begin with the idea that animals should be subject to the same moral principles as people, the latter with the idea that ecology is the standard of morality. I begin with the equal moral standing of each person. All one can demonstrate is that these principles are inconsistent. The choice is a matter of faith: if we believe in the equal standing of all people, we need an environmental ethic grounded in that belief. The rest of the chapter turns to this subject.

Future Generations

We saw earlier that the assertion of equal standing leaves many problems of justice unresolved. Chapter 1 considered in what respect equally worthy people must be treated equally, while chapter 9 asked whether the concepts of equal worth and equal treatment are applicable across national and other boundaries. This section turns to the question of future generations: Do they have equal standing with the present generation, and do they deserve equal treatment?[13] Do they deserve to be born into a world that is rich in biological and mineral resources, which has unspoiled wilderness areas, which has clean air and water? Do they deserve an earth that is at least as welcoming as the one onto which we were born? The heart of chapter 9's argument was that equal standing and equal treatment are separate concepts and that the former does not always imply the latter. While everyone in the world is of equal value, and while we have some obligations of justice to everyone, we do not always have equal obligations. These ideas are useful when thinking about future generations.

Take first the question of the equal moral worth of future people. It was once an almost universal belief — and it is still held by some — that all generations are equal in spiritual status, in their relationship to God.[14] God is revealed to people outside the dimension of time, and people go from this world to an eternal world in which time has no meaning and all souls are equal. Time is an illusion. If this is one's belief, then of course future people are equal in standing to today's people. We live in a more secular age, however, and religious faith can no longer be the basis for a shared understanding of justice.

Still, faith of some sort must lie at the foundation of a commitment to the principle of the equal standing of future generations. We must have faith that future people will exist and that they will be, in important respects, like us. We must have faith that we will be related to them, that we will be their ancestors, and that we are therefore responsible for them. Absent this sort of conviction, we might deny that future generations have equal — or any — moral significance. One way to think about the question is to try the thought experiment of reversibility.[15] Ask yourself whether you are as valuable as a person living in, say, 1600. Your answer is surely yes, and this is all that is needed to show that future generations are as valuable as we are.[16]

One might argue that future generations are not equally valuable because we do not know who they are, and we cannot know, since they do not exist. Most parents care deeply about their already living children and grandchildren and regard themselves as having a duty to those descendants, even after their own death. This is the basis for inheritance; we want to endow our successors with advantages. If pressed, most people would likely acknowledge that they share a similar if not quite as intense concern for their children and grandchildren who may not yet be born but who can reasonably be anticipated, even perhaps for grandchildren who may be born after one's death. As the chain moves further into the future, however, it frays; we lose our emotional connections. After perhaps two generations, future people are an abstraction to us.

Although we may feel this way, it is not an adequate basis for denying that future generations beyond the first few will have equal value. Future people do not yet exist, but we know that some people will exist. Or if we do not know with certainty that they will exist, we can say that if they do not exist, if there are no human beings on earth after a given date in the future, it will be a catastrophe, and we do not want to presume such a thing. We must believe that there will be future people. That being the case, the fact that we do not know who they are is irrelevant. We also do not know who most of the people now alive are. To my knowledge, I do not currently know a single person living in Nigeria, but this is irrelevant to my conviction that Nigerians are just as worthy as the people I do know. From reading and listening, I am convinced that over 100 million people live in Nigeria, and I am equally convinced that people will be living on the earth 400 years from now. In neither case is it necessary for me to know who they are in order to assign them equal worth.[17]

Since they are of equal worth, and since our treatment of the natural environment will affect their lives, we have obligations to them. In an old manuscript of Benedictine monks entitled *On the Conservation of Pine Forests,* is found: "[N]o one who plants a fir tree can hope to fell it when it is fully grown, no matter how youthful the person is. In spite of this the most sacred obligation is to replant and husband these pine forests. If we sweat for the benefit of posterity, we should not complain as we reap the results of the efforts of our forefathers."[18]

Although future generations have equal value, we cannot treat them the same as the current generation. We are incapable of affecting most aspects of the lives of people living, say, 400 years hence. What, then, can we say about our obligations to future generations? We can say one thing precisely: we must not harm them. This was one of the conclusions of chapter 9, that whatever else we do we must not diminish the quality of justice enjoyed by equally worthy people who are outside the jurisdictions in which we live. This turns out to be a strict requirement, when applied to future generations, because in the present, as we provide for ourselves and our children, we are changing the natural environment and in some respects diminishing it. This is not what future people deserve from us. They deserve to inherit a natural environment at least as good as the one we ourselves inherited.[19]

Neither democracy nor capitalism is completely up to the task of doing this. A serious problem with democracy is that future generations are not here to assert their needs.[20] Democratic governments are hardly oriented to the future at all, at least not to the long-run future, because only living people vote. To the extent that democratic governments operate well in the present, it is because they are a forum where different interests can be reconciled. If a person is absent from the bargaining table, his interest may go unheeded. Nothing about democracy, therefore, ensures that environmental policies will reflect the interests of future generations.

Neither does capitalism give the weight that is needed to the interests of future generations. It does, however, give some weight to the future. Think of an owner of a small factory who is nearing retirement age. Suppose he wants to sell his factory and live on the proceeds during his retirement. Although he will not be associated with the factory after he sells it, nevertheless, before he sells it he is very interested in its future profitability because the price he can get for it today depends upon the profits the factory is expected to generate in the future. Since expected future income is capitalized in the current prices of assets, people who own those assets are interested in preserving them into the future. It follows that the capitalist system is forward looking, even if the current owners of capital are not.

Still, the capitalist system has only a short-run concern for the future, paying no heed to the interests of people 400, or even 100, years hence. As we saw in chapter 3, capitalist markets discount the future. The discount factor can be thought of perhaps as the rate of interest or perhaps as the rate of time preference. Take the interest rate first. An investor does not think that $100 a year from now is worth as much as $100 today, because she can invest $100 today at a rate of interest, say 5 percent, and have $105 a year from now. Thus $100 a year from now is worth less than $100 today, perhaps just $95 at present. Thought of in terms of time preference, $100 a year from now is worth less than $100 today because we are more certain of our needs and desires today; events and needs a year from now seem less pressing to us. Therefore, in return for a promise of $100 a year from now, we might be willing to give up only $95 today. A discount rate of 5 percent does not lead to a huge difference in valuation over a year, but over a longer period it does. The claim to a sum of $100, 100 years from now, discounted at a 5 percent annual rate, would be worth only a few cents today. As it turns out, therefore, our factory owner who is approaching retirement may be interested in the expected value of his factory over the next ten to twenty years, but he will have no interest at all in its value 100 years hence, because its anticipated value that far in the future has virtually no effect on its current price.

Only a social rate of discount (or interest rate, or rate of time preference) of zero would give future benefits equal weighting with present benefits, indefinitely into the future. Capitalism cannot generate a zero rate of interest for a sustained period of time, however, because a positive rate of interest appears automatically in financial markets as a way of equilibrating sources and uses of funds.

In the way that capitalism gives some weight to the welfare of people in the near future, but not to people several generations hence, it matches our personal biases, thinking as we do of our children and grandchildren but not of their successors. If our system of production is organized, however, in such a way that it uses up the earth's resources within a century, leaving only a garbage dump behind, our descendants at that time will probably not find persuasive our explanation that their interests were of no moment to us because they were so heavily discounted by the rate of interest. They will understand their predicament as resulting from our selfishness. If the memory of our generation is not to be marred by such a condemnation, we must find ways of restraining capitalism's environmental rapaciousness.

A Humanist Approach to Environmental Protection

Let us see how far we can get by looking at environmental justice from the point of view of human beings, future as well as current, who are of equal value. Callicott denounces such an approach as "business as usual,"[21] but this is overly harsh. A serious, human-centered approach to the environment — based on the criteria of equality, freedom, and efficiency — can be demanding.

The central fact about people's relationship to the natural environment is that we depend upon it for the quality of our life, indeed for our survival. We are part of the earth's natural ecology, and we could not exist outside it. No person would last more than a few seconds in the natural environment of the Moon or Mars. We depend upon the earth for the air we breathe, the water we drink, the food we eat, and the goods we consume. Nature gives us many of our most profound pleasures. We delight in the changing seasons, in the wilderness areas, in the city parks, in the wild animals we encounter, in the pets we nurture, in the songs of the birds, in the hues of the leaves, and in the crashing surf at the seashore. For all these reasons, we must be stewards of nature.

The criterion of equality means that no person is privileged above anyone else. We must not leave a state of nature to our descendants that is less adequate to meet their needs than the one into which we were born. Among those now living, equality implies that groups or individuals are not entitled to advance their own interests by degrading the natural resources that are available to other people. It is unjust for me to increase the profits in my business, for example, by dumping my toxic wastes into your backyard.

True freedom, as chapter 1 described it, is the ability to pursue one's goals. It implies a lack of arbitrary restraints, but it also implies that we have the resources we need to pursue our goals. Laws and regulations that prevent us from despoiling nature may seem to restrict our freedom, but if they are appropriately tailored to the preservation of natural resources, they actually enhance our true freedom over the long run, since we need those natural resources to fulfill our goals.

Efficiency means getting the most and the best that we can out of our resources. Interpreted narrowly, this could lead to an exploitation of our resources, but it would be a mistake to interpret efficiency narrowly. Since we depend upon natural resources for what we want, we have to preserve them in usable form, not allow them to deteriorate, if we want to benefit from them to the maximum extent possible. The goal of efficiency over the generations points the way to sustainability as a guidepost to our interaction with nature. If we use our environment in ways that are not sustainable, it will lose its ability to give us what we need.

A human-centered approach to the environment can therefore be comprehensive; it is not an excuse for the business-as-usual of continued ecological destruction. It does, however, imply a tradeoff between economic activity and environmental preservation, with the welfare of people as the measure of the tradeoff. People would not be well served by either of two extremes: promoting economic production with no thought to its environmental impacts, on the one hand, or ceasing economic activity in order to avoid all environmental impacts, on the other. The ecocentrist view permits no tradeoff. If ecology is the criterion of justice, not people, anything that people do to degrade the environment is impermissible. If people are at the center of our consideration, however, if what must be honored is people's equality and liberty and their ability to do the best that they can for themselves, we find ourselves with conflicts that have to be resolved.

People want and deserve a comfortable standard of living, and we therefore engage in economic activity — but all economic activity alters our natural environment. We want to drive cars, for example, or at least ride the bus. Without cars, most of us would find our lives unduly limited. Yet the manufacture of cars uses up ores from the earth and their driving uses up nonrenewable fossil fuels. Their operation transforms those fuels into emissions that pollute our air. Should we therefore eliminate motorized transportation? The ecocentrists would probably say yes, but most of us would decline, because mobility is too important to us. Instead of banning cars, we try to improve the terms of the tradeoff by passing laws to promote greater fuel efficiency and to capture and reduce toxic emissions. These measures significantly reduce the environmental impact of cars, but they do not eliminate it completely. Cars still use scarce resources and pollute the air. We could go much further to reduce use of cars. We could impose a steep tax on cars, to discourage their purchase by people who do not have a very strong need for them (while recognizing that such a tax would discriminate against low-income people). We could ration gasoline, as was done in wartime, to reduce driving and to encourage the search for substitute fuels. We could impose restrictions on the number of cars bought each year. We could develop more incentives to induce the engineers to produce more fuel-efficient and nonpolluting vehicles. We may take some of these measures if we become more worried about the environmental impact of cars. Each measure has its cost, however, in terms of expense or convenience, so we have to ask at each point whether the cost is worth it.

There is nothing unique about cars in terms of this tradeoff. Every product we make and buy, and almost every activity in which we engage, has impacts that we can perhaps abate but seldom eliminate. We are constantly confronted with the question of how much we are willing to sacrifice for the sake of environmental protection.

The tradeoffs are complicated immeasurably because different people experience environmental impacts differently and because the costs of avoiding or abating the impacts fall upon us differently. The movement for environmental justice that arose at the end of the twentieth century documented the ways in which poor neighborhoods, people of color, women, third world countries, and other disadvantaged groups and areas have been environmentally exploited, not only by industrial polluters but in some cases by environmental activists themselves who have been less than completely sensitive to the inequalities that exist among human beings.[22] People living beside a toxic waste dump experience the pollution from that dump more severely than do people living miles away. Farmers who are told they must avoid the use of toxic pesticides bear more of the costs of pollution abatement than do nonfarmers. People living in rich countries consume more and therefore have a heavier impact on the environment, but they are also able to devote more resources to environmental protection than are people living in poor countries. In the real world in which we live, these sorts of environmental inequalities have to be worked out.

Economics and the Human-Centered Approach to the Environment

Modern economists have developed a way of thinking about environmental preservation within capitalism that is grounded in the human-centered approach. They see the problem as one of "external costs,"[23] which can be understood in contrast to the more common internal costs.

Think about a bicycle factory located beside a river. The factory uses processed inputs (steel, rubber, ball bearings, and so forth), and it hires workers. In each case it pays for these factors of production, and it therefore has an incentive to economize in its use of them. It will use as few of the factors as it can, consistent with its goal of maximizing its profits. The costs of these factors are internal costs, since the firm actually pays for them. A long tradition of economic analysis demonstrates that, if markets are functioning properly and if all costs are internal costs, not only do firms have an incentive to economize in the use of scarce resources, but they are actually led to use exactly the socially optimal amount of them. The assumptions behind this conclusion are stringent, to be sure, and a full understanding of it requires a level of economic analysis that is outside the limits of this chapter. The conclusion is based on the idea that the price of a factor of production is equal to its "opportunity cost," that is, its value in its next-most-important possible use. If our factory owner decides to pay for the resource, it must be because he has a use for it that is more valuable (where value is determined by the market) than the use that anyone else has for it. As a result of this process, resources are directed to their most useful social ends. A skeptic would naturally want to see the fine print before buying such a doctrine; my point in mentioning it here is not to defend it but to contrast it with the problem created by external costs.

External costs are costs that are imposed by a producer on society but that the producer does not have to pay for. Suppose that the process of making bicycles creates toxic wastes that are dumped into the river. By dumping the wastes, the factory imposes a cost on society, just as much as when it consumes scarce metal, uses ball bearings that other people have produced, or hires labor that could have been used in alternate pursuits. The difference is that it has to pay for the latter but not for the former. The market leads the factory to conserve in its use of labor but not to conserve in its use of the river as a garbage dump. The factory owners do not have to worry about the real costs imposed on the people downstream by their pollution, so they dump their waste into the river and ultimately destroy its value for other people.

To most economists, this is the way to understand pollution and other environmental problems, namely, as the consequences of a market failure, external costs. The solution suggests itself immediately: find a way to make the factory treat its waste disposal as if it were a matter of internal, not external, costs. Three strategies exist for achieving this: first, use moral suasion to convince the factory managers to act responsibly; second, regulate the waste disposal practices of the factory so that it does not destroy the river; and third, tax the emissions at a rate equal to the damage that each unit of pollution causes to the people located downstream. Each strategy has its strengths and weaknesses. Economists tend to prefer the third. A tax on pollution is sometimes derided as a license to pollute that will allow rich companies to continue with business as usual, but it actually has some merits. If the managers' goal is to maximize their profits, they will have an incentive to avoid the tax by abating emissions to the extent that the cost of abatement is less than the tax. If they decide to continue emitting some wastes, this must be because the value to the factory of continuing the emissions (that is, the saving from not abating the emissions) is greater than the cost of the pollution to those downstream. The tax rate can be set at any level the democratically elected government decides, and it can be changed as the value that people put on the cleanliness of the river changes.

Three features of this way of looking at environmental preservation should be obvious. First, it is based completely on the value of the environment to people. To the extent that people need clean water for drinking, swimming, irrigation, fishing, and other uses, and to the extent that they value the beauty of the river and its biota, they will impose restrictions on pollution.

Second, it calls not for the elimination of pollution but for *optimal pollution*, since all production creates pollution at some level, and we want both goods and services plus a clean environment. The reason the bicycle factory is in business is because we buy bicycles, and we buy them because we want and even need them, because they are valuable to us. A clean river is also valuable to us, so we are compelled to strike the right balance between the goods we value and the pollution we want to avoid.

Third, this approach to the environment requires the heavy regulatory hand of the government. If capitalism is understood simply as free markets, it is incompatible with even the most elementary forms of environmental protection. Chapter 2 argued, however, that government participation in the economy should not be seen as an attack upon or a retreat from capitalism; to the contrary, the capitalist system requires a partnership between government and the private market.

This sort of human-centered approach can take us a long way toward the environmental preservation we deserve, although not perhaps quite far enough. Earlier I argued that while we should reject the comprehensive doctrines associated with extensionism and ecocentrism, we should retain their insight that both animals and the natural ecology have inherent value, independent of their contribution to the welfare of human beings. We should remember this truth and hold ourselves responsible for our impacts upon the natural world.

Capitalism, Democracy, and Environmental Justice

How close will capitalism and democracy permit us to get to environmental justice? The answer depends partly on how we conceive of environmental justice. The ecocentrist prescription is obviously incompatible with capitalism, since it would require the dismantling of most of capitalism's material achievements. Progress can be made, however, toward the standard of environmental justice defended in this chapter, a standard that begins with a human-centered approach and that grants, in addition, independent moral value to animals and to the ecology as a whole.

Capitalist countries have made many environmental advances. To cite just one, the regulation of automobile and industrial emissions has led to a remarkable improvement in air quality in a number of regions of the United States, including the Los Angeles area, where once it was truly dangerous to breathe. The advances have occurred largely because of government regulation of the private sector; we have learned that the private sector can tolerate a lot of regulation and still thrive. Left to its own devices, on the other hand, the private sector would not be able to cope with the problem of external costs.

Part of the question, therefore, has to do with democracy. Is the democratic state capable of imposing the sort of regulations on capitalism's private sector that environmental justice requires? Unfortunately, the state is not completely up to the challenge, for three separate reasons: globalization, the future, and the power of money.

The most critical environmental problems are global in scope, and we lack not only a global government but even very many enforceable global treaties on the environment. National governments are reluctant to put their producers at a competitive disadvantage in international markets by imposing costly environmental restrictions that affect only their own country. The reluctance is understandably greater in the poor countries than in the rich. If we are to make progress with global warming, the ozone layer, ocean pollution, and a host of critical global environmental issues, we will need a regime of binding international treaties that is much more comprehensive than anything we have now. The democratic problem related to the future was discussed earlier in this chapter. Future generations have an equal stake in the world's natural environment, but they are unrepresented in the democratic state, so they have to rely upon the altruistic farsightedness of people now alive — and we are not always dependable. The money problem is that we are not all equal in the democratic state. Corporate interests typically oppose environmental regulations, and they have more than their fair share of influence in getting what they want.

These problems are all exacerbated when we go beyond the human-centered approach in an attempt to give some independent value to animals and to the ecology. Neither animals nor the ecology is represented in the state. Some have suggested solving the problem by appointing people to represent them,[24] but this would lead to obvious democratic problems, because it would create unequal voting privileges. If the Sierra Club, say, were appointed to speak for the ecology, would Sierra Club members get two votes to everyone else's one? If democracy is to be preserved, it is inescapable, I think, that animals and the ecology will remain unrepresented. Their independent value will be asserted, therefore, only to the extent that voters come to believe that those entities have independent value. This can result only from education and social action.

These are all serious problems, problems that lead one to the conclusion that full environmental justice is unlikely to be achieved within the system of capitalism regulated by a democratic state. The most serious problem, however, is economic growth. The capitalist system requires continuous growth. Is it possible that the growth could be sustainable, that the continually expanding economy could treat the natural environment in such a way that growth could continue indefinitely? It will be difficult. No doubt a great deal more can be done to promote sustainable agriculture, to find renewable and only lightly polluting energy sources, to advance our technology for abating and cleaning up polluting emissions, and in other ways to lighten the hand that we lay upon the land. Production requires the use of natural resources, however, and the earth is finite.

So far, exploration and discovery of most mineral resources have stayed ahead of usage. Our proven reserves of fossil fuels, to take one example, have increased over time in spite of the enormous amounts that have been extracted. This trend has to reverse at some point, because it is obvious that we are using fossil fuels faster than they are being replenished. Other mineral resources are in even more fixed supply. Even though we have not yet discovered all the useful ores in the earth's crust, and even though vast amounts of useful minerals that we have not yet found a way of extracting are dissolved in sea water, still we can be sure that the amounts, however large, are finite. Growth in production is sure to come up against physical limits at some point in the future. In the long run, therefore, we have to develop renewable energy sources, and we will have to depend upon recycling for our minerals. This may or may not be possible if production continues to increase.

It is not certain, therefore, that a large human population will be able to enjoy a growing economy into the indefinite future. The best hope for the human species living on a finite globe may be a declining population. If the birthrate falls to such an extent that deaths exceed births, our descendants may be able to settle into a relationship with the earth that is sustainable for a much longer period of time.

This book has been based largely on the prediction that capitalism will be with us into the future. How long into the future is a good question, though. In the very long run, if the capitalist economy continues to grow, it may run into inexorable physical limits. At that point it may have to be converted into a much more state-directed system with global controls imposed to prevent economic growth. Absent such a change, the human race may not survive. In light of our experiences with completely state-dominated societies, one must fear for the quality of justice in such a world.

Meanwhile, there is a great deal that we can do at the present time — locally, nationally, and internationally — to protect our environmental resources and to preserve the natural world. The environmental movement has had many successes, and its work has just begun.

Notes

1. For a comprehensive review of environmental ethics, see Joseph R. Desjardins, *Environmental Ethics: An Introduction to Environmental Philosophy,* 2d ed. (Belmont, Calif.: Wadsworth Publishing Co., 1997). A briefer introduction is contained in Robin Attfield, "Environmental Ethics, Overview," in *Encyclopedia of Applied Ethics* (San Diego: Academic Press, 1998), 2:73–81. A good website on the topic, with links to many of the important publications in the field, is http://www.cep.unt.edu/novice.html.

2. J. Baird Callicott, "The Search for an Environmental Ethic," in *Matters of Life and Death,* ed. Tom Regan (New York: Random House, 1986), 381–424.

3. See the following, all by Peter Singer: *Animal Liberation: Towards an End to Man's Inhumanity to Animals* (Wellingborough, England: Thorsons Publishers, 1975); "Not for Humans Only: The Place of Nonhumans in Environmental Issues," in *Ethics and Problems of the 21st Century,* ed. K. E. Goodpaster and K. M. Sayre (Notre Dame, Ind.: University of Notre Dame Press, 1979), 191–206; "Utilitarianism and Vegetarianism," *Philosophy and Public Affairs* 9 (1980): 325–37; *Practical Ethics,* 2d ed. (Cambridge: Cambridge University Press, 1993).

4. See Donald A. Graft, "Speciesism," in *Encyclopedia of Applied Ethics,* 4:191–205.

5. Singer, "Not for Humans Only," 195.

6. Singer, "Not for Humans Only," 196.

7. Tom Regan, "Utilitarianism, Vegetarianism, and Animal Rights," *Philosophy and Public Affairs* 9 (1980): 305–24; Tom Regan, *The Case for Animal Rights* (Berkeley: University of California Press, 1983). For an assessment of animal rights, see Evelyn Pluhar, "Animal Rights," in *Encyclopedia of Applied Ethics,* 1:161–72.

8. For more extensive treatments, see Desjardins, *Environmental Ethics,* and Kate Rawles, "Biocentrism," in *Encyclopedia of Applied Ethics,* 1:275–83.

9. Aldo Leopold, *A Sand County Almanac with Essays on Conservation from Round River* (New York: Oxford University Press, 1949).

10. Callicott, "Search for an Environmental Ethic."

11. The term "deep ecology" was introduced by Arne Naess in "The Shallow and the Deep, Long-Range Ecology Movement: A Summary," *Inquiry* 16 (1973): 95–100.

12. For example, Callicott, "Search for an Environmental Ethic," and James Sterba, "Environmental Justice," in *Morality in Practice,* 5th ed., ed. James P. Sterba (Belmont, Calif.: Wadsworth Publishing Co., 1997), 480–86.

13. For a survey of approaches to the moral standing of future generations, see Robin Attfield, *The Ethics of Environmental Concern,* 2d ed. (Athens: University of Georgia Press, 1991), chapter 6. For collections of papers on the subject, see R. I. Sikora and Brian Barry, eds., *Obligations to Future Generations* (Philadelphia: Temple University Press, 1978), and Ernest Partridge, ed., *Responsibilities to Future Generations: Environmental Ethics* (Buffalo: Prometheus Books, 1981).

14. Peter Laslett, "The Conversation between the Generations," in *Philosophy, Politics, and Society,* 5th ser., ed. Peter Laslett and James Fishkin (Oxford: Basil Blackwell, 1979), 36–56.

15. Lawrence Kohlberg, "Justice as Reversibility," in *Philosophy, Politics, and Society,* 257–72. Rawls's original position is a similar thought experiment; see John Rawls, *A Theory of Justice* (Cambridge, Mass.: Harvard University Press, 1971).

16. I am claiming in this section that future people who will exist have equal moral standing to people who currently exist. This argument has nothing to

do with the right of any particular people to be born. That is another question entirely, so my argument has no bearing on the moral debate over abortion.

17. Gregory Kavka, "The Futurity Problem," in Sikora and Barry, *Obligations to Future Generations*, 186–203.

18. Quoted in Van Rensselaer Potter, "Evolving Ethical Concepts," *BioScience* 27 (1977): 251.

19. For other philosophical routes to roughly the same conclusion, see Mary B. Williams, "Discounting versus Maximum Sustainable Yield," in Sikora and Barry, *Obligations to Future Generations*, 169–85, and Robert Elliot, "The Rights of Future People," *Journal of Applied Philosophy* 6 (1989): 159–69.

20. See Dennis C. Mueller, "Intergenerational Justice and the Social Discount Rate," *Theory and Decision* 5 (1974): 263–73.

21. Callicott, "Search for an Environmental Ethic."

22. Carl Talbott, "Environmental Justice," in *Encyclopedia of Applied Ethics*, 2:93–105. One of the best accounts of environmental exploitation is Robert D. Bullard, *Dumping in Dixie: Race, Class, and Environmental Quality* (Boulder, Colo.: Westview Press, 1990).

23. Externalities were introduced into the economics literature by A. C. Pigou, *The Economics of Welfare* (London: Macmillan, 1920). For a modern treatment of environmental problems using externalities as the organizing principle, see William J. Baumol and Wallace E. Oates, *Economics, Environmental Policy, and the Quality of Life* (Englewood Cliffs, N.J.: Prentice-Hall, 1979).

24. Christopher D. Stone, "Should Trees Have Legal Standing? Toward Legal Rights for Natural Objects," *Southern California Law Review* 45 (1972): 450–501.

EPILOGUE

THE CAPITALIST SYSTEM places constraints around our ability to achieve a just world, but capitalism is malleable. Movements for social justice in our time have transformed people's lives: the labor movement, the civil rights movement, the women's movement, and many others. The social security system, the war on poverty, the minimum wage, the progressive income tax, and other legislative achievements have brought us closer to a just society, within the confines of capitalism. We still have a long agenda in front of us. We should work for a just income distribution, justice for poor people, justice for minorities, justice for foreigners, justice for immigrants, justice for generations yet to come, and many other forms of justice.

We can succeed, although not completely. "If death defines the human condition," Stanley Hoffman writes, "injustice defines the social one. There is a duty, national and international, to reduce it as much as possible. But there is no definitive victory."[1] Indeed there is no definitive victory, but there are partial and contingent victories. One of Pete Seeger's most rousing songs ends, "And when we sing another little victory song, precious friend you will be there, singing in harmony."*

I come, in the end, to the Covenant of the Unitarian Universalist Association:

We covenant to affirm and promote:
The inherent worth and dignity of every person
Justice, equity, and compassion in human relations
Acceptance of one another and encouragement to spiritual
  growth....
A free and responsible search for truth and meaning
The right of conscience and the use of the democratic process...
The goal of world community...
And respect for the interdependent web of all existence of which
  we are a part.[2]

---

*PRECIOUS FRIEND, YOU WILL BE THERE by Pete Seeger © Copyright 1974, 1982 by STORMKING MUSIC, INC. All rights reserved. Used by permission.

Notes

1. Stanley Hoffman, *Duties beyond Borders: On the Limits and Possibilities of Ethical International Relations* (Syracuse, N.Y.: Syracuse University Press, 1981), 187.

2. Unitarian Universalist Association, *1998–1999 Directory* (Boston: Unitarian Universalist Association, 1998), 10.

SELECT BIBLIOGRAPHY

The select bibliography contains most of the references in the book to theories, philosophy, and arguments. I recommend that people interested in reading further about social justice begin with articles in the *Encyclopedia of Applied Ethics,* 4 vols. (San Diego: Academic Press, 1998). I have not listed the *Encyclopedia* articles separately in the select bibliography.

Ackerman, Bruce A. *Social Justice in the Liberal State.* New Haven, Conn.: Yale University Press, 1980.

Ackerman, Bruce A., and Susan Alstott. *The Stakeholder Society.* New Haven, Conn.: Yale University Press, 1999.

Aristotle. *The Nichomachean Ethics.* Translated by David Ross. Revised by J. L. Ackrill and J. O. Urmson. Oxford: Oxford University Press, 1980.

Arneson, Richard J. *The Ethics of Environmental Concern.* 2d ed. Athens: University of Georgia Press, 1991.

———. "Liberalism, Distributive Subjectivism, and Equal Opportunity for Welfare." *Philosophy and Public Affairs* 19 (1990): 159–94.

———. "What Do Socialists Want?" In John E. Roemer, *Equal Shares: Making Market Socialism Work,* edited by Erik Olin Wright, 209–30. London: Verso, 1996.

Barry, Brian. *Democracy, Power, and Justice: Essays in Political Theory.* Oxford: Clarendon Press, 1989.

Beitz, Charles R. *Political Theory and International Relations.* 2d ed. Princeton, N.J.: Princeton University Press, 1999.

———. "Social and Cosmopolitan Liberalism." *International Affairs* 75 (1999): 515–29.

Bishop, John Douglas, ed. *Ethics and Capitalism.* Toronto: University of Toronto Press, 2000.

Bolick, Clint. *The Affirmative Action Fraud: Can We Restore the American Civil Rights Vision?* Washington, D.C.: Cato Institute, 1996.

Bowen, William G., and Derek Bok. *The Shape of the River: Long Term Consequences of Considering Race in College and University Admissions.* Princeton, N.J.: Princeton University Press, 1998.

Buchanan, Allen. "Recognitional Legitimacy and the State System." *Philosophy and Public Affairs* 28 (1999): 46–78.

Cahn, Steven M., ed. *Affirmative Action and the University: A Philosophical Inquiry.* Philadelphia: Temple University Press, 1993.

———, ed. *The Affirmative Action Debate.* New York: Routledge, 1995.

Callicott, J. Baird. "The Search for an Environmental Ethic." In *Matters of Life and Death*, edited by Tom Regan, 381–424. New York: Random House, 1986.

Campbell, Tom. *Justice*. London: Macmillan Education, 1988.

Carens, Joseph H. "Aliens and Citizens: The Case for Open Borders." *Review of Politics* 49 (1987): 251–73.

———. "Open Borders and Liberal Limits: A Response to Isbister." *International Migration Review* 34 (2000): 636–43.

———. "Reconsidering Open Borders." *International Migration Review* 33 (1999): 1082–97.

Chester, Ronald. *Inheritance, Wealth, and Society*. Bloomington: Indiana University Press, 1982.

———. "Inheritance in American Legal Thought." In *Inheritance and Wealth in America*, edited by Robert K. Miller Jr. and Stephen J. McNamee, 23–43. New York: Plenum Press, 1998.

Cohen, G. A. "Robert Nozick and Wilt Chamberlain: How Patterns Preserve Liberty." *Erkenntnis* 11 (1977): 5–23.

———. *Self-Ownership, Freedom, and Equality*. Cambridge: Cambridge University Press, 1995.

Cohen, Marshall, Thomas Nagel, and Thomas Scanlon, eds. *Equality and Preferential Treatment*. Princeton, N.J.: Princeton University Press, 1977.

Copp, David. "The Idea of a Legitimate State." *Philosophy and Public Affairs* 28 (1999): 2–45.

Daly, Herman E. *Steady-State Economics*. 2d ed. Washington, D.C.: Island Press, 1991.

Desjardins, Joseph R. *Environmental Ethics: An Introduction to Environmental Philosophy*. 2d ed. Belmont, Calif.: Wadsworth Publishing Co., 1997.

Drakich, Janice, Marilyn Taylor, and Jennifer Bankier. "Academic Freedom Is the Inclusive University." In *Beyond Political Correctness: Toward the Inclusive University*, edited by Stephen Richer and Lorna Weir, 118–35. Toronto: University of Toronto Press, 1995.

Dworkin, Ronald. *Taking Rights Seriously*. Cambridge, Mass.: Harvard University Press, 1977.

———. "What Is Equality? Part 1: Equality of Welfare," and "Part 2: Equality of Resources." *Philosophy and Public Affairs* 10 (1981): 185–246 and 283–345, respectively.

Elliot, Robert. "The Rights of Future People." *Journal of Applied Philosophy* 6 (1989): 159–69.

Elster, Jon. *Solomonic Judgements: Studies in the Limitations of Rationality*. Cambridge: Cambridge University Press, 1989.

Ezorsky, Gertrude. *Racism and Justice: The Case for Affirmative Action*. Ithaca, N.Y.: Cornell University Press, 1991.

Fair, Ray C. "The Optimal Distribution of Income." *The Quarterly Journal of Economics* 85 (1971): 551–79.

Fried, Barbara. "Wilt Chamberlain Revisited: Nozick's 'Justice in Transfer' and the Problem of Market-Based Distribution." *Philosophy and Public Affairs* 24 (1995): 226–45.

Friedman, Milton. *Capitalism and Freedom.* Chicago: University of Chicago Press, 1962.

Goodin, Robert E. "What Is So Special about Our Fellow Countrymen?" *Ethics* 98 (1988): 663–86.

Green, Leslie. "Concepts of Equity in Taxation." In *Fairness in Taxation: Exploring the Principles,* edited by Allan M. Maslove, 87–103. Toronto: University of Toronto Press, 1993.

Gutmann, Amy, and Dennis Thompson. *Democracy and Disagreement.* Cambridge, Mass.: Belknap Press of Harvard University Press, 1996.

Harman, Gilbert. "Moral Relativism Defended." *Philosophical Review* 84 (1975): 3–22.

Haslett, D. W. "Is Inheritance Justified?" *Philosophy and Public Affairs* 15 (1986): 122–55.

Hausman, Daniel M., and Michael S. McPherson. *Economic Analysis and Moral Philosophy.* New York: Cambridge University Press, 1996.

———. "Taking Ethics Seriously: Economics and Contemporary Moral Philosophy." *Journal of Economic Literature* 31 (1993): 671–731.

Held, Virginia. *Feminist Morality: Transforming Culture, Society, and Politics.* Chicago: University of Chicago Press, 1993.

Hoffman, Stanley. *Duties beyond Borders: On the Limits and Possibilities of Ethical International Relations.* Syracuse, N.Y.: Syracuse University Press, 1981.

Holmes, Stephen, and Cass R. Sunstein. *The Cost of Rights: Why Liberty Depends on Taxes.* New York: W. W. Norton, 1999.

Isbister, John. "Are Immigration Controls Ethical?" In *Immigration: A Civil Rights Issue for the Americas,* edited by Susanne Jonas and Suzie Dod Thomas, 85–98. Wilmington, Del.: Scholarly Resources, 1999.

———. "A Liberal Argument for Border Controls: Reply to Carens." *International Migration Review* 34 (2000): 629–35.

Justinian. *Institutes.* Translated by Thomas Collett Sandars. London: Longmans, Green and Co., 1922.

Kilby, Christopher. "Aid and Sovereignty." *Social Theory and Practice* 25 (1999): 79–92.

Kincheloe, Joe L. "The Struggle to Define and Reinvent Whiteness: A Pedagogical Analysis." *College Literature* 26 (1999): 162–75.

Korten, David C. *When Corporations Rule the World.* West Hartford, Conn.: Kumarian Press, 1995.

Laslett, Peter, and James Fishkin, eds. *Philosophy, Politics, and Society.* 5th ser. Oxford: Basil Blackwell, 1979.

Leopold, Aldo. *A Sand County Almanac, with Essays on Conservation from Round River.* New York: Oxford University Press, 1949.

Lerner, S., C. M. A. Clark, and W. R. Needham. *Basic Income: Economic Security for All Canadians.* Toronto: Between the Lines, 1999.

Levine, Andrew. "Rewarding Effort." *Journal of Political Philosophy* 7 (1999): 404–18.

Locke, John. *The Second Treatise of Government.* 1690. Reprint, Indianapolis: Bobbs-Merrill, 1952.

Marcuse, Herbert. *One Dimensional Man: Studies in the Ideology of Advanced Industrial Society.* Boston: Beacon Press, 1964.

McMurtry, John. *Unequal Freedoms: The Global Market as an Ethical System.* West Hartford, Conn.: Kumarian Press, 1998.

Mead, Lawrence M. *The New Politics of Poverty: The Nonworking Poor in America.* New York: Basic Books, 1992.

Meilaender, Peter C. "Liberalism and Open Borders: The Argument of Joseph Carens." *International Migration Review* 33 (1999): 1062–81.

Mill, John Stuart. *On Liberty.* Edited by Currin V. Shields. New York: Liberal Arts Press of New York, 1956.

———. *Utilitarianism.* Edited by Oskar Priest. New York: Macmillan Publishing Co., 1957.

Mink, Gwendolyn. *Welfare's End.* Ithaca, N.Y.: Cornell University Press, 1998.

Moore, G. E. *Principia Ethica.* Cambridge: Cambridge University Press, 1903.

Musgrave, Richard A. "Progressive Taxation, Equity, and Tax Design." In *Tax Progressivity and Income Inequality,* edited by Joel Slemrod, 341–56. Cambridge: Cambridge University Press, 1994.

———. *The Theory of Public Finance.* New York: McGraw-Hill, 1959.

Naess, Arne. "The Shallow and the Deep, Long-Range Ecology Movement: A Summary." *Inquiry* 16 (1973): 95–100.

Nagel, Thomas. "A Defense of Affirmative Action." In *Ethical Theory and Business,* edited by Tom L. Beauchamp and Norman E. Bowie, 370–74. 5th ed. Upper Saddle River, N.J.: Prentice Hall, 1997.

Nardin, Terry, and David R. Marpel, eds. *Traditions of International Ethics.* Cambridge: Cambridge University Press, 1992.

Nozick, Robert. *Anarchy, State, and Utopia.* New York: Basic Books, 1974.

O'Neill, Onora. "Distant Strangers, Moral Standing, and State Boundaries." In *Current Issues in Political Philosophy: Justice in Society and World Order,* edited by Peter Koller and Klaus Paul, 119–32. Vienna: Verlag Holder-Pichler-Tempsky, 1997.

Opeskin, Brian R. "The Moral Foundations of Foreign Aid." *World Development* 24 (1996): 21–44.

Partridge, Ernest, ed. *Responsibilities to Future Generations: Environmental Ethics.* Buffalo: Prometheus Books, 1981.

Pigou, A. C. *The Economics of Welfare.* London: Macmillan, 1920.

Plato. *The Laws.* Translated by A. E. Taylor. London: J. M. Dent and Sons, 1934.

Posner, Richard A. *The Economics of Justice.* Cambridge, Mass.: Harvard University Press, 1981.

Putterman, Louis, John E. Roemer, and Joaquim Silvestre. "Does Egalitarianism Have a Future?" *Journal of Economic Literature* 31 (1998): 861–902.

Rachels, James. *The Elements of Moral Philosophy.* Philadelphia: Temple University Press, 1986.

Rawls, John. *The Law of Peoples.* Cambridge, Mass.: Harvard University Press, 1999.

———. *A Theory of Justice.* Cambridge, Mass.: Harvard University Press, 1971.

Regan, Tom. *The Case for Animal Rights.* Berkeley: University of California Press, 1983.

———. "Utilitarianism, Vegetarianism, and Animal Rights." *Philosophy and Public Affairs* 9 (1980): 305–24.

Roberts, Robert C. "Will Power and the Virtues." *Philosophical Review* 93 (1984): 227–47.

Roemer, John E. *Theories of Distributive Justice.* Cambridge, Mass.: Harvard University Press, 1996.

Ross, W. D. *The Right and the Good.* London: Oxford University Press, 1930.

Scanlon, Thomas. "Equality of Resources and Equality of Welfare: A Forced Marriage?" *Ethics* 97 (1986): 111–18.

Schlegel, Stuart A. *Wisdom from a Rainforest: The Spiritual Journey of an Anthropologist.* Athens: University of Georgia Press, 1998.

Sen, Amartya. *On Ethics and Economics.* Oxford: Basic Blackwell, 1987.

———. *Inequality Reexamined.* Cambridge, Mass.: Harvard University Press, 1992.

Sher, George. "Diversity." *Philosophy and Public Affairs* 28 (1999): 85–104.

Sikora, R. I., and Brian Barry, eds. *Obligations to Future Generations.* Philadelphia: Temple University Press, 1978.

Singer, Peter. *Animal Liberation: Towards an End to Man's Inhumanity to Animals.* Wellingborough, England: Thorsons Publishers, 1975.

———. "Not for Humans Only: The Place of Nonhumans in Environmental Issues." In *Ethics and Problems of the 21st Century,* edited by K. E. Goodpaster and K. M. Sayre, 191–206. Notre Dame, Ind.: University of Notre Dame Press, 1979.

———. *Practical Ethics.* 2d ed. Cambridge: Cambridge University Press, 1993.

———. "Utilitarianism and Vegetarianism." *Philosophy and Public Affairs* 9 (1980): 325–37.

Slemrod, Joel, and Jon Bakija. *Taxing Ourselves: A Citizen's Guide to the Great Debate over Tax Reform.* Cambridge, Mass.: MIT Press, 1996.

Smith, Harlan M. *Understanding Economics.* Armonk, N.Y.: M. E. Sharpe, 1999.

Solow, Robert M. *Work and Welfare.* Princeton, N.J.: Princeton University Press, 1998.

Steele, Shelby. *The Content of Our Character: A New Vision of Race in America.* New York: St. Martin's Press, 1990.

Sterba, James P. "Environmental Justice." In *Morality in Practice,* edited by James P. Sterba, 480–86. 5th ed. Belmont, Calif.: Wadsworth Publishing Co., 1997.

———. "Recent Work on Alternative Conceptions of Justice." *American Philosophical Quarterly* 23 (1986): 1–22

Stone, Christopher D. "Should Trees Have Legal Standing? Toward Legal Rights for Natural Objects." *Southern California Law Review* 45 (1972): 450–501.

Sumberg, Theodore A. *Foreign Aid as Moral Obligation?* Washington Papers 1. Beverly Hills, Calif.: Sage Publications, 1973.

TenBroek, Jacobus. *Equal under the Law.* New York: Collier, 1969.

Tisch, Sarah J., and Michael B. Wallace. *Dilemmas of Development Assistance: The What, Why, and Who of Foreign Aid.* Boulder, Colo.: Westview Press, 1994.

Tucker, Robert W. *The Inequality of Nations.* New York: Basic Books, 1977.

United Nations Center for Human Rights. *The Rights of Migrant Workers.* Human Rights Fact Sheet 24. New York: United Nations, 1995.

Valls, Andrew. "The Libertarian Case for Affirmative Action." *Social Theory and Practice* 25 (1999): 299–323.

Van Parijs, Philippe. *Real Freedom for All: What (If Anything) Can Justify Capitalism?* Oxford: Clarendon Press, 1995.

———. "The Second Marriage of Justice and Efficiency." *Journal of Social Policy* 19 (1990): 1–25.

———. "Why Surfers Should Be Fed: The Liberal Case for an Unconditional Basic Income." *Philosophy and Public Affairs* 20 (1991): 101–31.

Van Wyk, Robert N. "World Hunger and the Extent of Our Positive Duties." In *Social and Personal Ethics,* edited by William H. Shaw, 472–80. 3d ed. Belmont, Calif.: Wadsworth Publishing Co., 1999.

Walzer, Michael. *Just and Unjust Wars: A Moral Argument with Historical Illustrations.* New York: Basic Books, 1977.

———. "The Moral Standing of States: A Response to Four Critics." *Philosophy and Public Affairs* 9 (1980): 209–29.

———. *Spheres of Justice: A Defense of Pluralism and Equality.* New York: Basic Books, 1983.

Wasserstrom, Richard. "One Way to Understand and Defend Programs of Preferential Treatment." In *The Moral Foundations of Civil Rights,* edited by Robert K. Fullinwider and Claudia Mills. Totowa, N.J.: Rowman and Littlefield, 1986.

Williams, Bernard. *Morality: An Introduction to Ethics.* New York: Harper and Row, 1972.

Wolf, Susan. "Moral Saints." *Journal of Philosophy* 79 (1982): 419–39.

Wolff, Edward N. *Top Heavy: The Increasing Inequality of Wealth in America and What Can Be Done about It.* New York: New Press, 1996.

Wong, David B. *Moral Relativity.* Berkeley: University of California Press, 1984.

INDEX

KATIE ISBISTER

About the Author

John Isbister is a professor of economics at the University of California, Santa Cruz. He was raised in Ottawa, Canada, and studied history as an undergraduate at Queen's University in Kingston, Ontario. He received his doctorate in economics from Princeton University in 1969 and joined the faculty of the University of California, Santa Cruz, as a founding fellow of one of its ten interdisciplinary, liberal arts colleges, Merrill College. From 1984 to 1999 he was the provost of Merrill College. He is the author of three other books: *Promises Not Kept: The Betrayal of Social Change in the Third World*, now in its fourth edition, and *The Immigration Debate: Remaking America*, both published by Kumarian Press, and *Thin Cats: The Community Development Credit Union Movement in the United States*. He teaches courses on economic theory, economic development, and ethics. He is married to the writer Roz Spafford and has four children and one grandson.

 Kumarian Press is dedicated to publishing and distributing books and other media that will have a positive social and economic impact on the lives of peoples living in "Third World" conditions no matter where they live.

Kumarian Press publishes books about Global Issues and International Development, such as Peace and Conflict Resolution, Environmental Sustainability, Globalization, Nongovernmental Organizations, and Women and Gender.

To receive a complimentary catalog or to request writer's guidelines call or write:

Kumarian Press, Inc.
1294 Blue Hills Avenue
Bloomfield, CT 06002
U.S.A.

Inquiries: (860) 243-2098
Fax: (860) 243-2867
Order toll free: (800) 289-2664

e-mail: kpbooks@aol.com
Internet: www.kpbooks.com